IMAGES
of America

AROUND CANANDAIGUA

IMAGES
of America

AROUND CANANDAIGUA

Nancy H. Yacci

ARCADIA
PUBLISHING

ISBN 978-0-7385-3455-8

Published by Arcadia Publishing
Charleston, South Carolina

Printed in the United States of America

Library of Congress Catalog Card Number: Applied for

For all general information contact Arcadia Publishing at:
Telephone 843-853-2070
Fax 843-853-0044
E-mail sales@arcadiapublishing.com
For customer service and orders:
Toll-Free 1-888-313-2665

Visit us on the Internet at www.arcadiapublishing.com

Contents

INTRODUCTION

History has been good to the Canandaigua area. Our heritage abounds with statesmen, entrepreneurs, and common people. The early settlers to this area worked to develop a thriving community in which to make a living and to foster and build families. Those who were especially fortunate often gave back to the community by building public facilities for all to enjoy. Many of these gifts are depicted in this book.

The photographic images presented here were drawn from the collection of the Ontario County Historical Society. The society, founded in 1902, has had over 16,000 images donated to its collection over the years. Many of the pictures presented were found in old family photo albums. Some were part of the Boyce collection. Still others were discovered by chance while conducting historical research. Every one offers a unique view into the past.

It is our hope that this book will reveal a part of Canandaigua many do not know. With the assistance of these fascinating images, we see grand steamboats, important community events, and the historic face of downtown Canandaigua, but best of all, we get to know its people. It was these strong individuals and the lives they created here which shaped and molded this wonderful region.

The board of trustees are pleased to present this book to the community. Special thanks to trustee Nancy Yacci and her several helpers, who labored long and hard in the archives, loving almost every minute of it, to produce this book. Also a word of thanks to the historical society's president, John R. Kennedy, who believed in the project from the beginning, and has never faltered in his support.

We know you and your family will enjoy this picture book and cherish it as a reminder of this community's past.

One

NATIVE AMERICAN HERITAGE

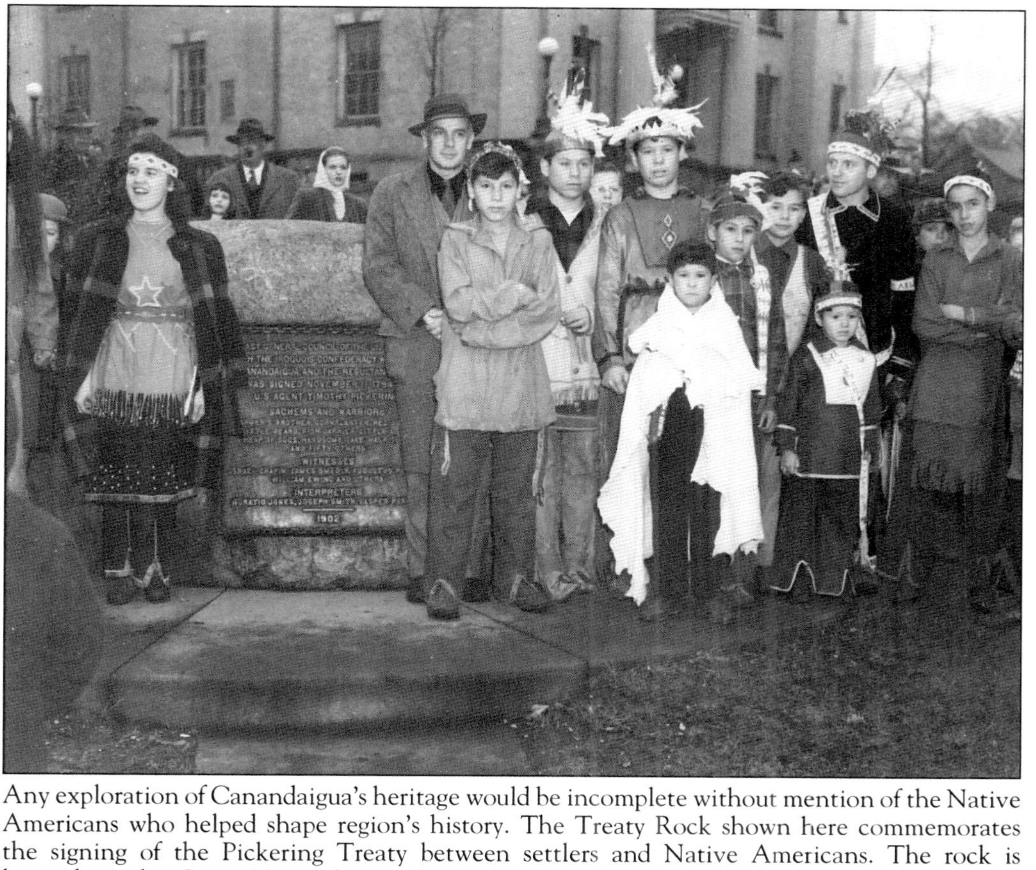

Any exploration of Canandaigua's heritage would be incomplete without mention of the Native Americans who helped shape region's history. The Treaty Rock shown here commemorates the signing of the Pickering Treaty between settlers and Native Americans. The rock is located on the Court House lawn, where the original treaty was signed on November 11, 1794. The 30-ton boulder was placed with great ceremony on May 30, 1903, and was given by Dr. Dwight Burrell.

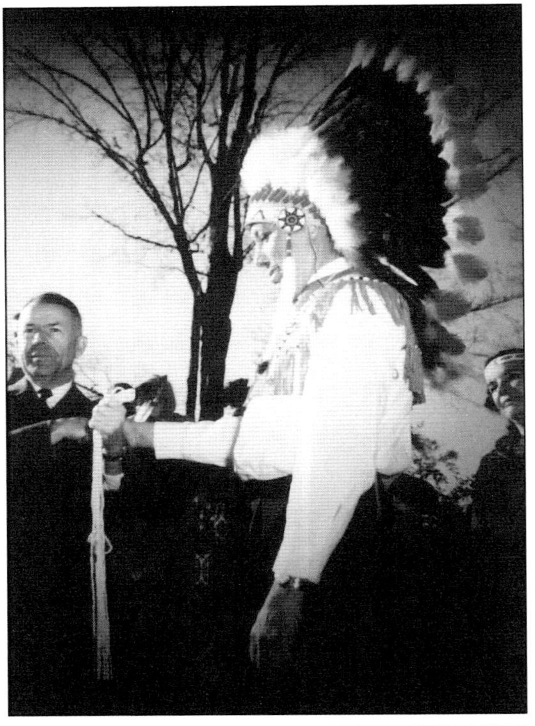

This image was taken in 1960, and it shows Mayor Arthur Munson holding strings of Wampum that represent the commitment to friendship and to the Pickering Treaty of 1794. The signing of the treaty is celebrated every year on November 11, with a reading of the treaty and a gift of fabric to the Native Americans as was written in the original treaty. (Photograph by Sheldon Fisher.)

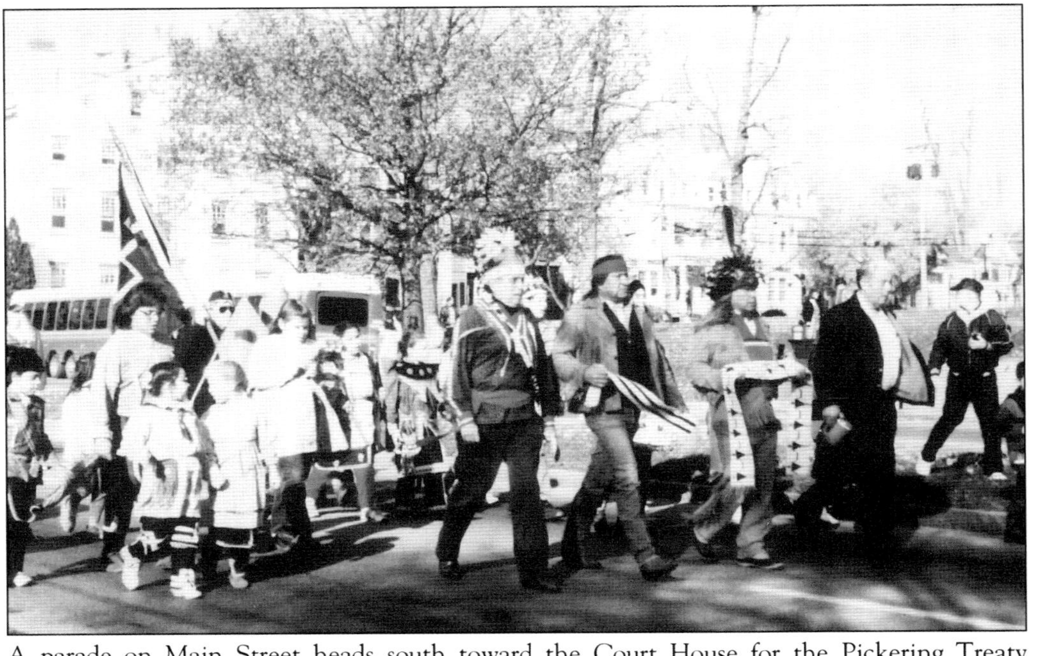

A parade on Main Street heads south toward the Court House for the Pickering Treaty commemoration. Leading the marchers are, from left to right: Chief Leo Henry from the Tuscarora Nation, Faithkeeper Clayton Logan with the Two Row Wampum belt from the Cattaraugus Reservation, Vernon Jimerson with the George Washington belt from Seneca, and Ben Cusick from Tuscarora. (Photograph by Robert Gorall.)

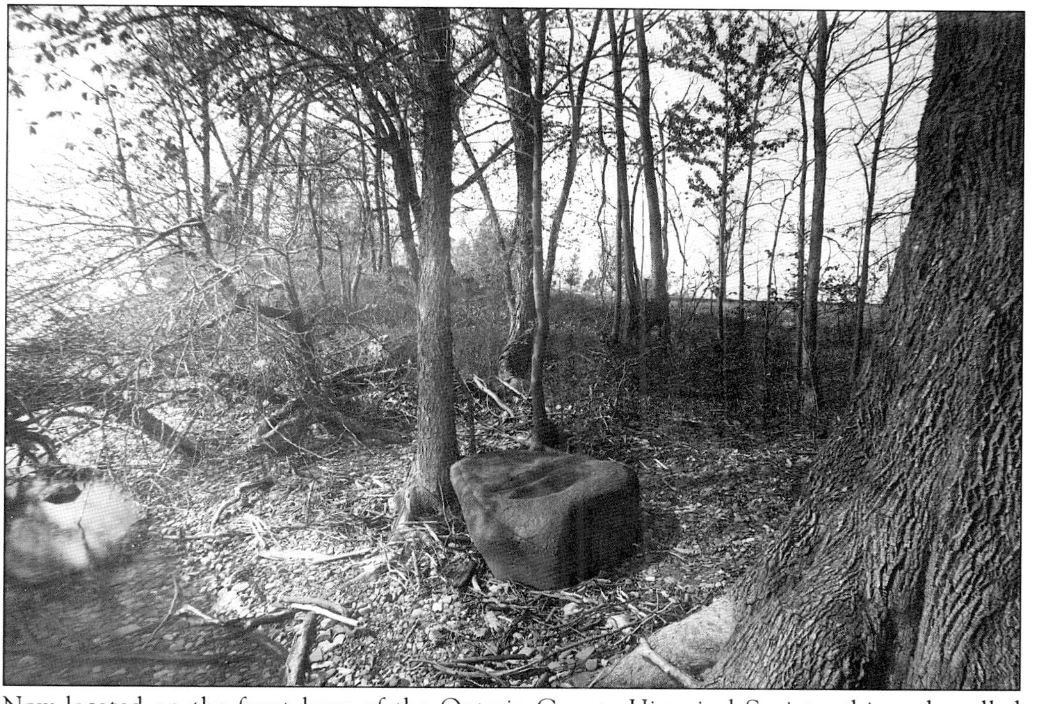

Now located on the front lawn of the Ontario County Historical Society, this rock, called Osteaha Gahnigahia (rock mortar), was used by the Seneca Indians in shaping and finishing their stone implements. It was originally located along the shore of Canandaigua Lake.

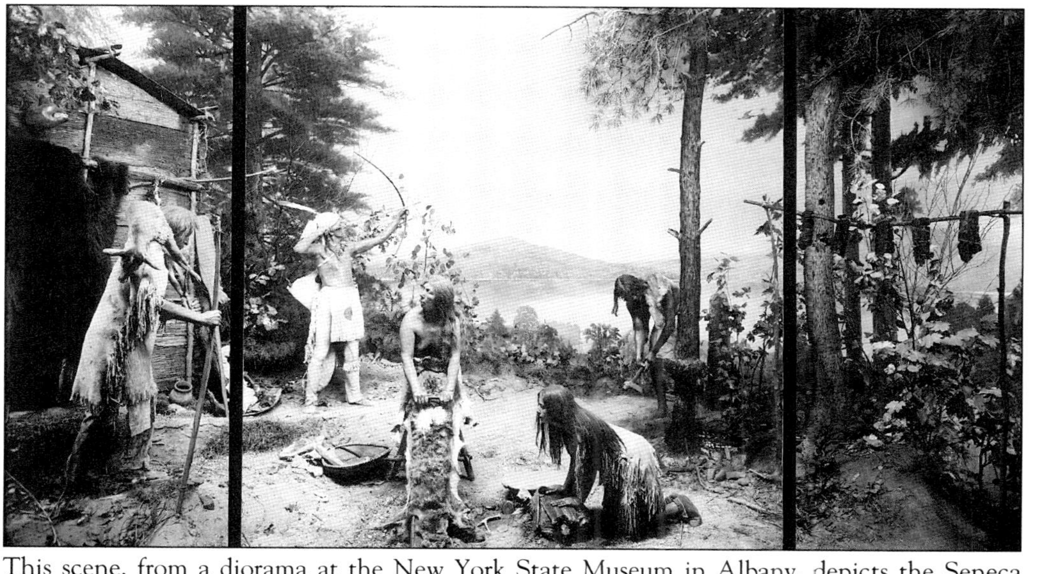

This scene, from a diorama at the New York State Museum in Albany, depicts the Seneca partaking in daily activities along the west side of Canandaigua Lake. Bare Hill, which is significant to the Seneca, can be seen in the distance.

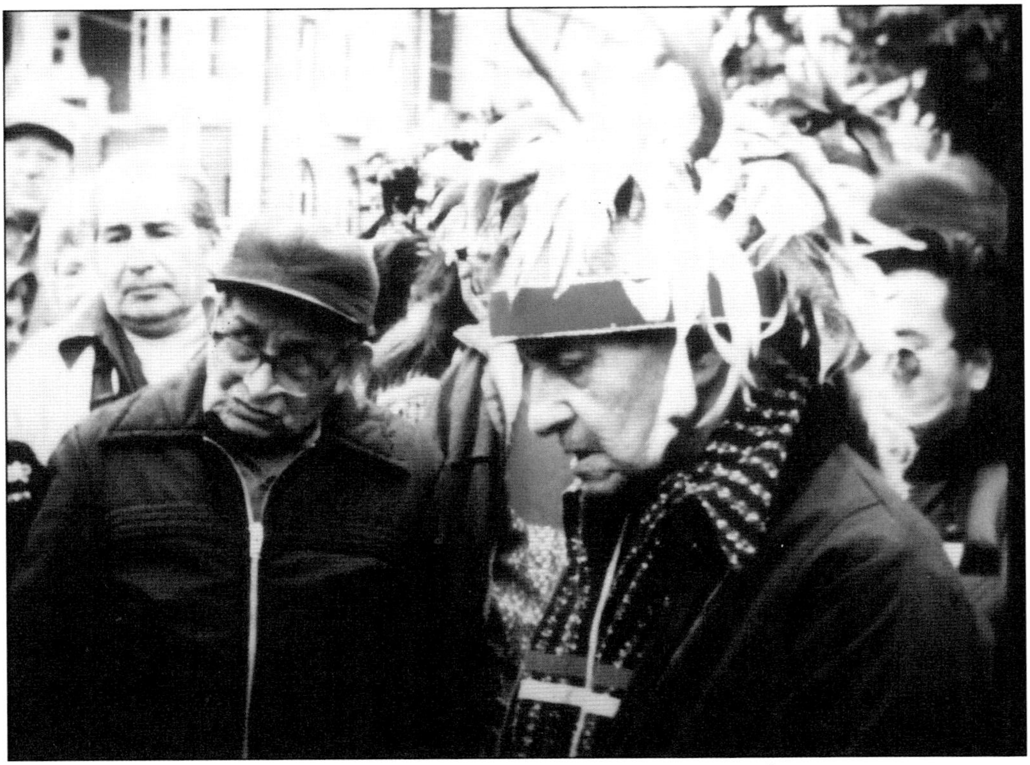

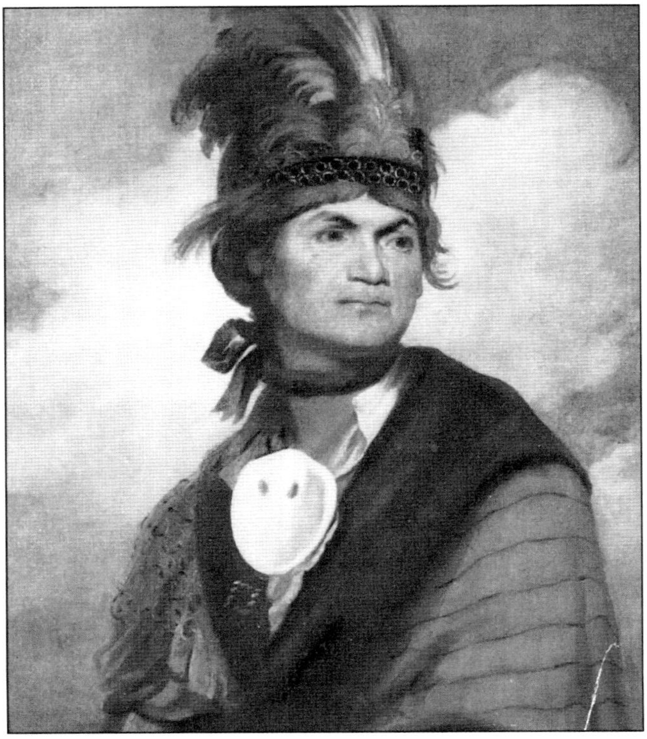

During the treaty ceremony of 1985, a white pine tree was planted. Shown are: Oren Lyons (Faithkeeper from Onondaga), Chief Corbett Sundown (Hawk Clan from Tonawanda), and Chief Leon Shenandoah (Eel Clan from Onondaga). Chief Shenandoa is wearing a Gus-To-Weh with deer antlers, indicating his high position within the six nations of Iroquois. (Photograph by Robert Gorall.)

This is a painted portrait of Chief Joseph Brant. Brant was a Mohawk Indian who befriended Englishman Sir William Johnson at the time of the American Revolution. Chief Brant was instrumental in persuading the Mohawks to side with the British during the Revolutionary War.

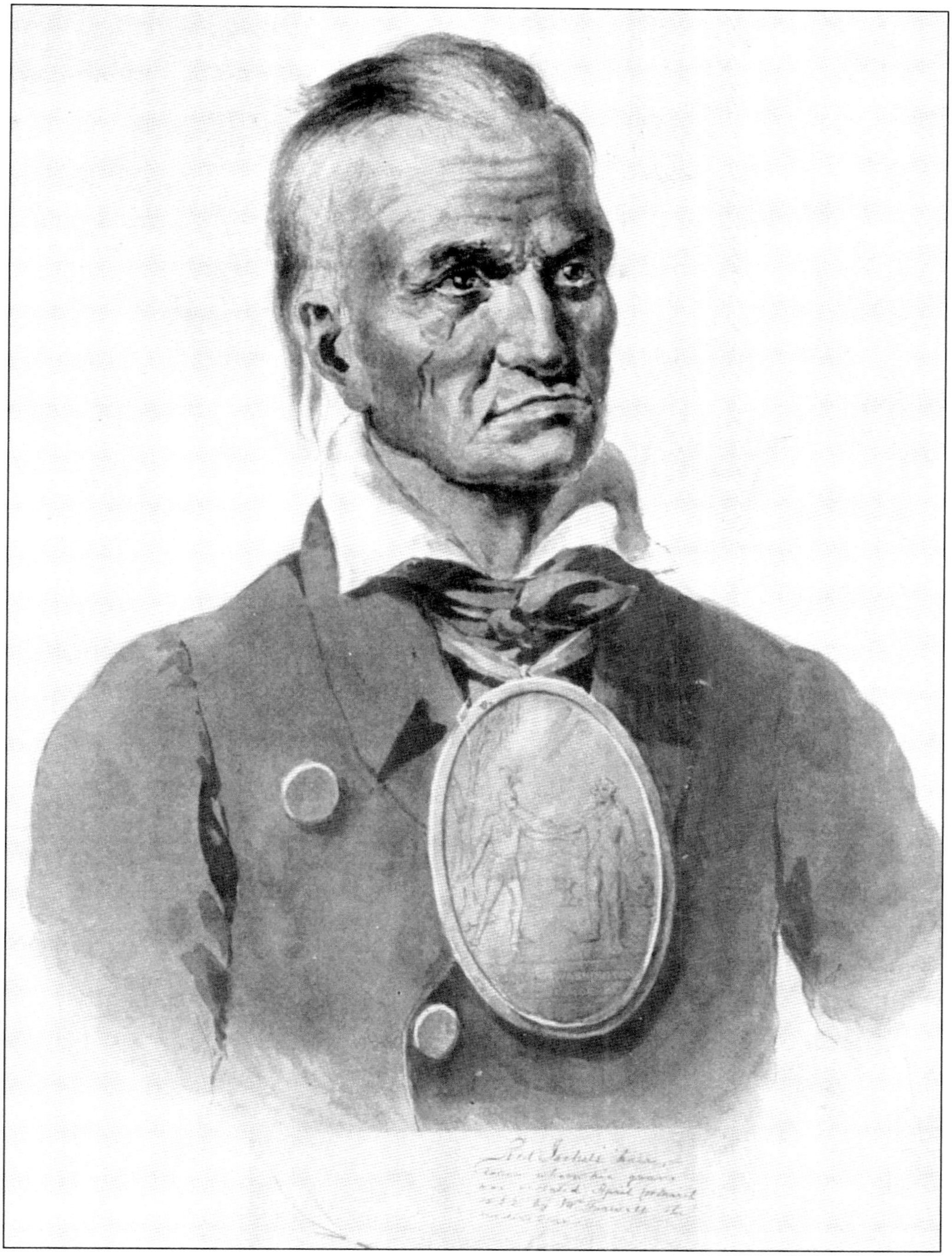

Red Jacket, a Seneca Indian from either Seneca Castle or Cayuga Lake, became a famous orator for the Iroquois. Originally named Sagoyewatha, he was quoted as saying, "I am an orator. I was born an orator." He was named Red Jacket based on his preference for wearing scarlet clothing. Medals were sometimes given to the leaders of the Iroquois by the U.S. government. The Peace Medallion around Red Jacket's neck was a gift from George Washington.

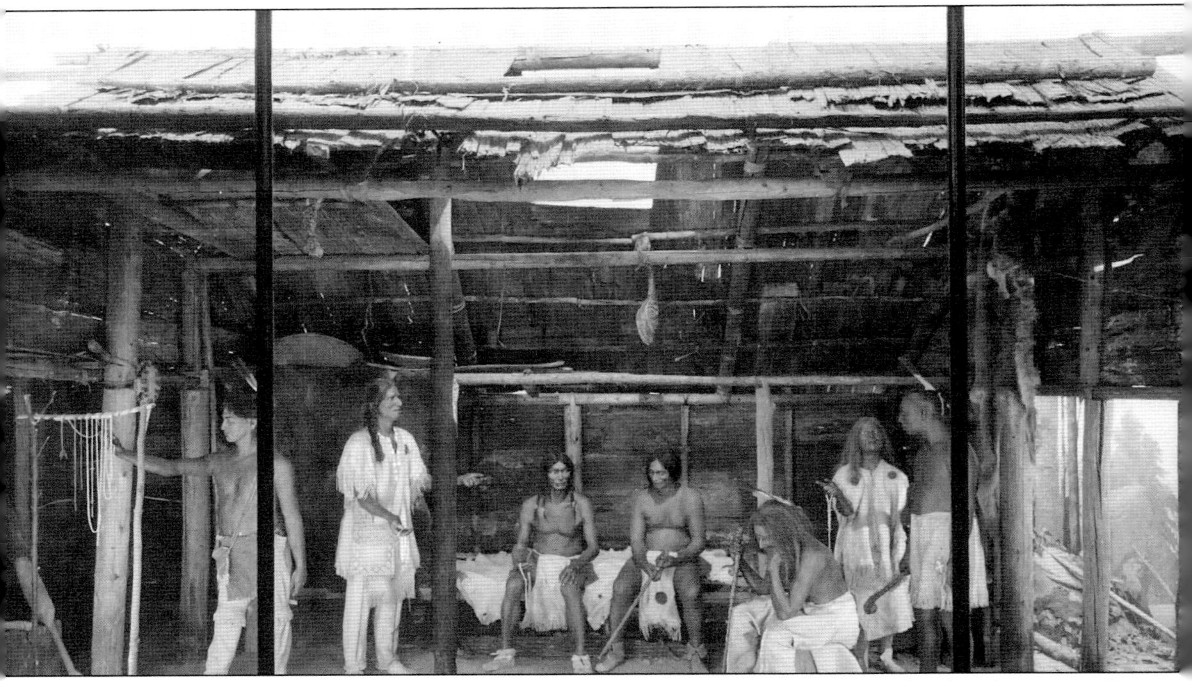

This Native American scene shows several interesting details. Iroquois lived in longhouses made of wood. Extended families lived in one house, sharing food and child-rearing responsibilities. Fires were built inside the home for cooking and warmth. Smoke from the fire would escape through an opening in the roof. Shelving along the walls stored dried foods and tools. Tools were fashioned from bone, wood, and stone. Beds lined the walls alongside the shelving. Animal hides provided warmth during the cold winters.

Two

RECREATION

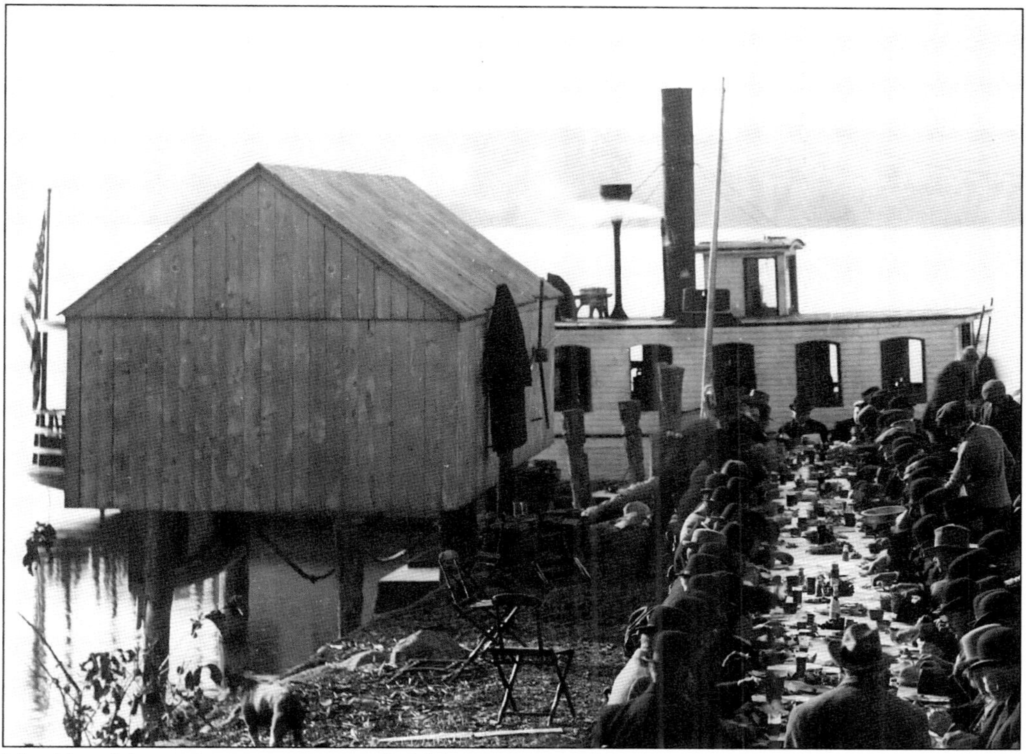

The Republican Party picnic was held by Senator John Raines on the Lincoln property in October 1909. Born in Canandaigua in 1840, Raines served in the Civil War and practiced law in Geneva. He later moved to Canandaigua, residing at 116 Gorham Street—the well-known Octagon House. He died in 1909.

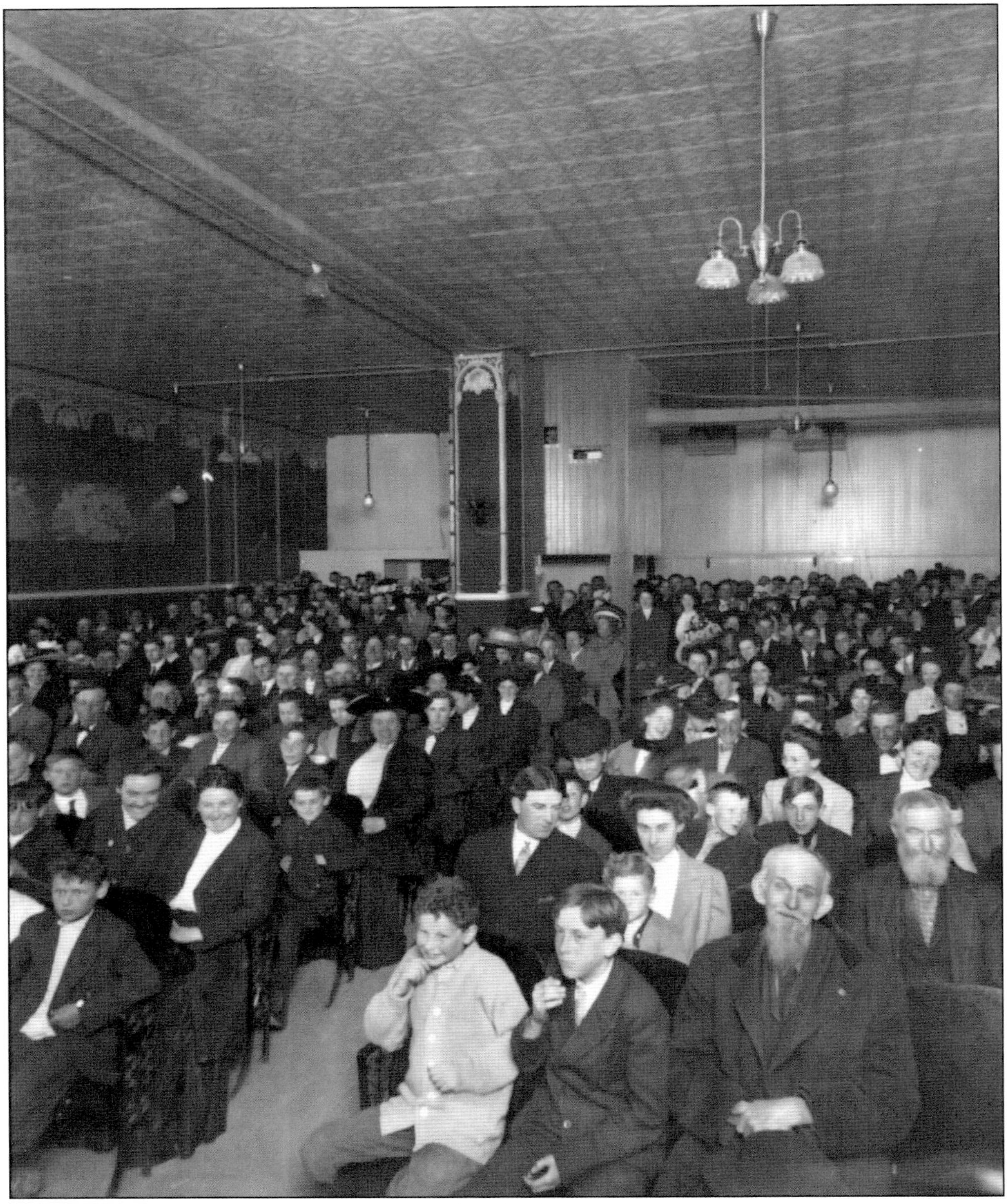

People await a motion picture at the Hubbell Block's Bijou Theater. Notice the projection booth in the back of the theater. (Photograph taken by Crandall Studios in Canandaigua.)

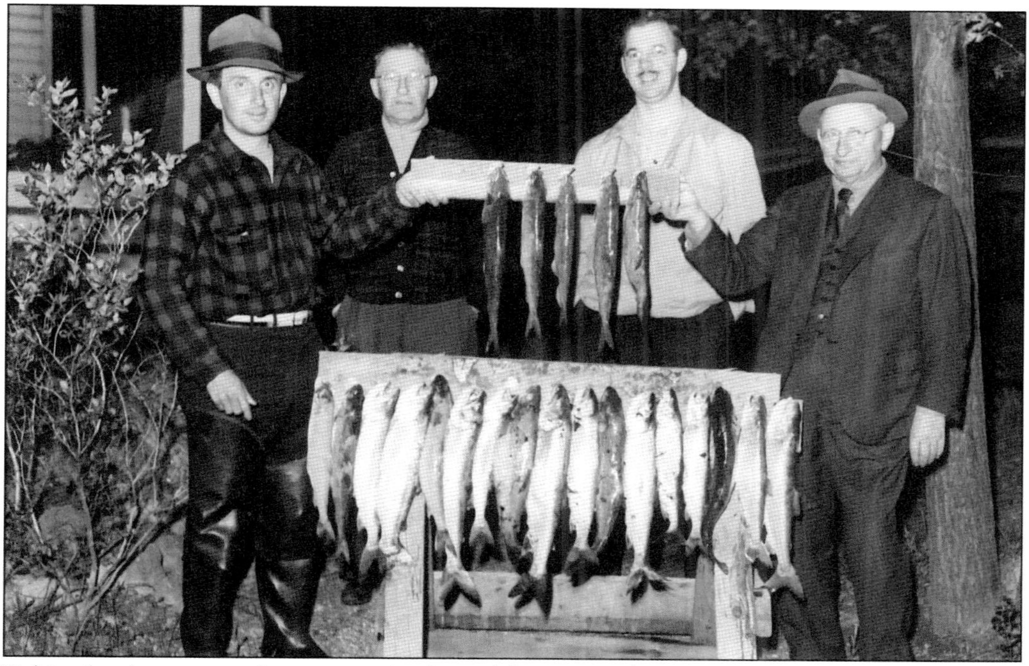

Fishing has been a popular sport in the finger lakes region for a long time. Pictured here in May 1945 are, from left to right: G. Henry Boyce (the well-known area photographer), George L. Boyce, an unknown gentleman, and Dr. Simpson.

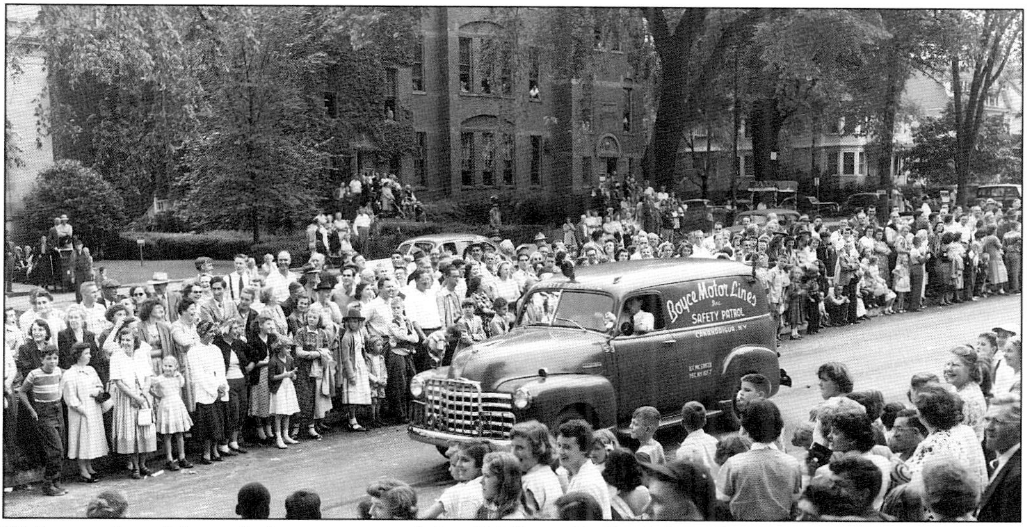

This parade celebrated the opening of the "Million Dollar Main Street" on August 18, 1950. The project improved the downtown district by widening and paving the formerly brick street. The Union Free School can be seen in the background. The parade opened with a speech by Bertram D. Tallamy, state superintendent of public works, who claimed Main Street as a highway of peace: "Hitler built great highways as a means to fight war. We are developing highways for the social and economic benefit of everyone." Over 30,000 people attended the spectacle, which included a ribbon cutting by Mayor Urstadt, forty floats, sixteen marching bands, water sports, a street dance, and a fireworks display.

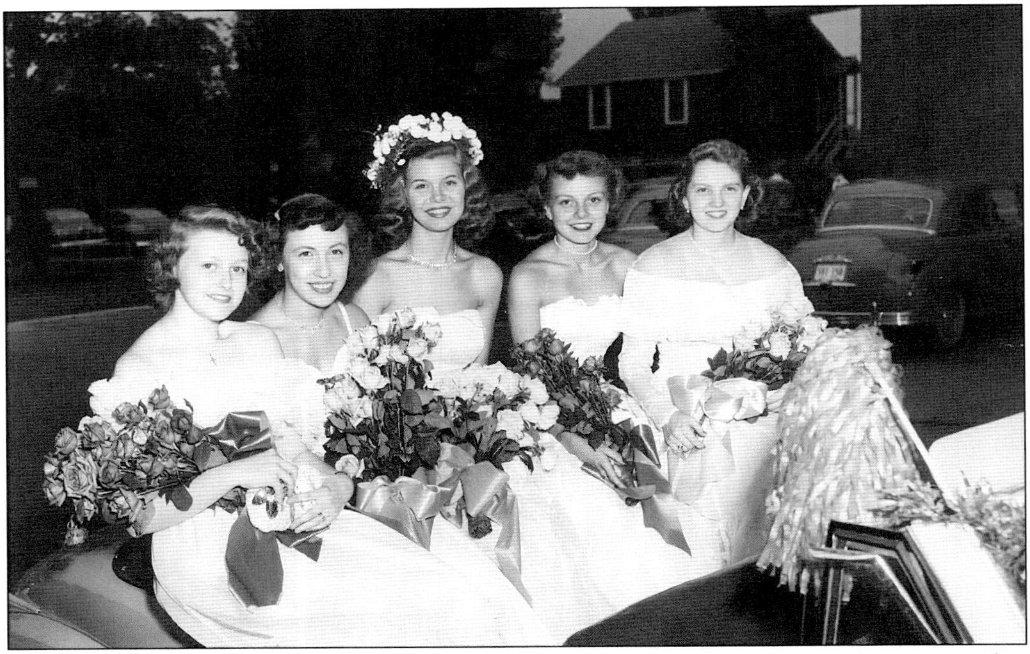

The 1950 opening of Main Street also included the crowning of the Queen of the Finger Lakes and her court. Shown, from left to right, are: Dorothy Mumerow, Norma Ross, Queen Katy Caulkins (known then as Kathleen Van Voohren), Janet Beyea, and Janet McCarthy.

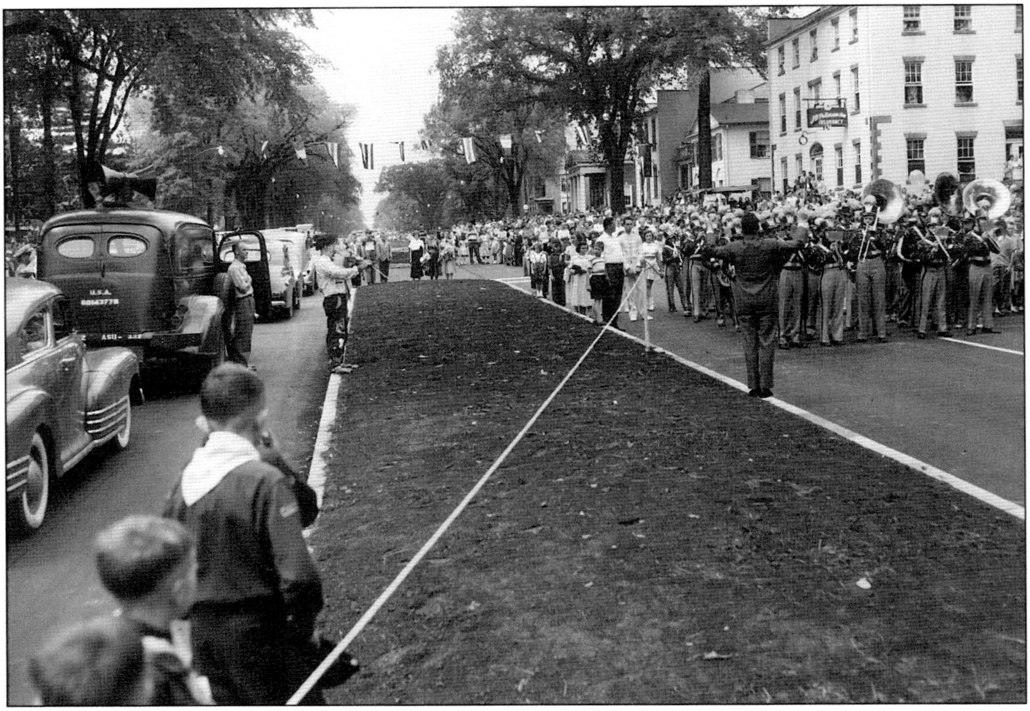

Main Street's opening day parade headed south on Main Street using the eastern two lanes. Here, the Canandaigua Marching Band stops in front of the reviewing stand for judging.

People are gathered on the south lawn of the Granger Place School for an unknown ceremony. Plays were often given in this outdoor setting.

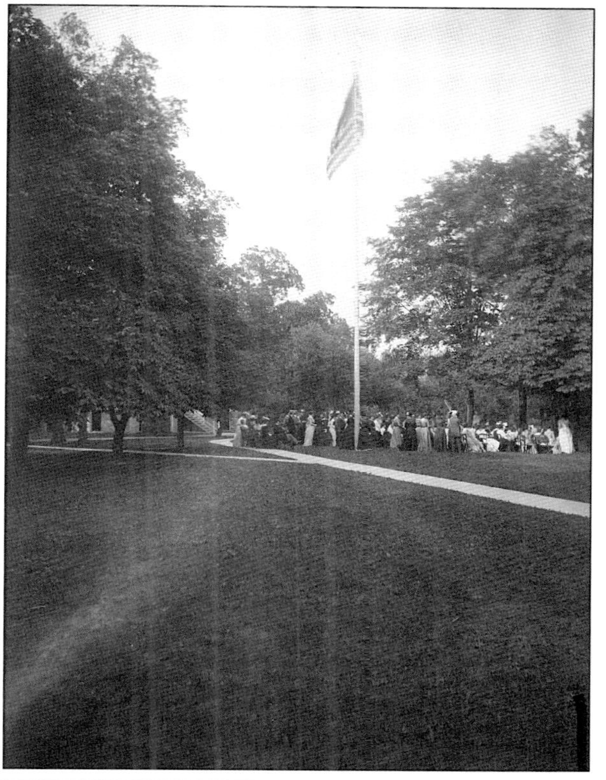

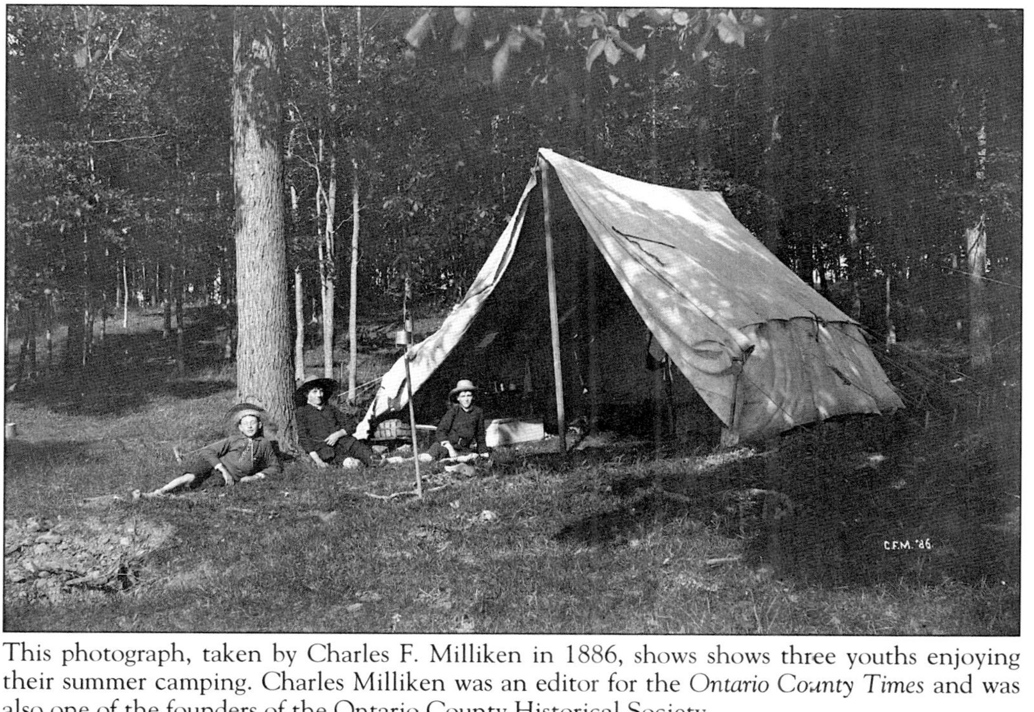

This photograph, taken by Charles F. Milliken in 1886, shows shows three youths enjoying their summer camping. Charles Milliken was an editor for the *Ontario County Times* and was also one of the founders of the Ontario County Historical Society.

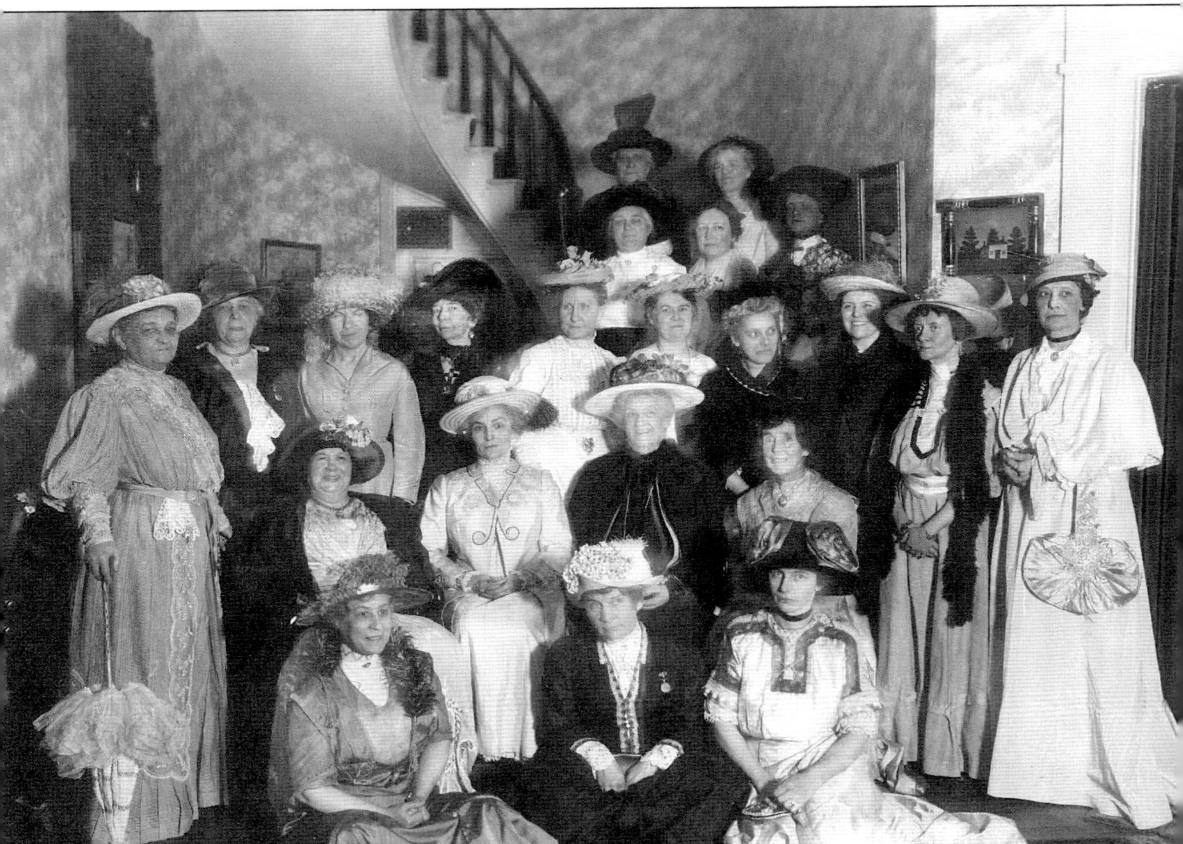

Women's clubs have always been popular in Canandaigua. The Current Events Club is still active today. Among those listed as members are the McKechnies, owners of a local brewery and bank. In this image, taken January 29, 1934, the women are dressed in period costumes. Listed on the back of the photograph are: Minnie Selover, Eloise DePew, Anna McKechnie, Mrs. Herbert Gaylord, Carrie Campbell, Helen Adams, Jessie Burt, Mrs. Belle Croucher, Mrs. Gertrude Masten, Mary Holmes, May Hamlin, Edith Johnson, Lilliam Baines, Blanche Stetson, Mary Sutherland, Mrs. William Lewis, Alice L. Anderson, Bertha Burgess, Gratia Harrall, Mrs. Lois Beeman, and Mrs. Gertrude McKechnie.

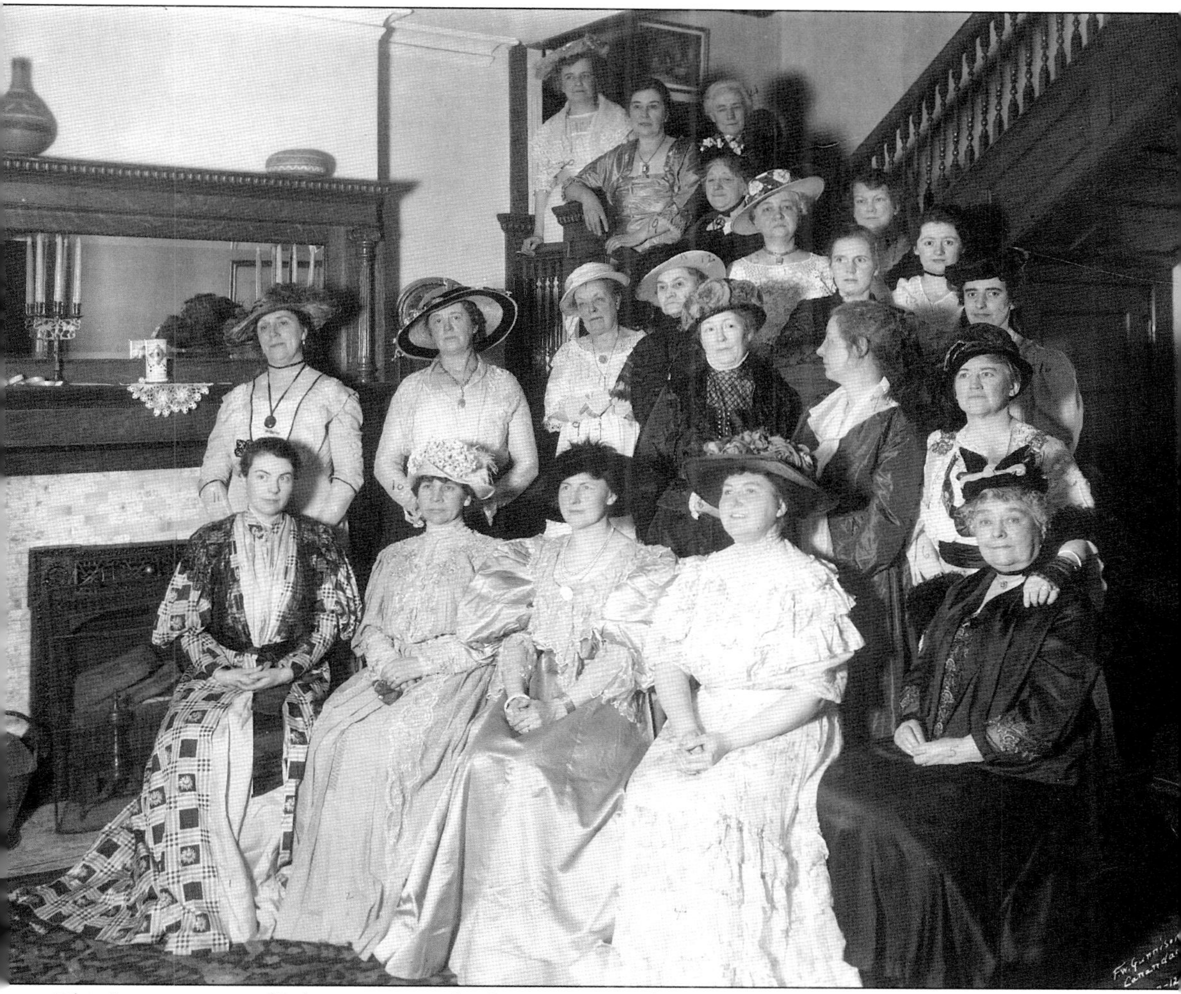

This Interrogation Club meeting took place on December 12, 1934. The club was founded in 1896 to promote intellectual improvement and sociability among its members. Its motto is: "Who asks, errs not." These ladies are also dressed in period costumes. Listed as members are: Mrs. Clifford Strait, Mrs. James Green, Mrs. Rodney Pease, Mrs. Earle Hutton, Mrs. Edwin Gardner, Mrs. Gordon Lewis, Mrs. A.W. Armstrong, Mrs. Frank E. Fisk, Mrs. Louis Browne, Mrs. Theodore Hugo, Mrs. Gooding Packard, Mrs. F.D. Weeks, Mrs. John Bohlmann, Mrs. Horace Fitch, Mrs. Philip H. Sisson, and Mrs. Richard Conyne.

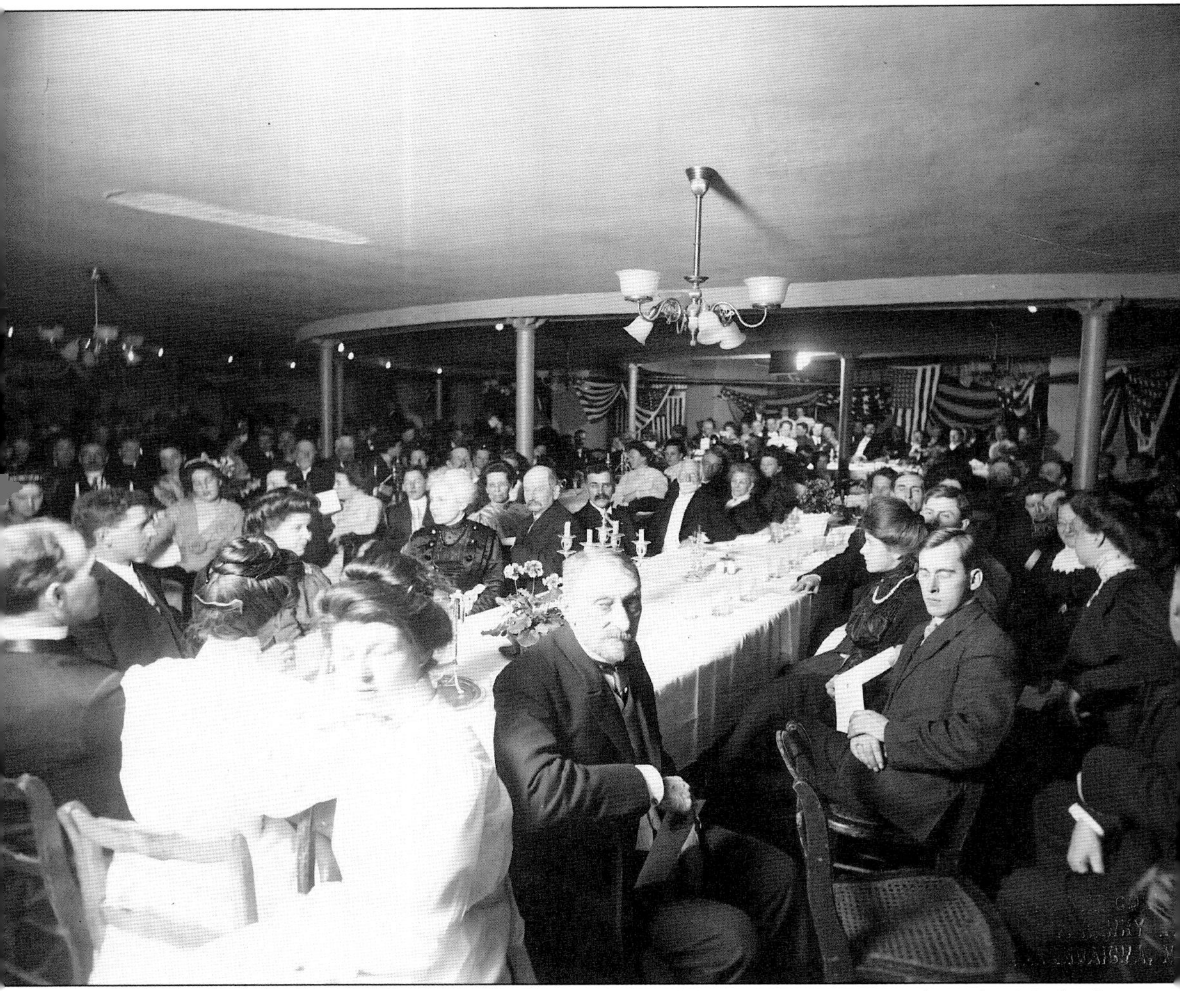

A large group assembles for a political dinner (possibly for Senator Raines) at the Methodist church. Notice the beautiful table settings and linens used.

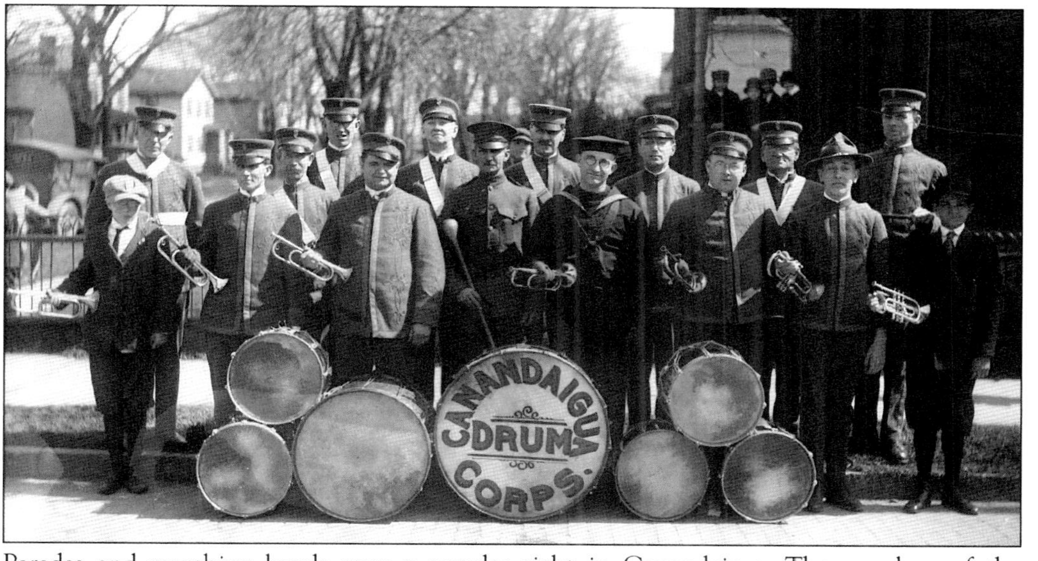

Parades and marching bands were a popular sight in Canandaigua. The members of the Canandaigua Drum Corps posed with their instruments and fine uniforms in April 1919, at the corner of Beeman and Center Streets.

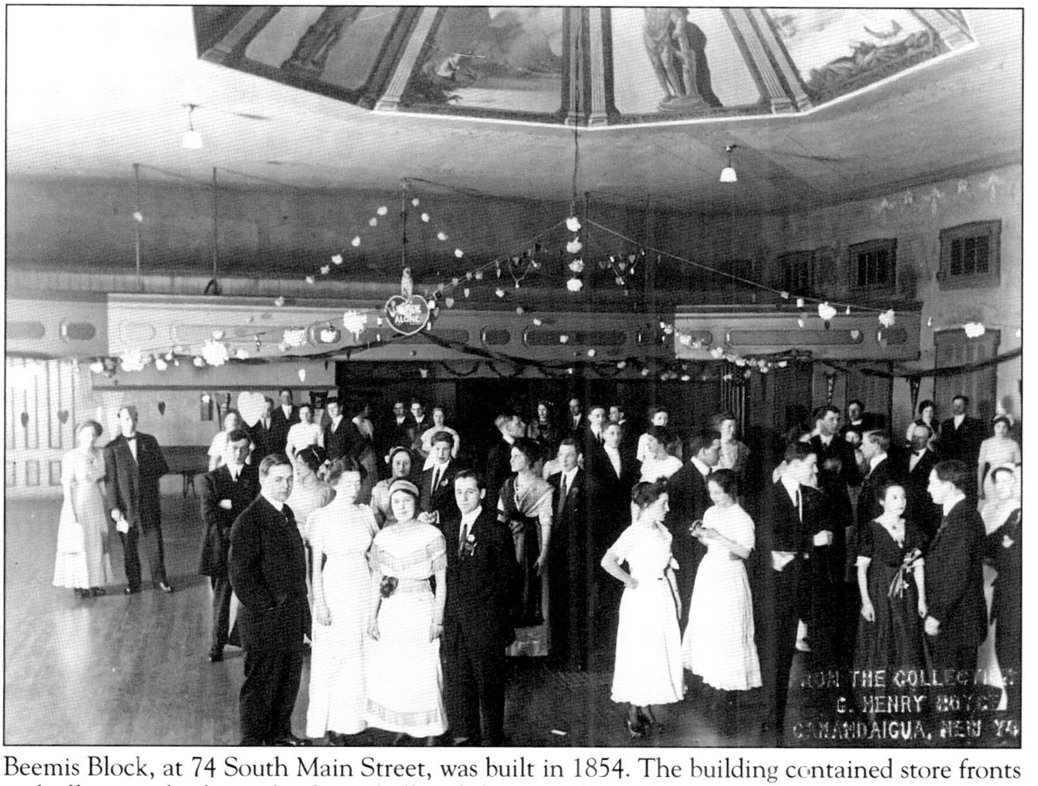

Beemis Block, at 74 South Main Street, was built in 1854. The building contained store fronts and offices, and it housed a dance hall and theater. The ceiling of the third-floor dance hall is domed and painted with twelve different scenes. The paintings remain intact today, but the dance hall is in a state of disrepair.

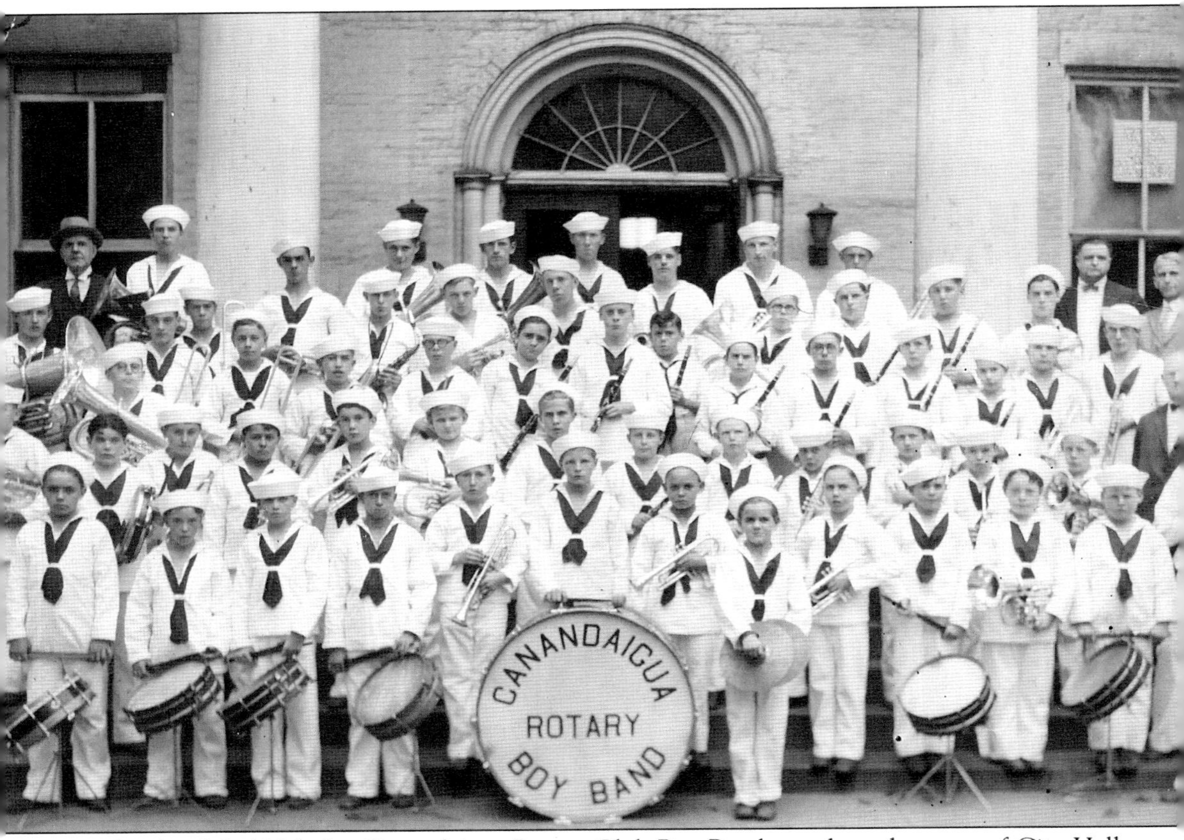

On April 7, 1926, the Canandaigua Rotary Club Boy Band posed on the steps of City Hall, dressed in their sailor-like uniforms. Members included: John Collins, Robert Wright, Fred Clapp, R.M. Dorin, Ed Bates, Jack Phalen, Roswell Wheeler, Clark Holcomb, Bud Dawson, James Ciocci, Stewart Much, William Keyes, Peter Reed, John Olschewoke, Virgil Goff, Edmund Kallina, Howard VanAuken, Bill Schreck, Leo Westley, William Searles, Robert Case, Jas. Reed, Clarence Stanley, Hollis Murphy, Earl Clausen, Theo Avery, Burton Stanley, Gordon Holcombr Jr., Bob Eisiline, Homer Fiero, Charles Tuttle, Gus Milton, George Packard, Ed Herendeen, Gene Baker, Everett Pierce, Homer Combs, Leland Holcomb, Edgar Fisk, Jas McClure, Kenneth Lord, Jackie Butler, Jas Dudley, Hugh Knapp, Carl McVane, John McCabe, Eugen Masten, Dave Wilson, Jack Masten, and John Jucque.

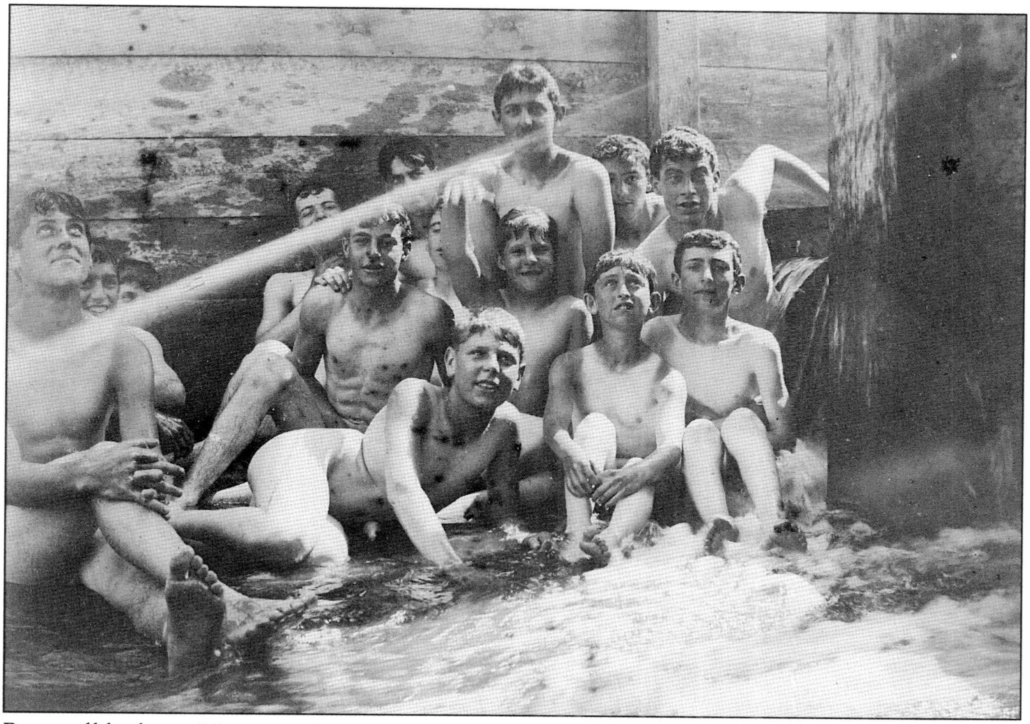

Boys will be boys. "A souvenir of our trip to the Outlet at Canandaigua Lake," wrote Clarence Bernheimer after partaking in the taxidermy class picnic on August 4, 1897.

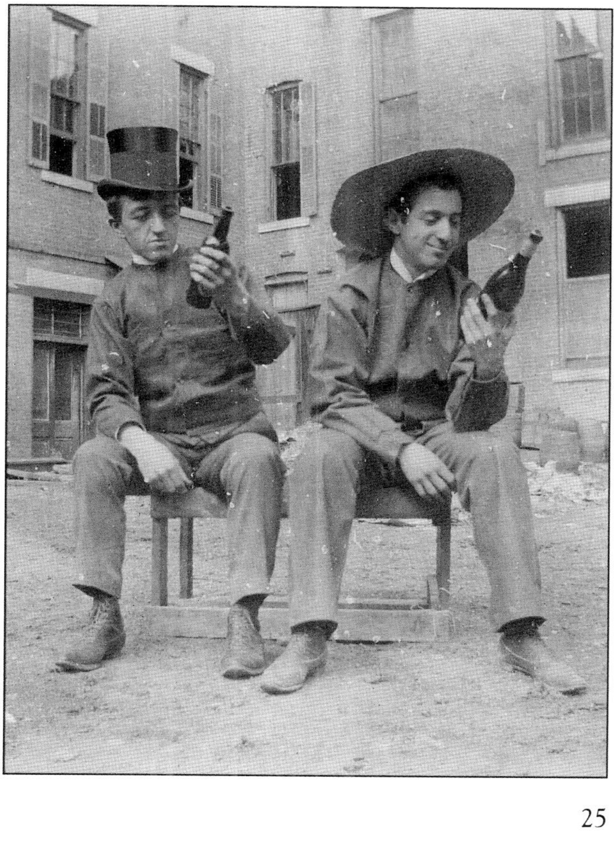

Henry Weisenbeck and an unidentified friend enjoy a sip behind the Weisenbeck and Son clothing and furniture store. The store, started by the family in the 1870s, featured men's and boys' clothing as well as hats and furnishing goods. It was located at 166 South Main Street in what was described as a spacious double store.

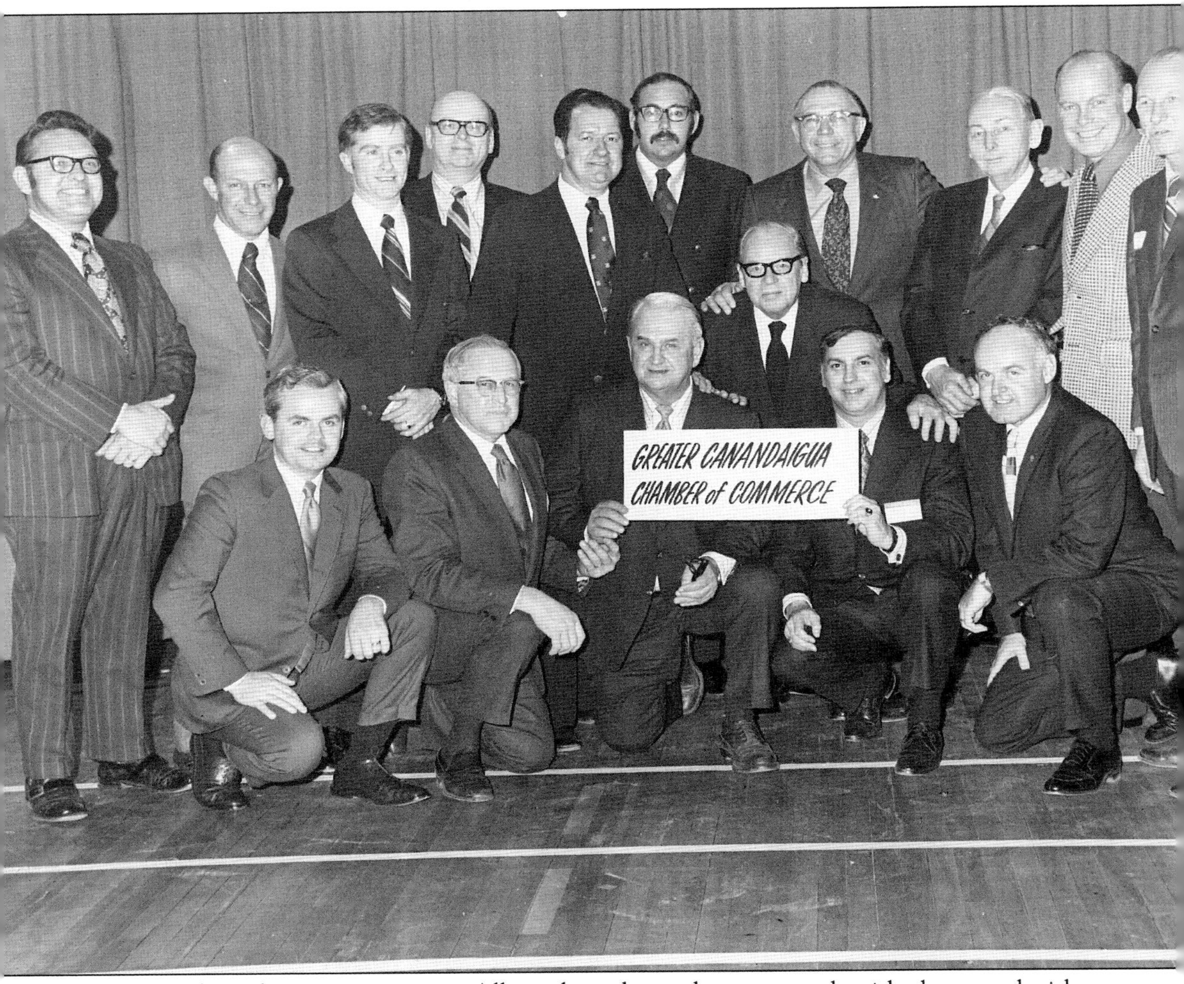

A chamber of commerce trip to Albany brought students to speak with the state legislators. Pictured are, from left to right: (front row) James Dorn, Burral Case, William Mitchel, Bernard Hagerman, Jim Emery, and Robert Craugh; (back row) unknown, Cy Moranda, Bruce Kennedy, Ted Avery, Robert Quigley, Richard Boyce, Louis Kieswetter, unknown, Ted Shepard, and unknown.

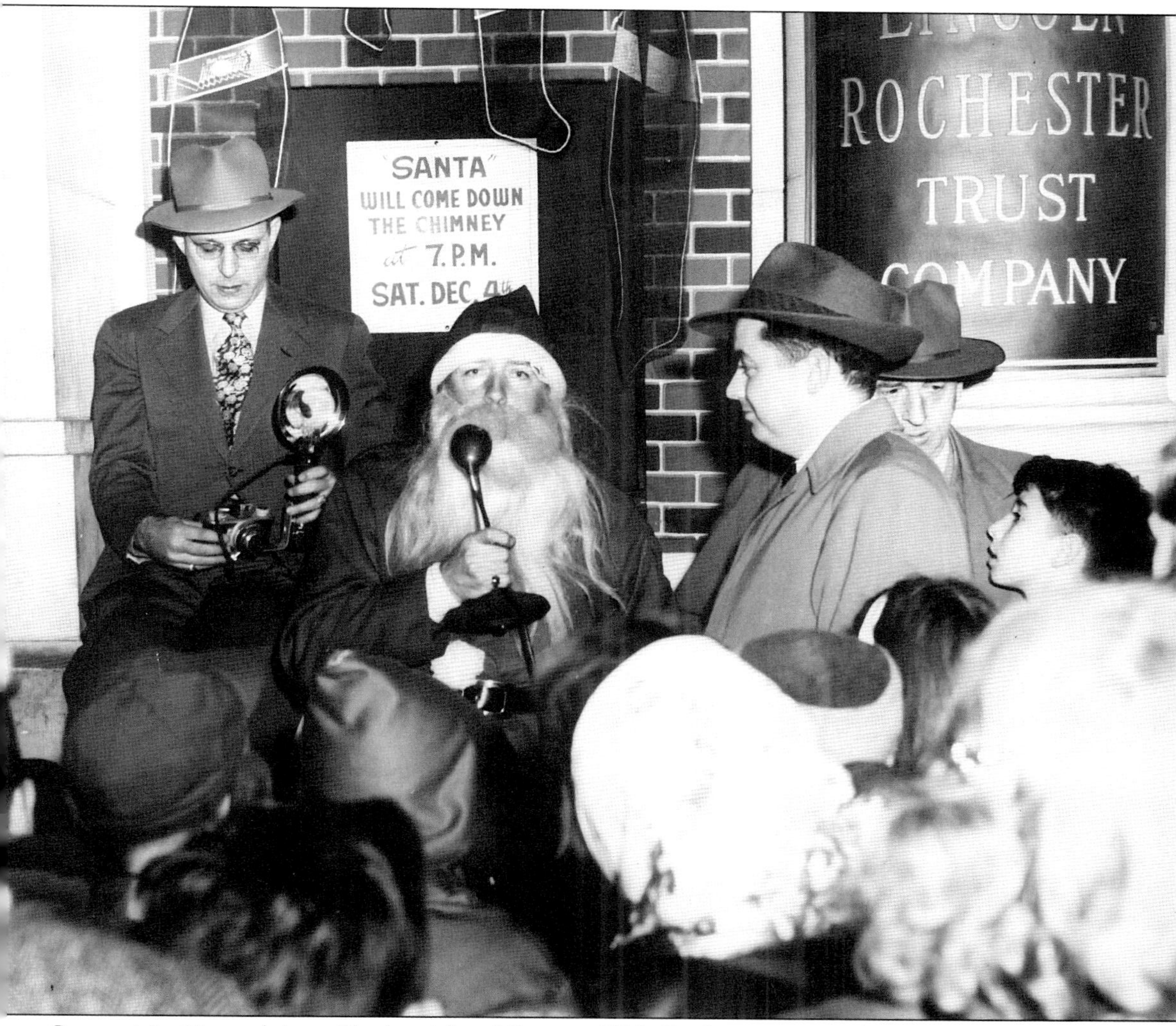

Santa visits Canandaigua. To the right of Santa is Walt Benham, mayor of Canandaigua from 1956 to 1957, greeting children in front of the Lincoln Rochester Trust Company at 130 South Main Street. Burral Case is to the left of Santa, ready to capture a magical moment between Santa and a child.

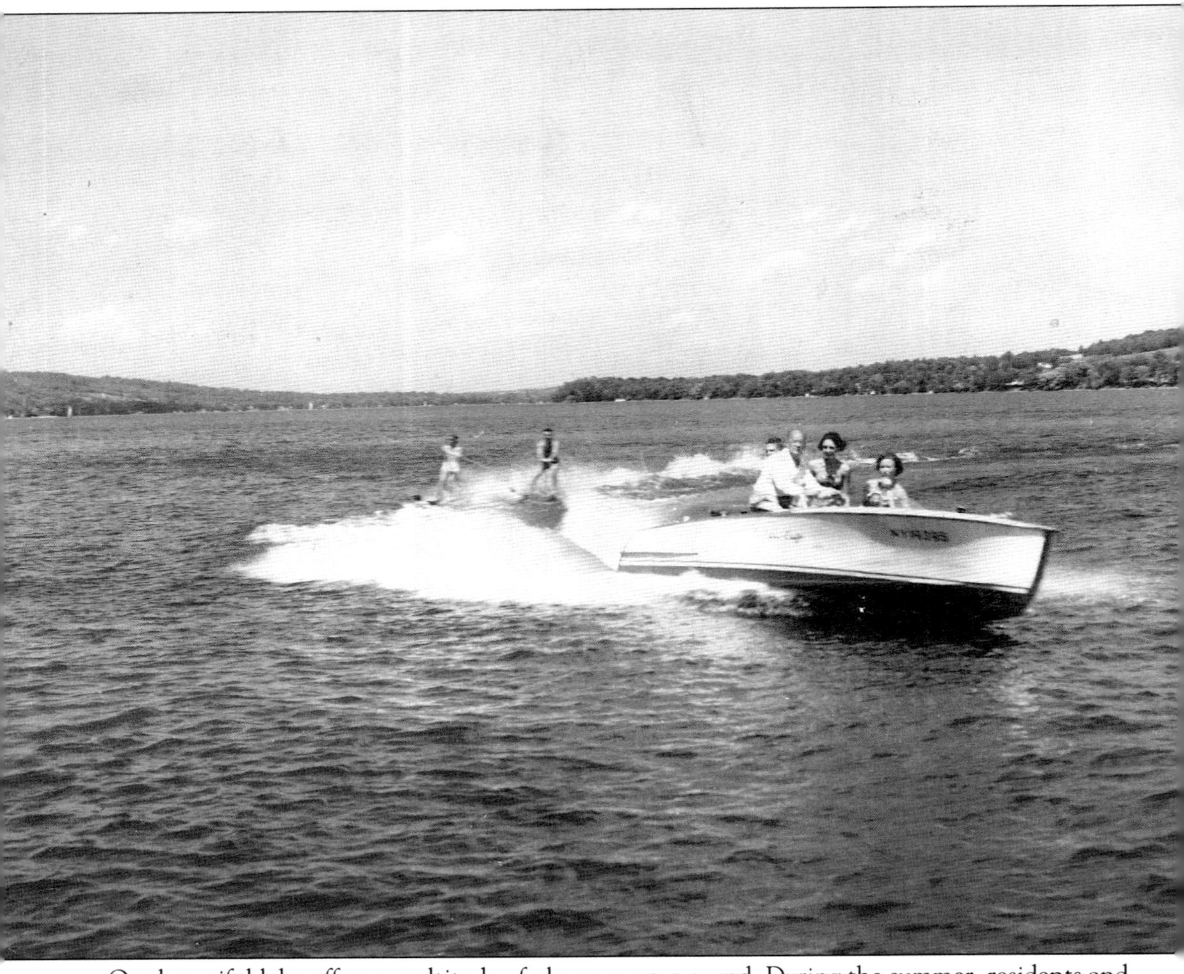

Our beautiful lake offers a multitude of pleasures year-round. During the summer, residents and visitors enjoy swimming, fishing, and boating. Here is one of the Shepard twins (is it Ted or Dick?) enjoying a beautiful day on the lake.

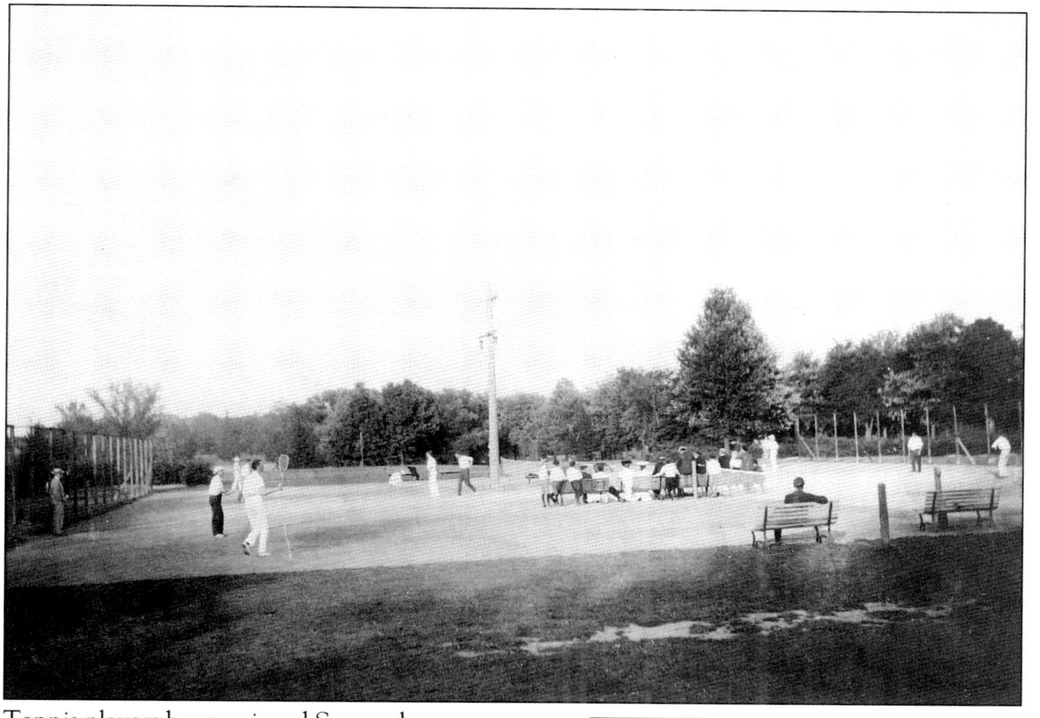

Tennis players have enjoyed Sonnenberg Playground for many years. The playground opened around 1903 for the benefit of the community's children, and was a gift from area philanthropist Mary Thompson. Notice the formal attire worn by the players.

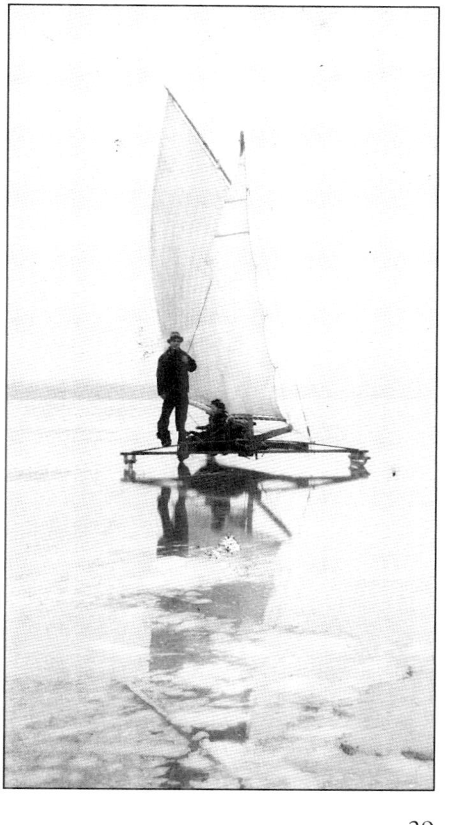

Hardy individuals enjoy braving the cold as they iceboat and fish on the lake during winter. The ice looks as if it is melting on the surface.

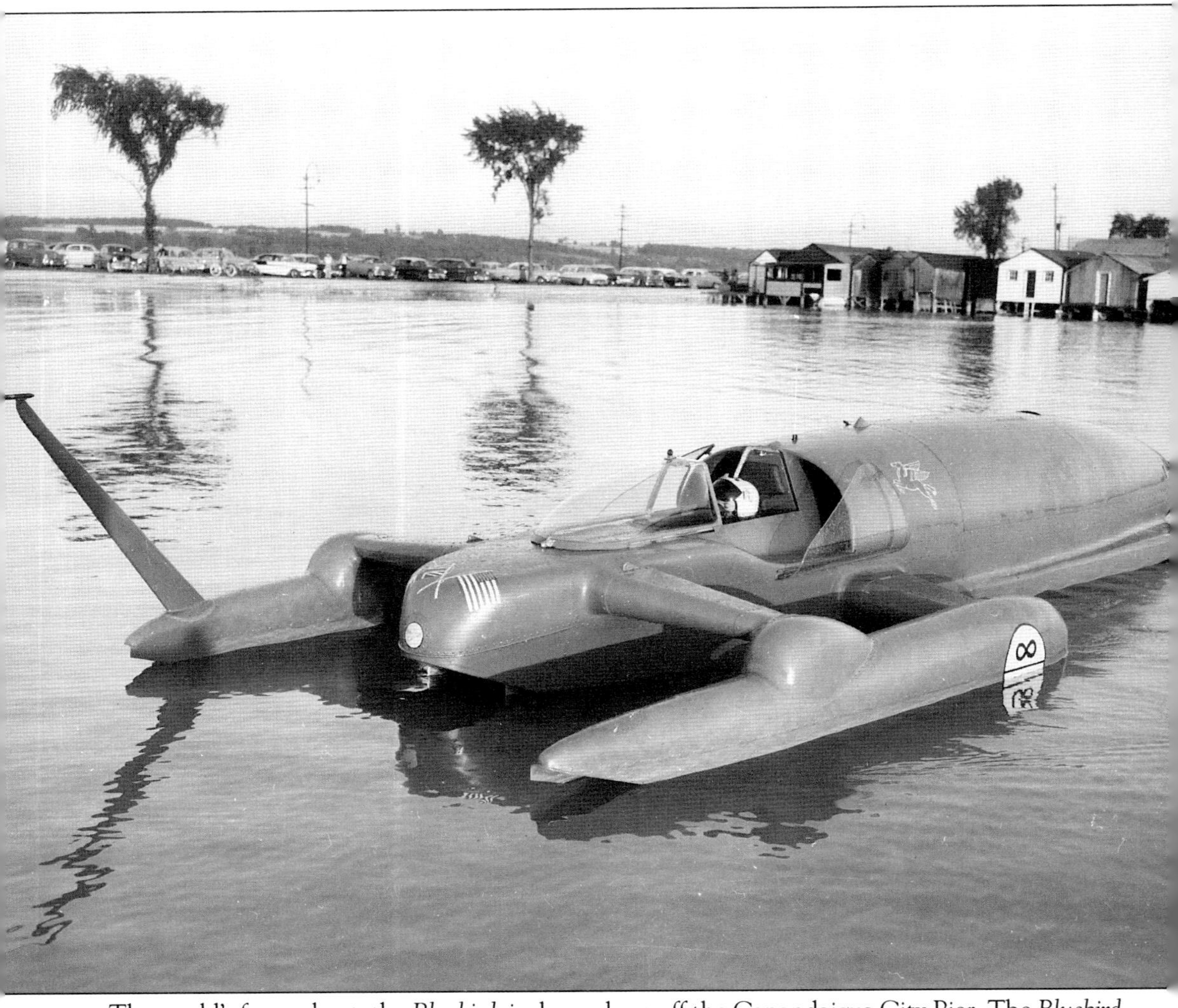

The world's fastest boat, the *Bluebird*, is shown here off the Canandaigua City Pier. The *Bluebird* was a jet-powered hydroplane that attempted to break its own record of 225.63 mph one summer in Canandaigua. Barely visible in the cockpit is England's Donald Malcolm Campbell, preparing for an assault on his record. The bar projecting from the *Bluebird's* right float is Campell's air-speed indicator. The *Bluebird* was unsuccessful in attaining its speed goal, however, leaving many in the community disappointed. Campbell later died in a boat explosion in Europe.

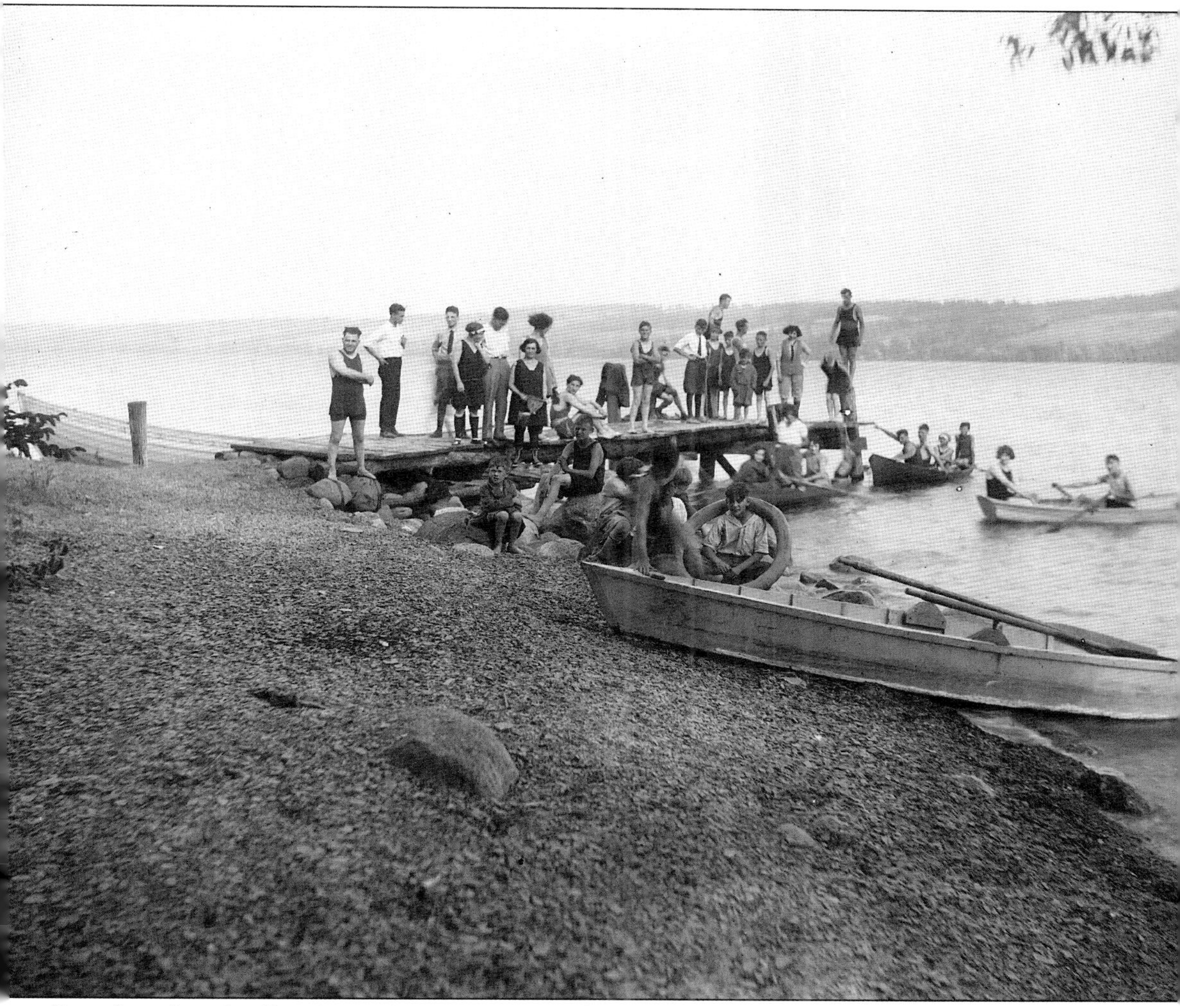
Friends gathered at Boy Scout Camp Tarion, on the east side of the lake, in August 1927.

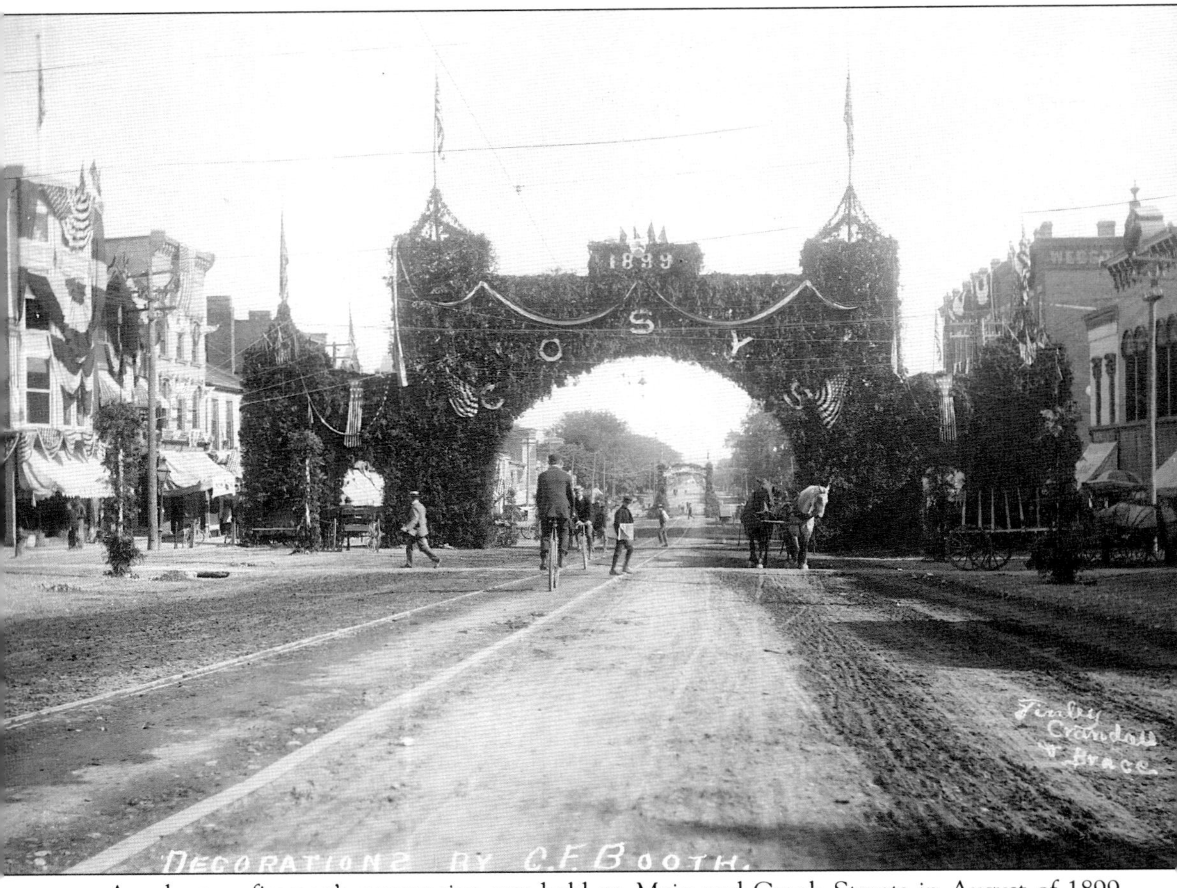

A volunteer firemen's convention was held on Main and Coach Streets in August of 1899. Notice the the tall bicycle rolling down Main Street, as well as the banners beautifully hung on the buildings. At this time the street was not yet paved. The initials "C.O.S.Y.S." stand for Chemung, Ontario, Schuyler, Yates, and Seneca Counties. The photograph is signed "Crandall" in the lower right-hand corner.

Three

WEATHER AND DISASTERS

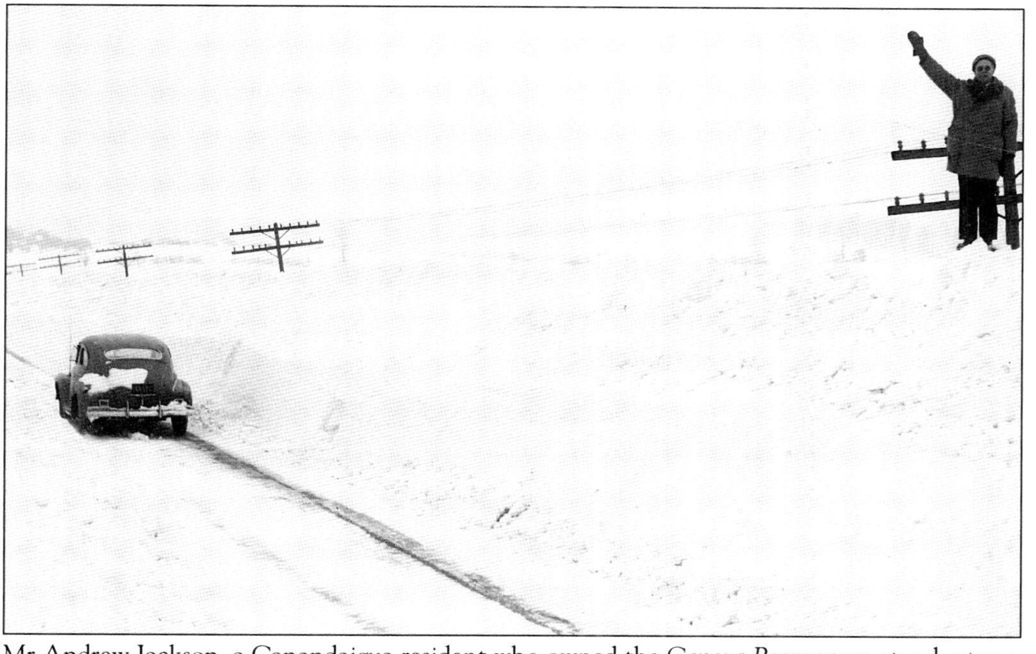

Mr Andrew Jackson, a Canandaigua resident who owned the *Geneva Pennysaver*, stands atop a snowbank on Freshour Road. The snow nearly reached the tops of the telephone poles during the winter of 1945.

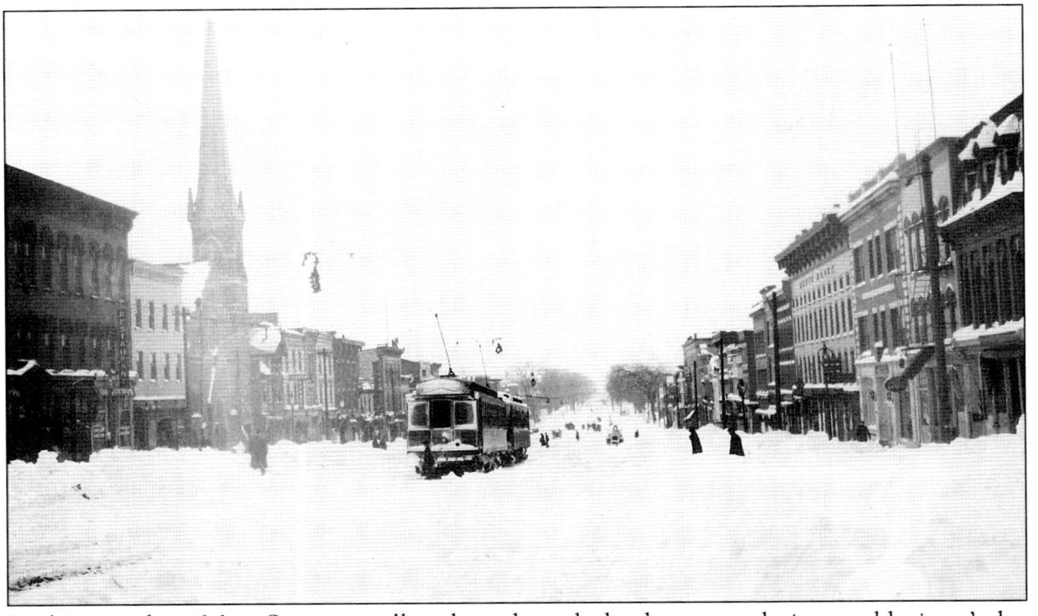

Looking south on Main Street, a trolley plows through the deep snow during a cold winter's day in 1925. The tall steeple on the east side of Main Street belonged to the Baptist church, which later burned. Note the people crossing the street.

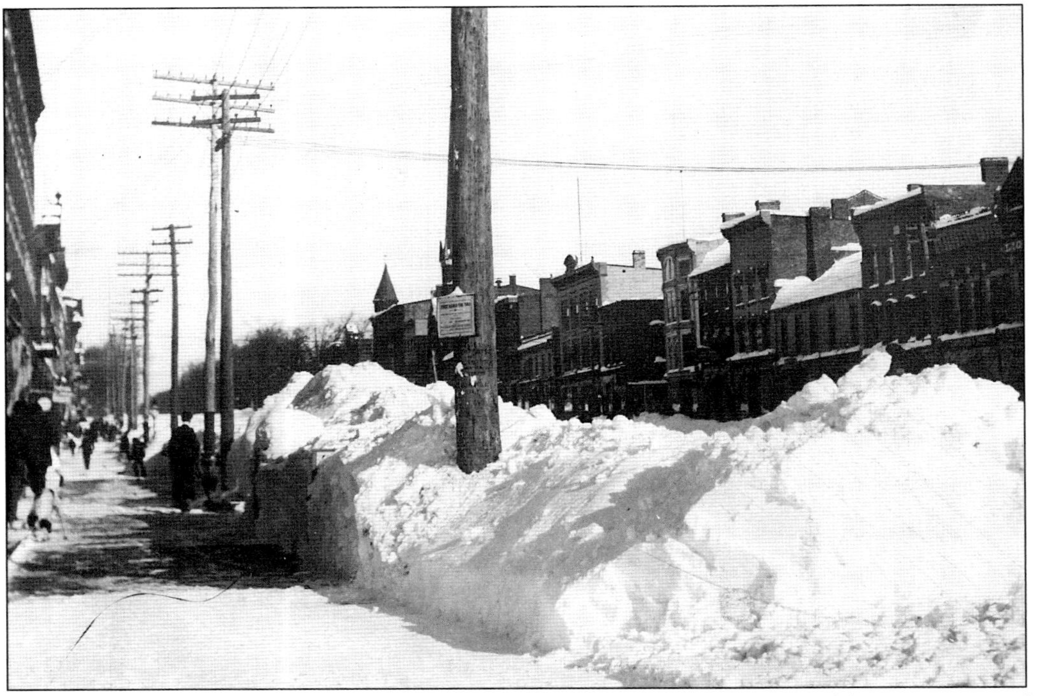

Dated "Winter of 1888" on the back of the photograph, this storm produced huge amounts of snowfall in Canandaigua. Sidewalks were narrow paths. Merchants did not have modern-day conveniences such as snow blowers to clear their entryways. Note the spire of the McKechnie Bank in the distance.

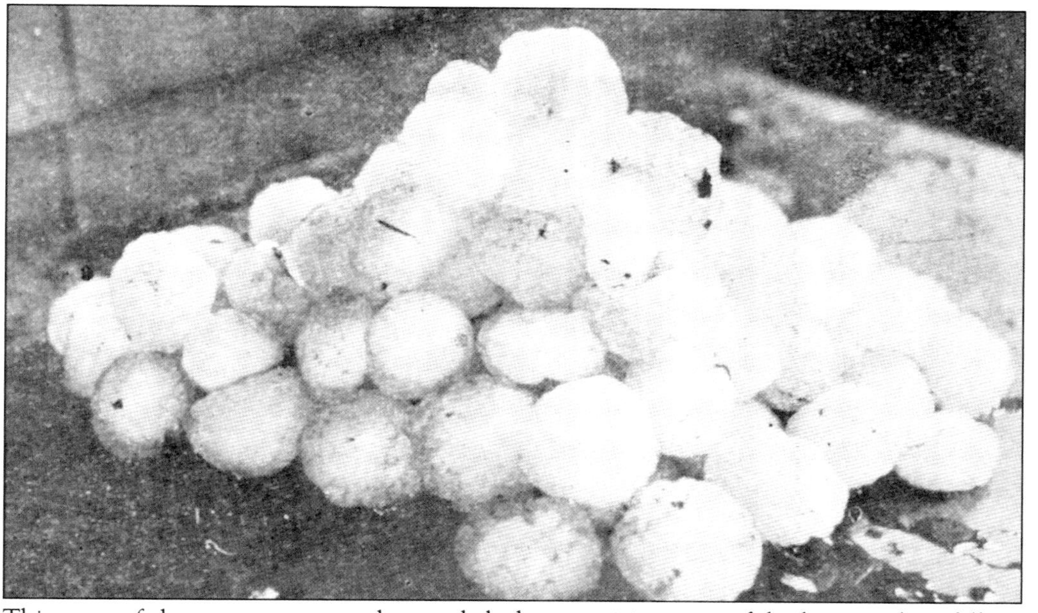

This turn-of-the-century postcard recorded the surprising size of hailstones that fell in Canandaigua on June 10, 1906. Stones were recorded as being 9 to 11 inches in diameter. The newspaper reported that some stones reached 6 to 7 inches in diameter, while "some were larger than hen's eggs." Damage from the storm reached into the hundreds of thousands of dollars. To the west of the village of Canandaigua where the storm was more severe, cattle, horses, and sheep were killed in the fields. "Dead songsters covered the parks and streets." Crops were destroyed, and many of the churches' stained-glass windows were damaged, as well as the greenhouses at Sonnenberg. In some areas, hailstones reached a depth of 2 feet.

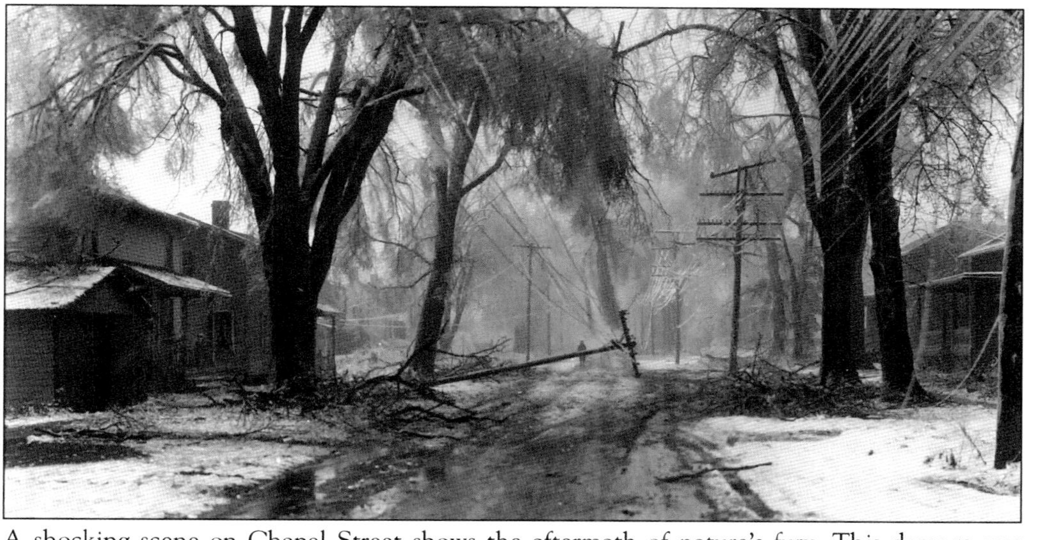

A shocking scene on Chapel Street shows the aftermath of nature's fury. This damage was caused when an ice storm hit Canandaigua on March 18, 1936, knocking out communications and power. The Webster Hotel on Main Street advertised in the *W.H. Hawley Pennysaver*, "If you are without heat drop in the Web." A similar ice storm hit Canandaigua fifty-five years later in March of 1991.

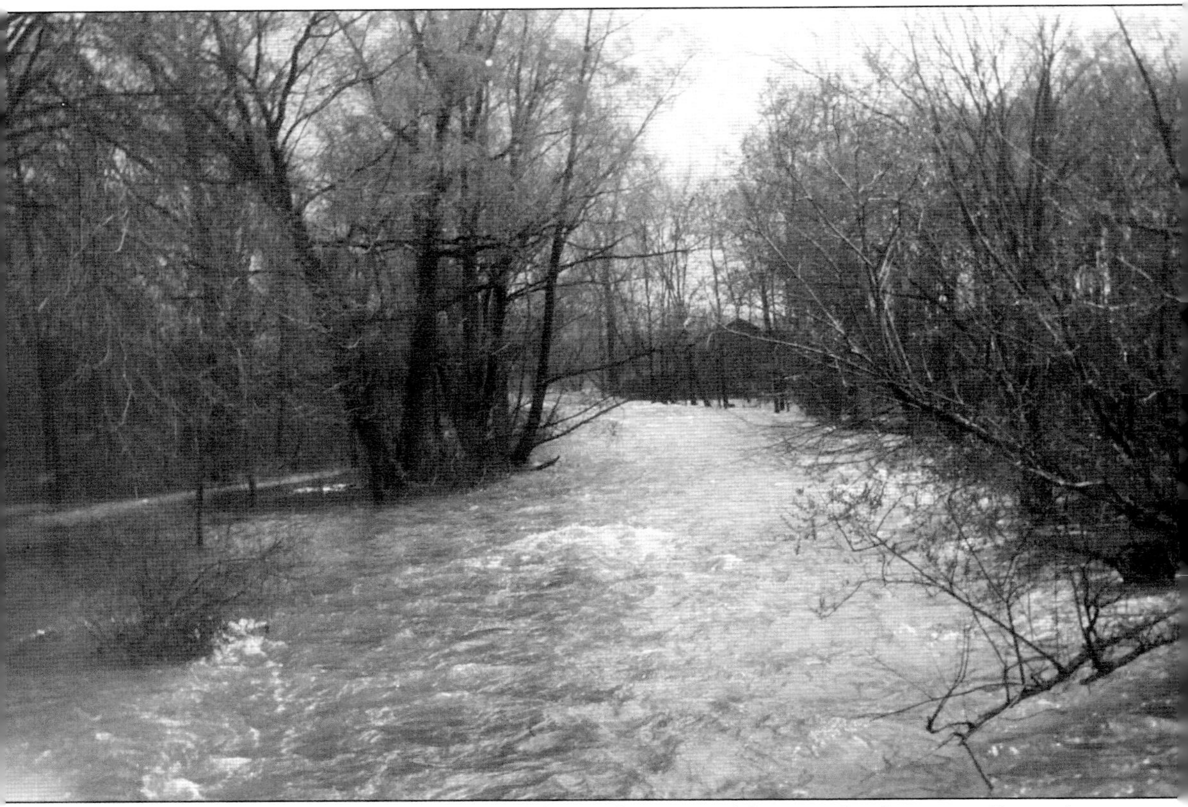

The Canandaigua Outlet serves as the lake's only source of drainage for the entire Canandaigua watershed basin. Each spring the Canandaigua Outlet is subject to flooding as winter snow and ice melt and fill the lake. Flood control gates at the entrance of the outlet on Lakeshore Drive control the lake level by releasing water into the outlet. This undated photograph shows a common spring scene.

The Smith Brothers' Mill was once located on Mill Street in Canandaigua. Notice the burlap sacks filled with grain on the sleighs. The Smith Brothers' Mill was very successful, selling grain throughout New York State.

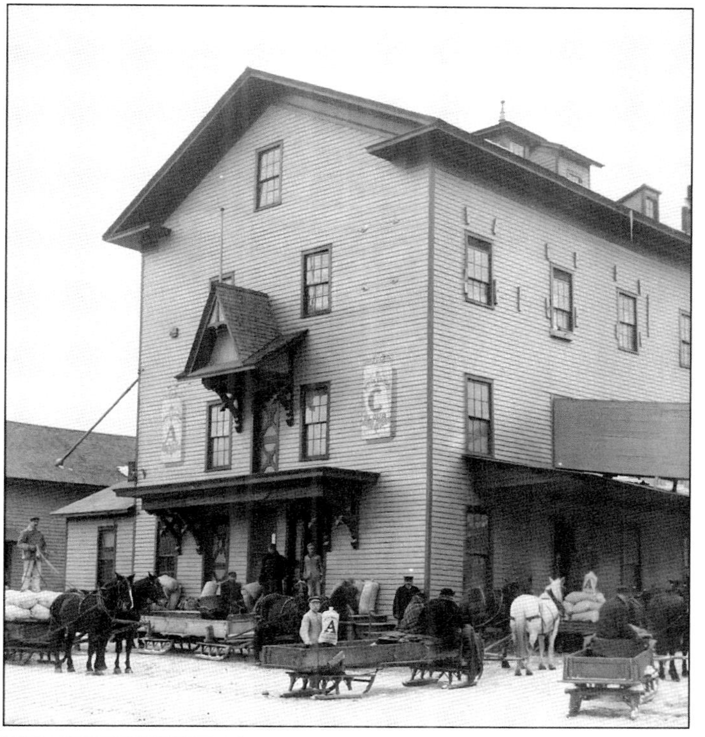

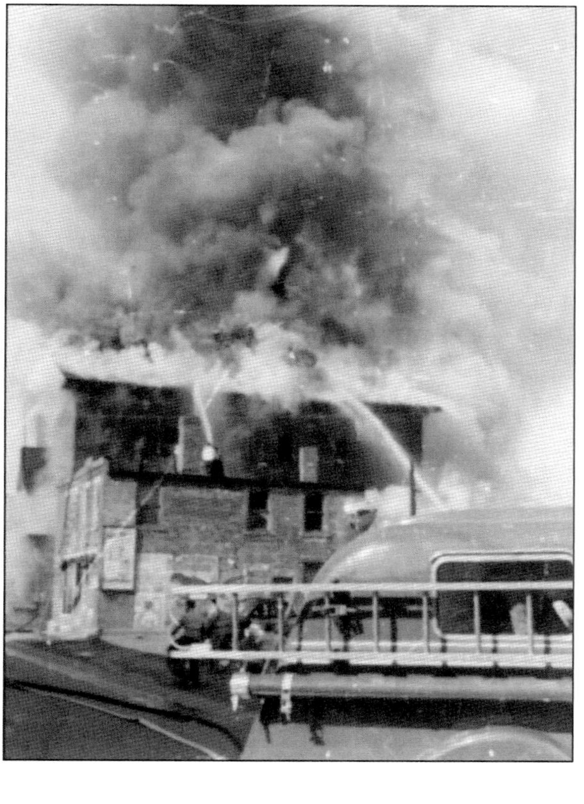

The Merril Hose Fire Company responds, but could not save the Smith Brothers' Mill from destruction. This photograph shows the devastation the fire caused the mill.

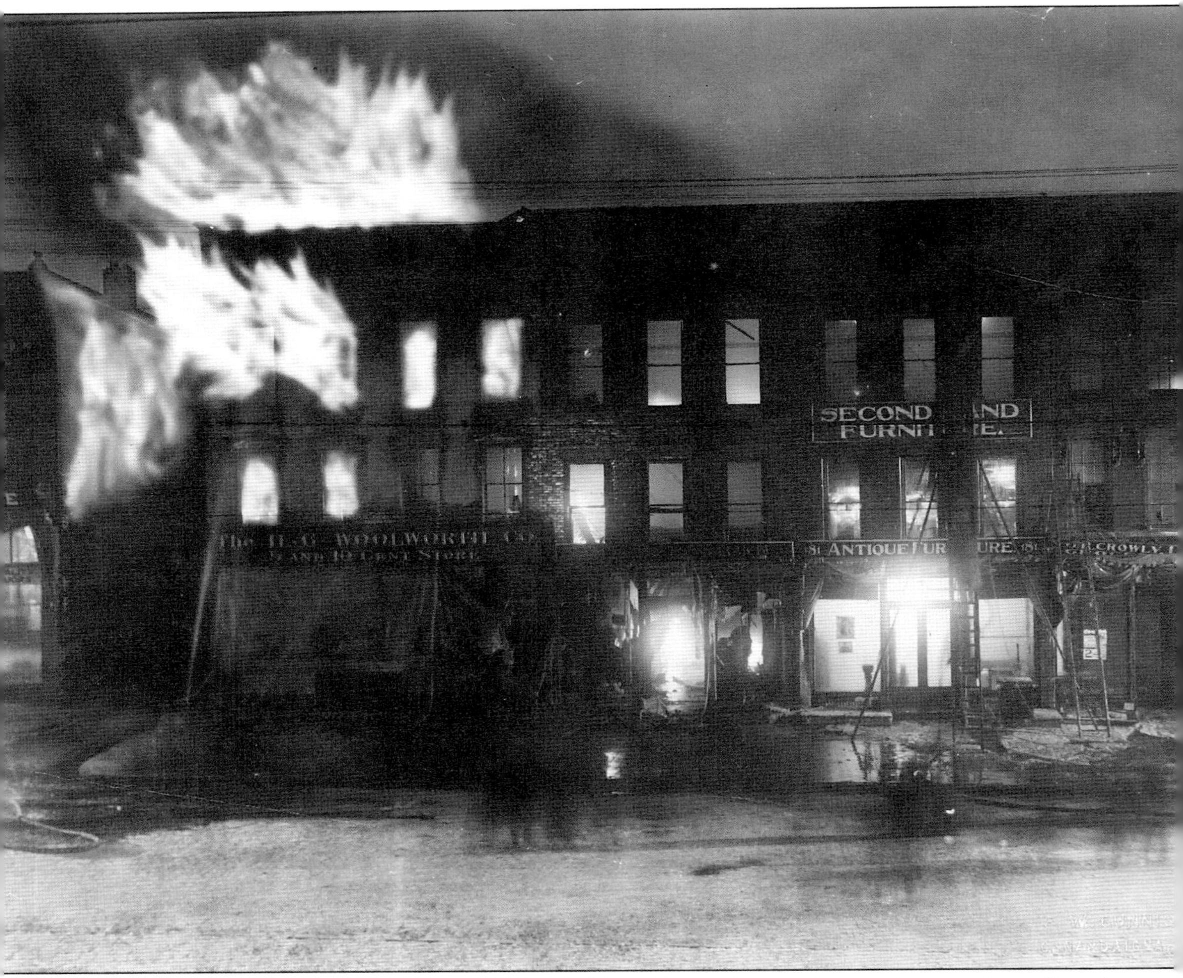

The Woolworth's Fire of 1915 at 175 South Main Street damaged several stores, including the Fair Store at 179 South Main, and J.W. Dale, a second-hand furniture store at 181 South Main. The flames appear to have crossed the alleyway over to Burke Brothers' Wine and Liquors. This block later housed Newberry's Department Store, which also suffered a fire.

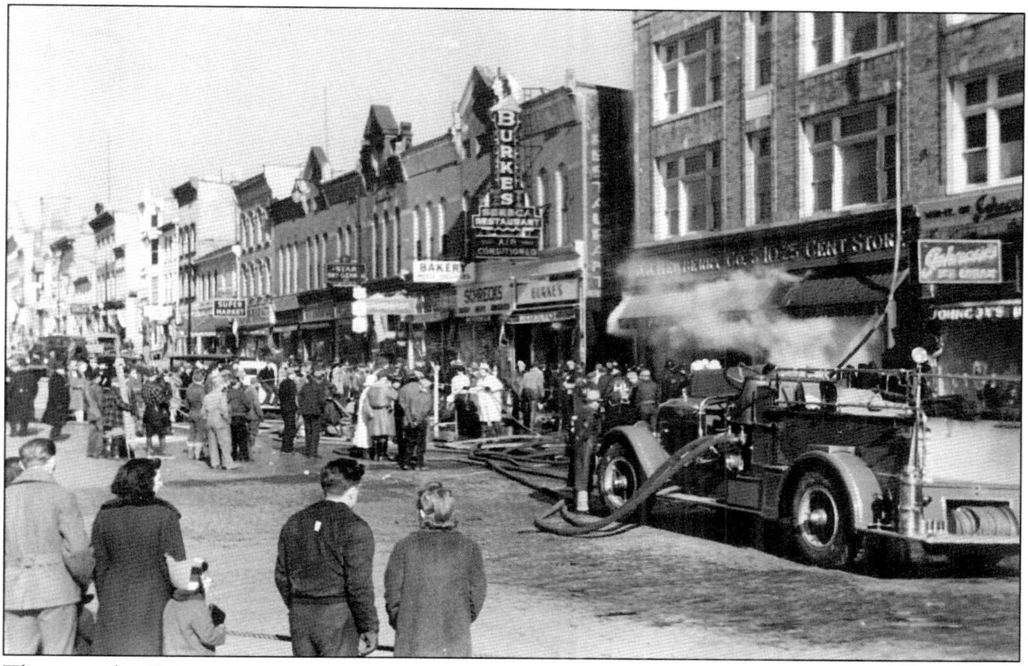

This popular 5 & 10¢ store in Canandaigua was damaged by fire. Located at 175 South Main Street, Newberry's provided Canandaigua residents with a variety of items as well as a soda counter. Patrons could purchase household items, cosmetics, paper goods, clothing, and fabric. Newberry's was later rebuilt to serve the residents of Canandaigua until the 1960s, when larger department stores such as Nichols on Routes 5 & 20 came to town. Concerned citizens gathered to watch the scene of the fire.

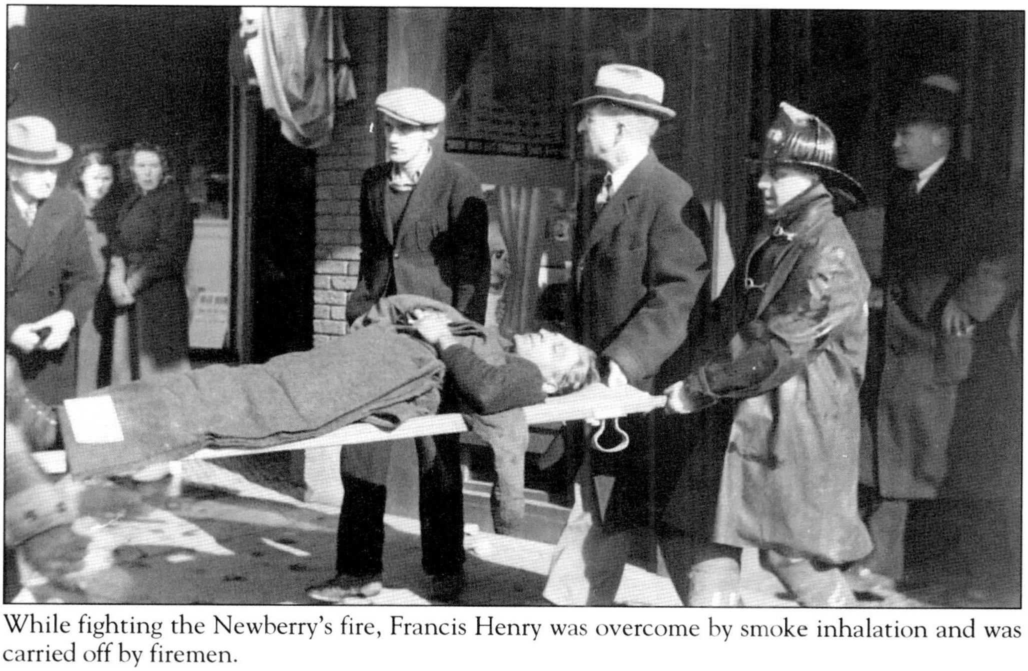

While fighting the Newberry's fire, Francis Henry was overcome by smoke inhalation and was carried off by firemen.

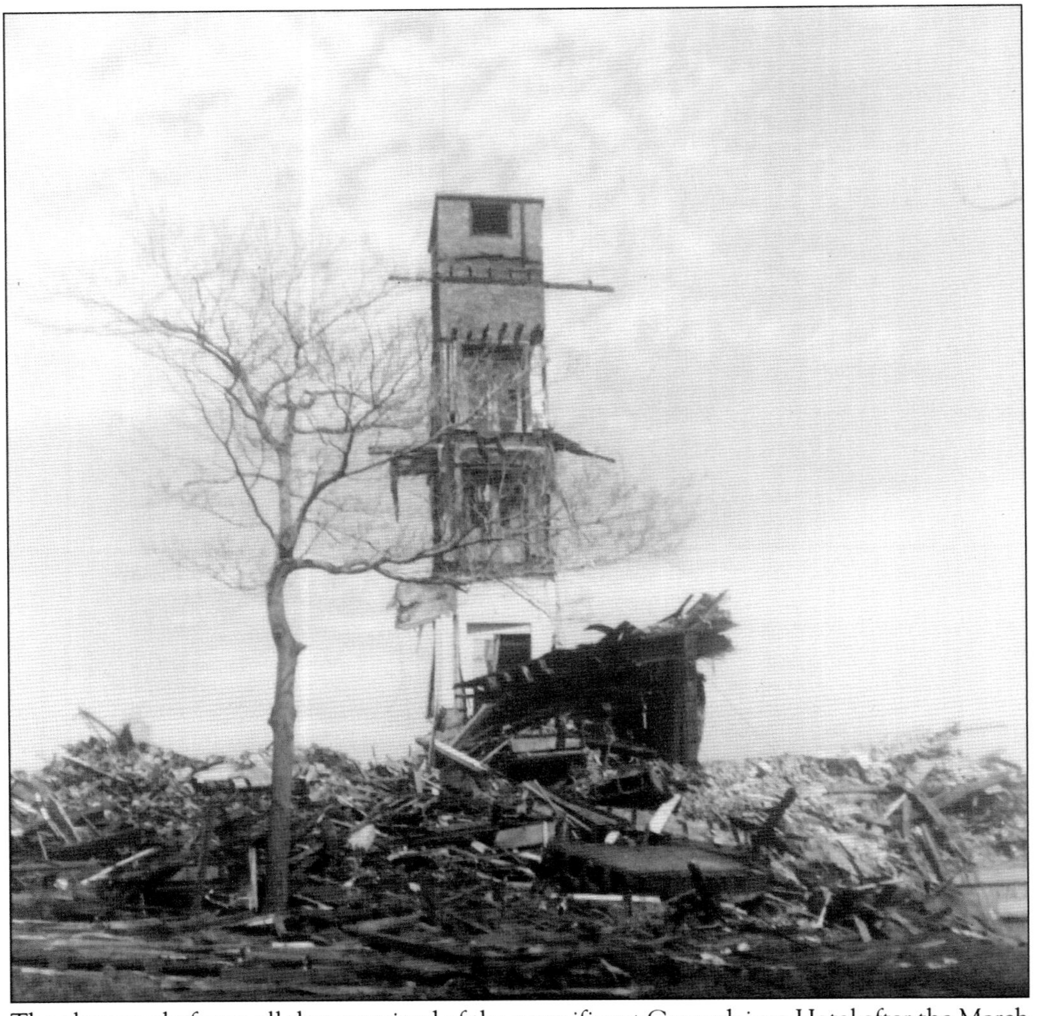

The elevator shaft was all that remained of the magnificent Canandaigua Hotel after the March 1971 blaze that destroyed the building. The origin of the fire was never determined, but it was believed to have started near the banister between the third and fourth floors. This historic building in the center of town had several fires during its rich history. Originally called the Blossom House, it burned to the ground in 1851 and was later rebuilt with money from wealthy villagers. Mrs. Frederick Ferris Thompson purchased the property in 1921 and spent over $315,000 in improvements and restoration of the property. In 1958 the building, then known at the Treadway Inn, suffered over $200,000 in damage due to another fire. It was repaired, and renamed the Canandaigua Hotel in 1960. Finally, in March 1971, a fire that killed several residents also ended the life of the hotel. The Canandaigua Police Station now sits on the former site of the once-grand structure.

Four

HOTELS

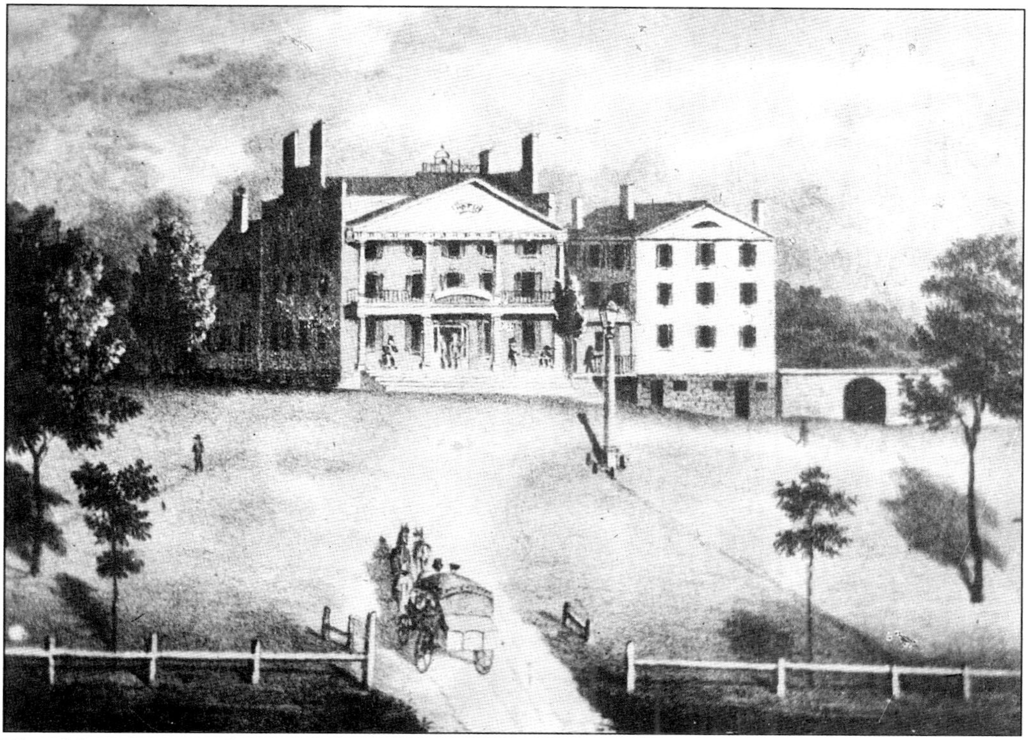

The Blossoms Hotel on Main and Ontario Streets was also known as the Canandaigua Hotel. It served as a station for stagecoach travelers. People wishing to go to Syracuse could ride the Eagle, which departed every morning at 4 am. Other destinations were Geneseo, Buffalo, and Palmyra.

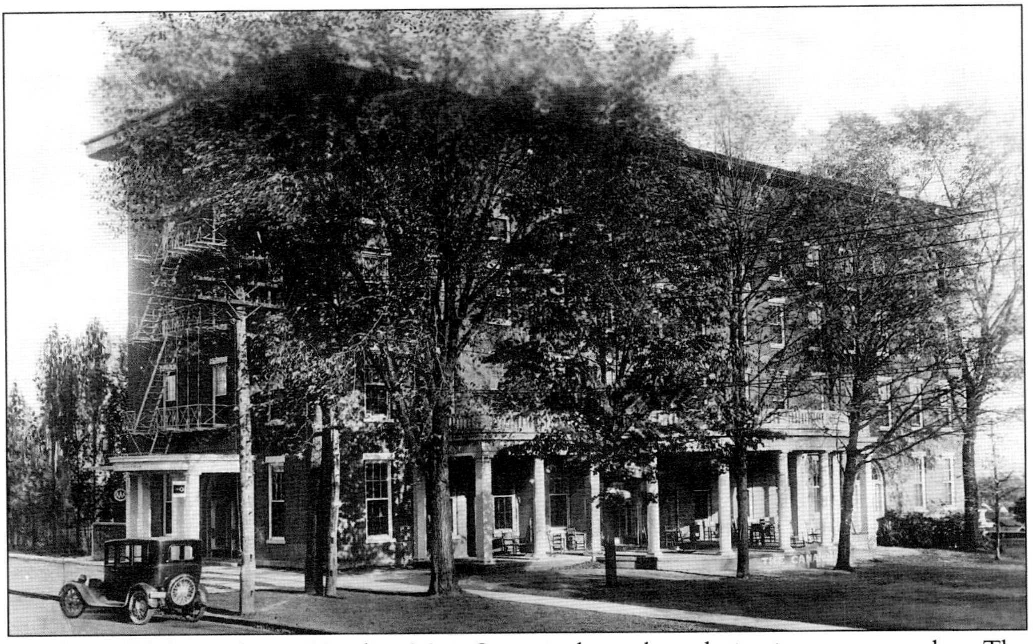

The beautiful Canandaigua Hotel on Main Street is shown here during its prosperous days. The hotel was a popular site for travelers as well as residents. This *c.* 1920 photograph shows the very inviting front porch. Travelers could enjoy a comfortable room for $2 per night.

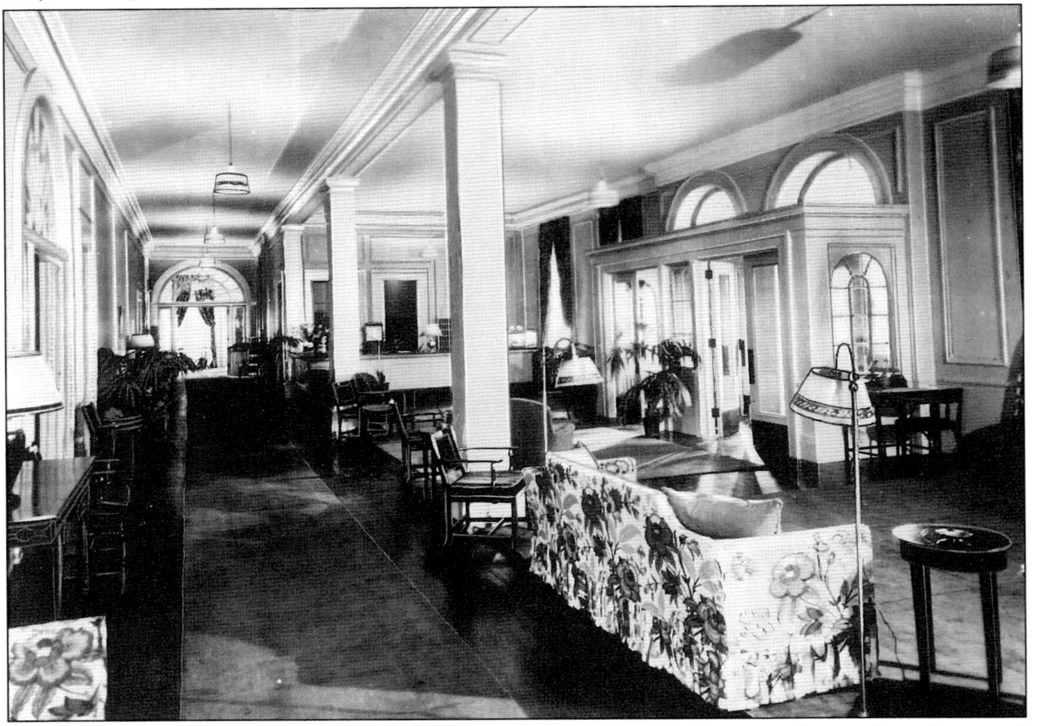

Windows on the east side of the Canandaigua Hotel's lobby gave visitors plenty of sunshine and a lovely view of the front lawn and fountain outside.

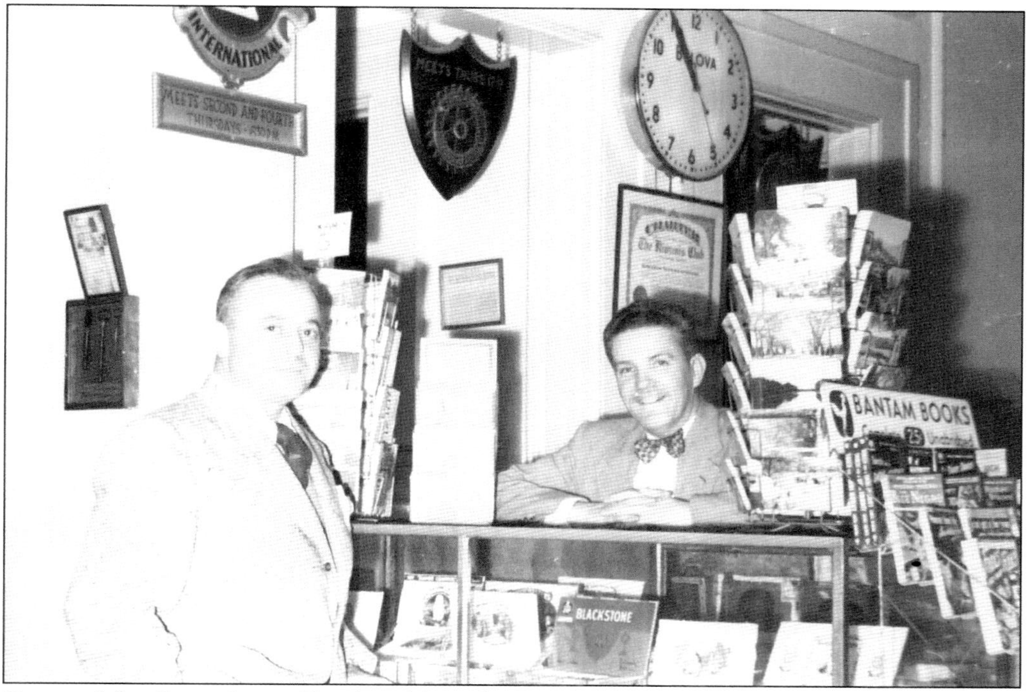

Guests of the Canandaigua Hotel could purchase items and learn of the local attractions at the newsstand within the lobby of the hotel. Notice the price of the postcards on the counter.

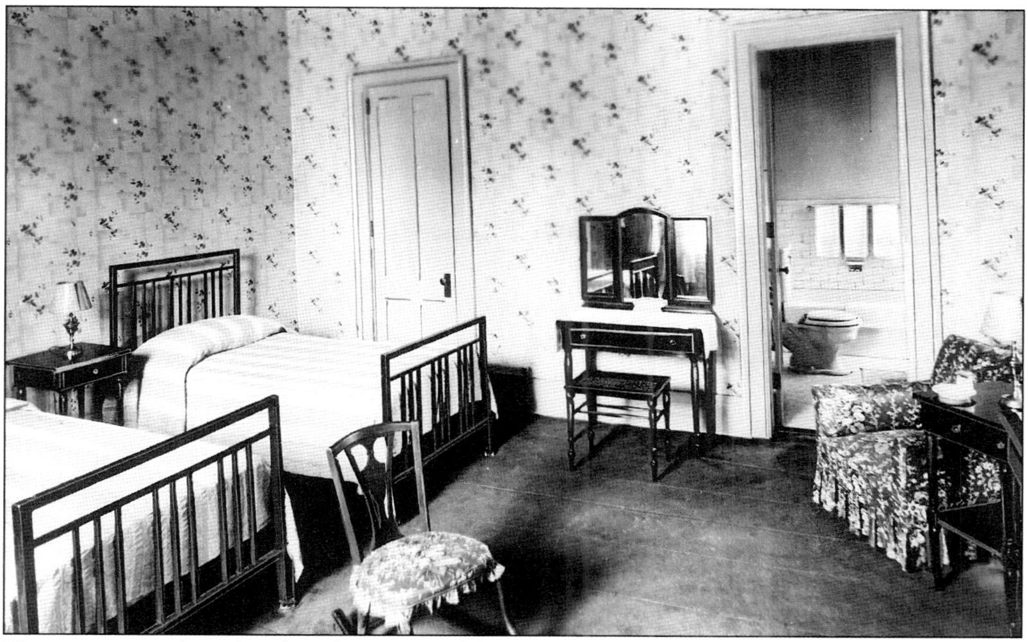
Elegant in its day, this hotel room could have been seen on a brochure promoting the hotel. A private bathroom and comfortable furnishings were available to guests at the Canandaigua Hotel.

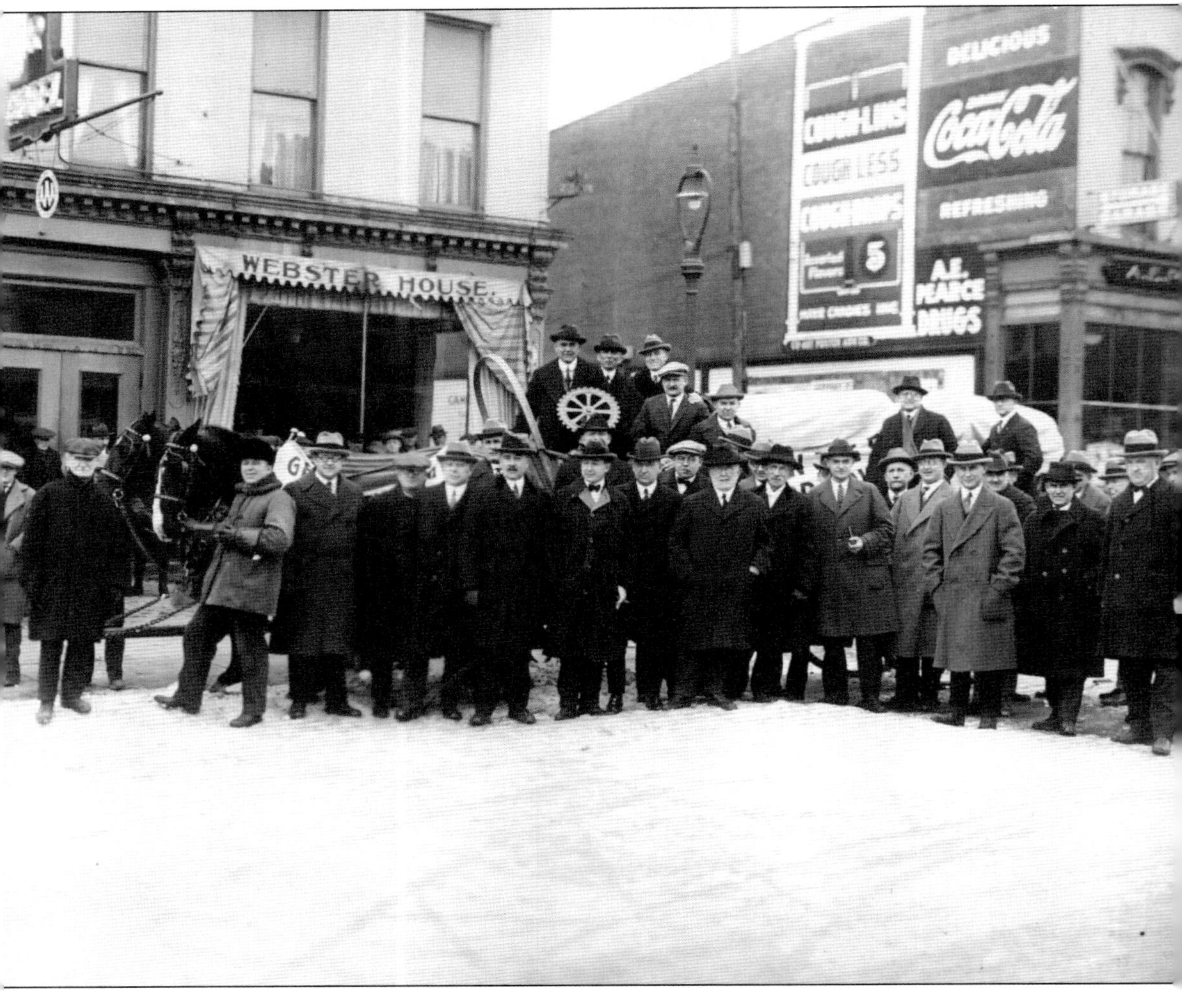

The Canandaigua Rotary Club poses outside the Webster House Hotel on February 28, 1924. "The Web" was located at 152 South Main Street. The photograph lists the following: (front row) David Wilson, Frank DeGraff, Bert Class, Mike, Glenn Lord, Charles Milliken, Rodney Pease, Art Thompson, Frank Cougevan, and Fred Kershaw; (standing at the rear) Charles Sackett and William F. Schreck. The others in the photograph are unidentified.

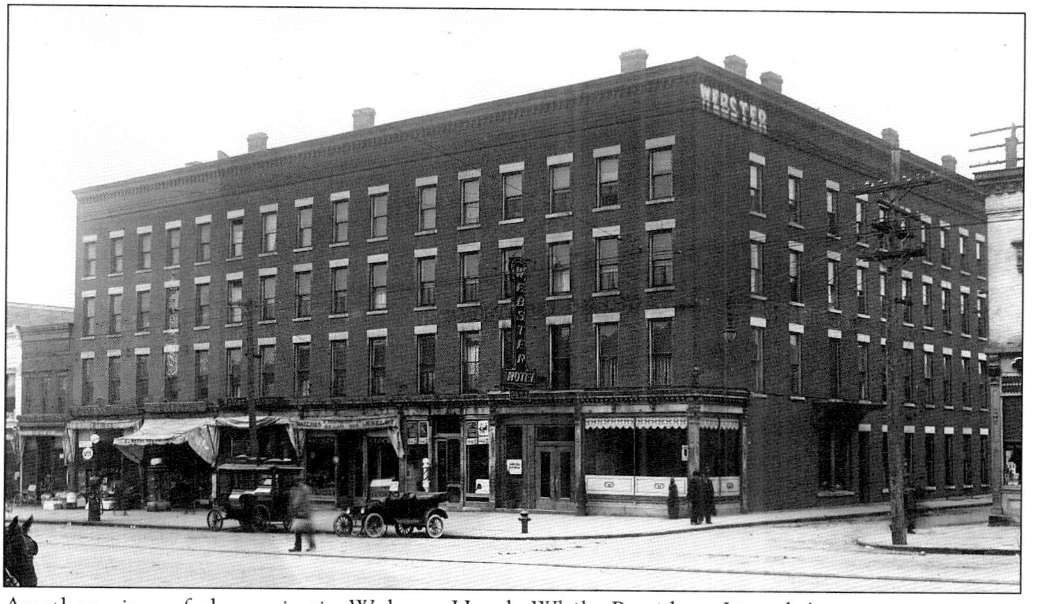

Another view of the majestic Webster Hotel. While President Lincoln's assassination was being investigated, a suspect in the slaying, John Harrison Surrat, proved his innocence by his signature of registration at the Webster Hotel on the day of the shooting.

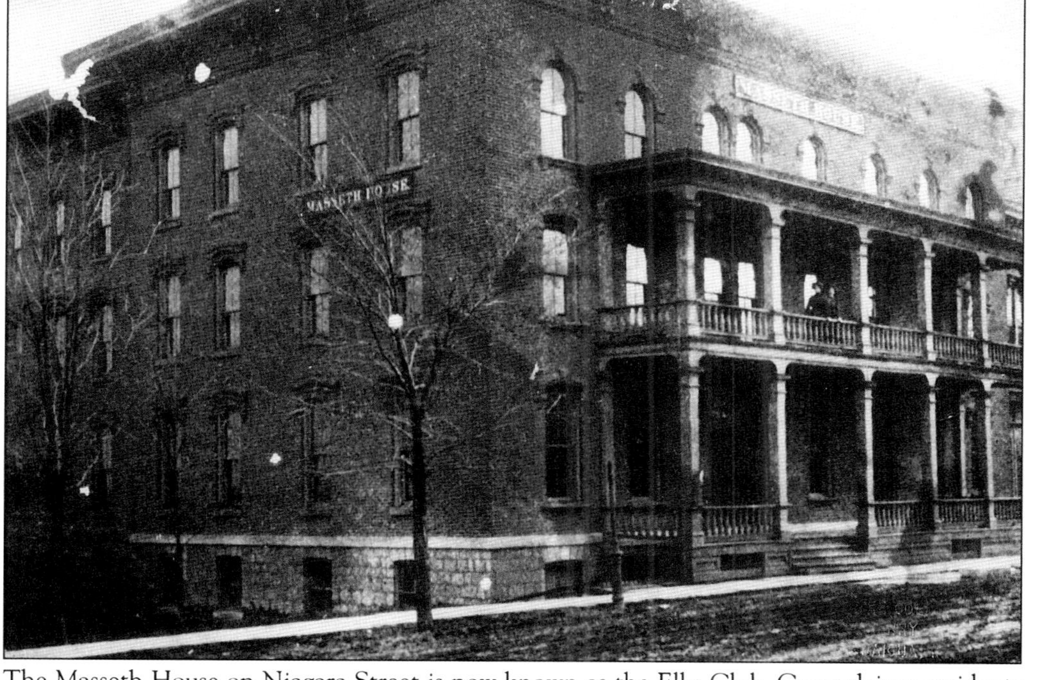

The Masseth House on Niagara Street is now known as the Elks Club. Canandaigua residents Elizabeth Pierce and Barbara Wright's mother, Josephine Rula Masseth, were born here. This hotel remained in their family until it became the Imperial Hotel in the early 1900s. The first floor had a dining hall and tavern, the second floor was reserved for the owners' living quarters, while the third floor housed the guest quarters.

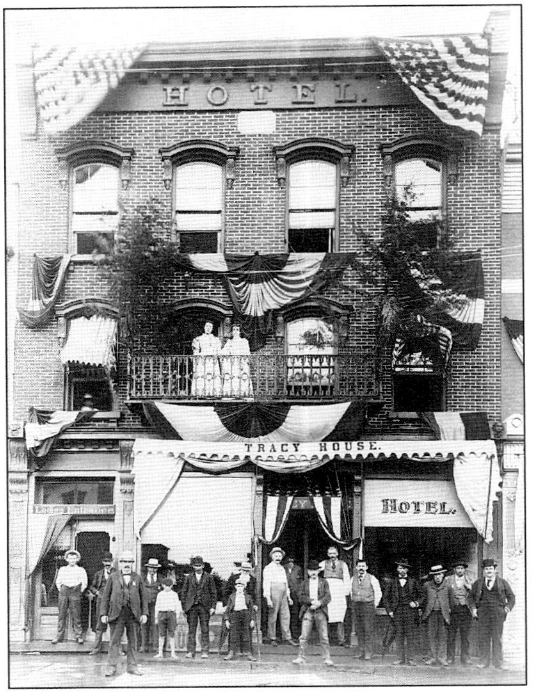

The Tracy House at 151 South Main is decorated with a patriotic flair in this July 4, 1897 photograph. Observe the proud employees standing out front, and the ladies entrance on the left side. The hotel was managed by Elisha Gulick, an owner of fast race horses which were stabled on Mill Street.

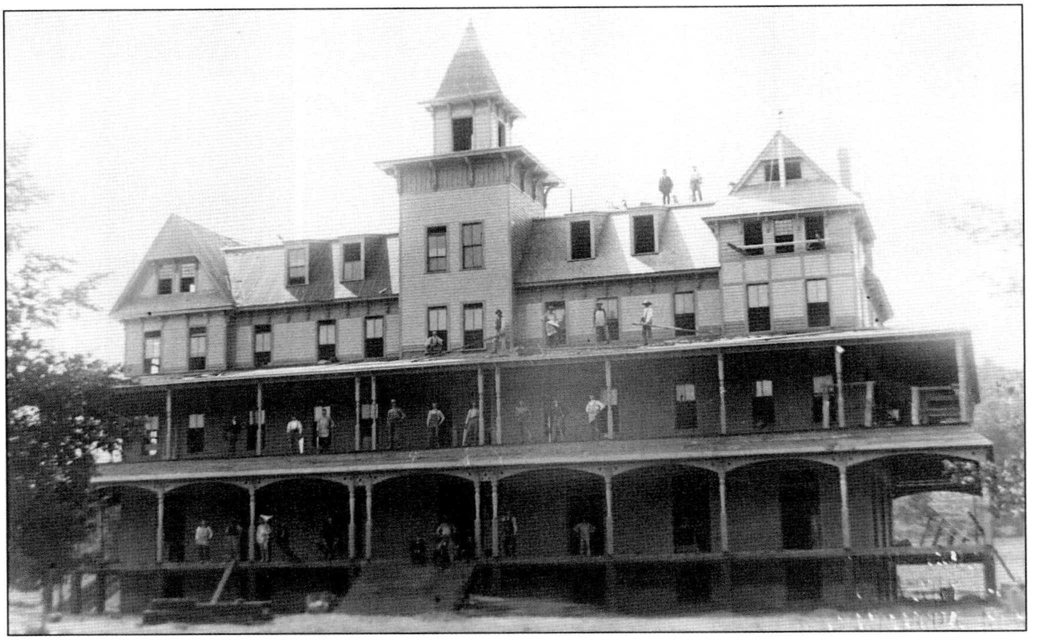

The construction of the Seneca Point Hotel is shown here in 1886. A brochure announcing the hotel's opening described it as, "situated near lake and glen and hill, open to constant breezes that temper the summer heat, removed from all danger of malaria." The hotel could serve several hundred guests, and featured fire alarms, electric bells, and other modern conveniences. Guests of the hotel could enjoy billiards, dancing, a safe sailing pond for children, tennis, and baseball. A fire in the laundry room on August 17, 1899, destroyed the hotel.

Five

Downtown

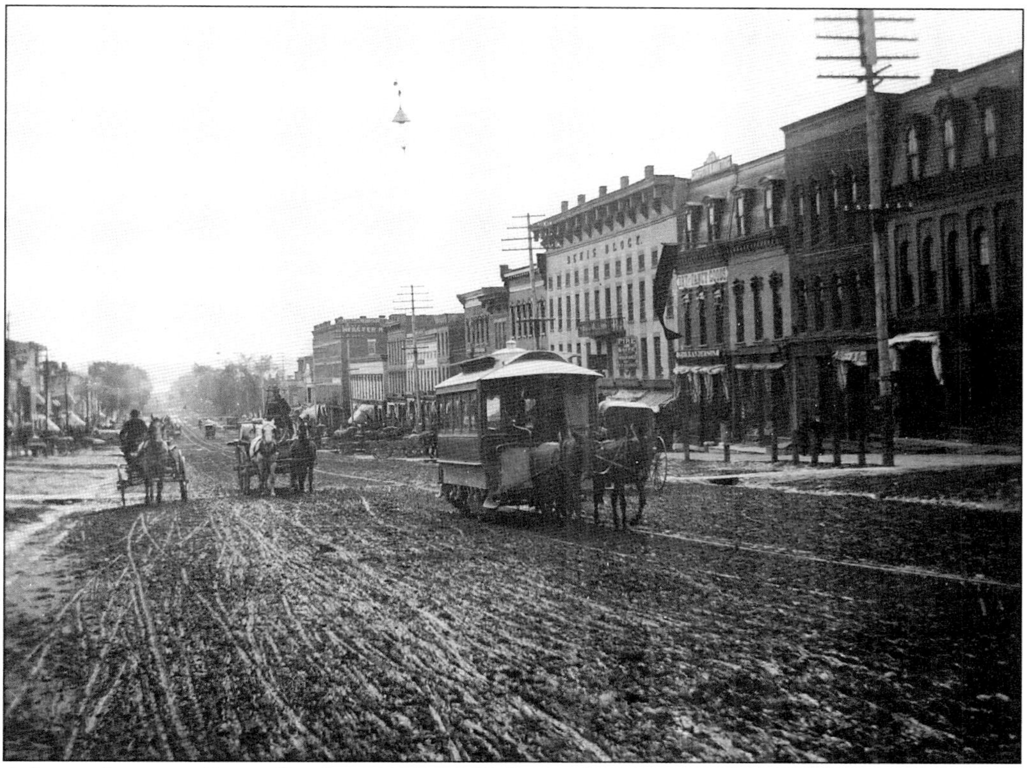

A horse-drawn trolley pulls its cargo through the mud near City Hall. This photograph shows the trolley using the center lane while private coaches pass on the unpaved street. The street was paved with bricks in 1904. Trolley service began in 1887, tracing a route from the lake dock, up Main Street, and ending north of Buffalo Street. The early trolleys were horse-drawn; the first electric trolley ran in 1893.

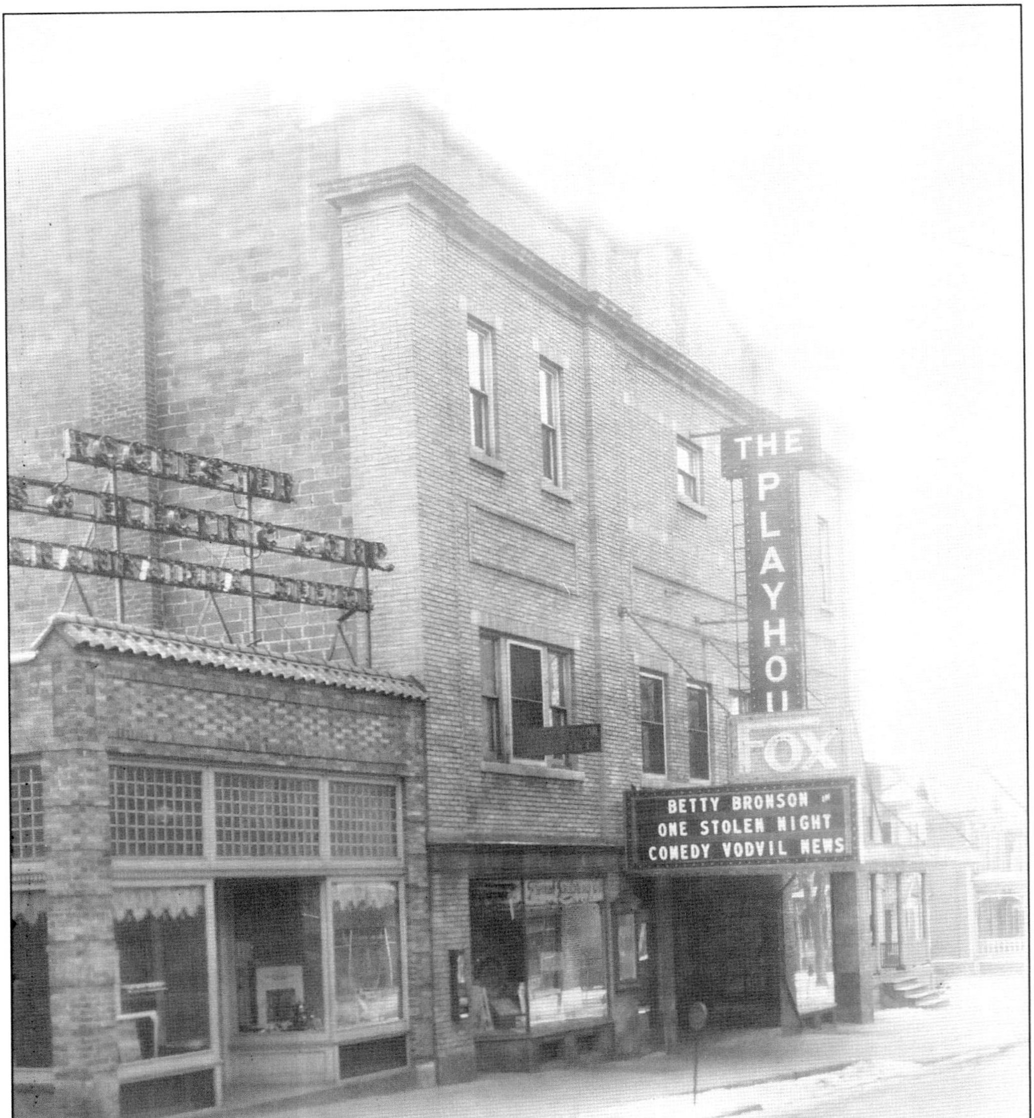

Canandaigua's Playhouse Theater on Chapin Street was an entertainment center. The Merril Hose Fire Company staged minstrel shows here as a fund-raiser for many years, employing a producer from New York City, and showcasing elaborate costumes and scenery. The theater also showed motion pictures. It was demolished in 1972, after several years of declining attendance.

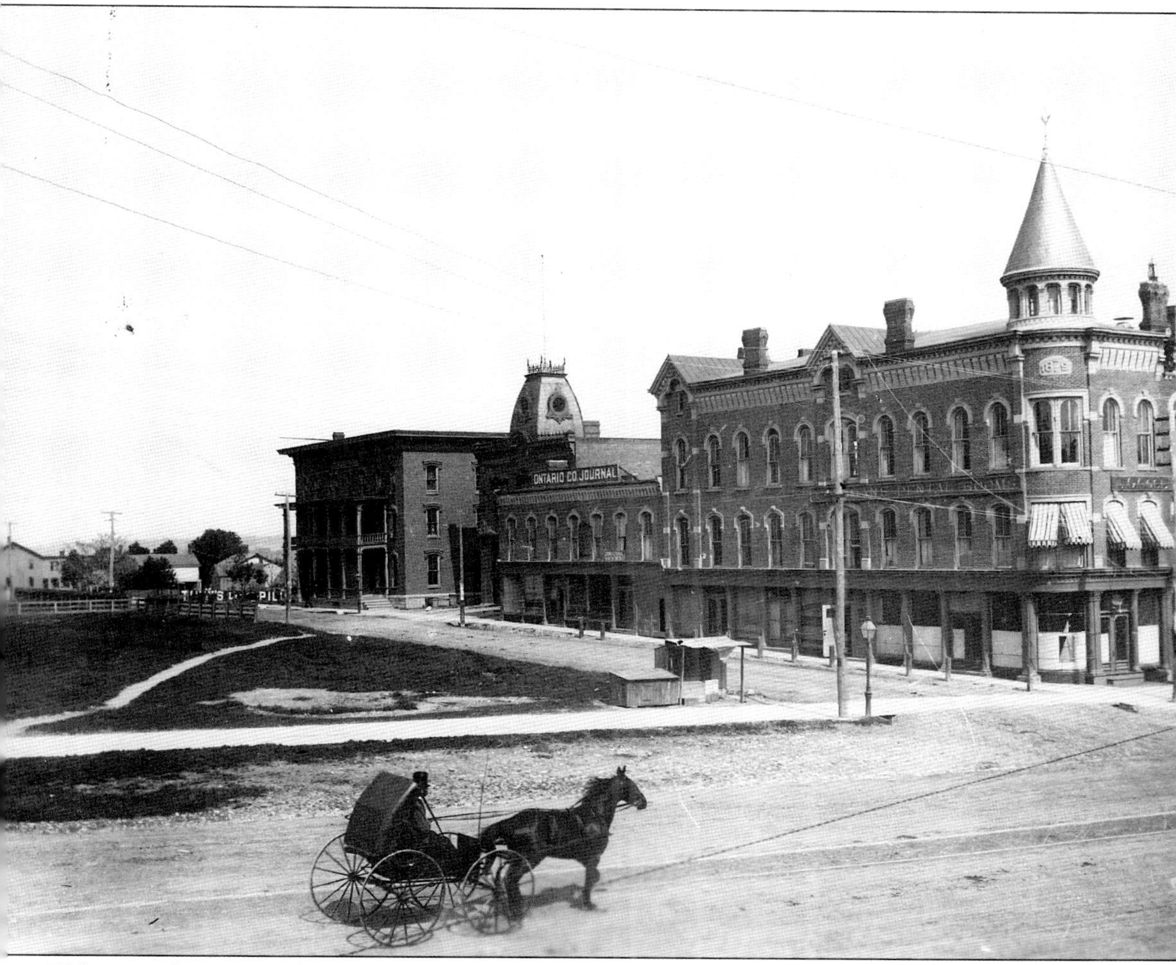

Taken in the 1880s, this unique photograph shows the east side of Main Street before the Flannigan Block was constructed. There is a clear view to the Masseth House Hotel as well as the Erina Hose Fire Company and *Ontario County Journal* building. The corner building is the McKechnie Bank with several storefronts. Upstairs is a dental office. This building, which burned down in 1954, is the current location of Bruno's Italian Restaurant. Notice the trolley tracks running down Main Street and the buggy driver in his stovepipe hat.

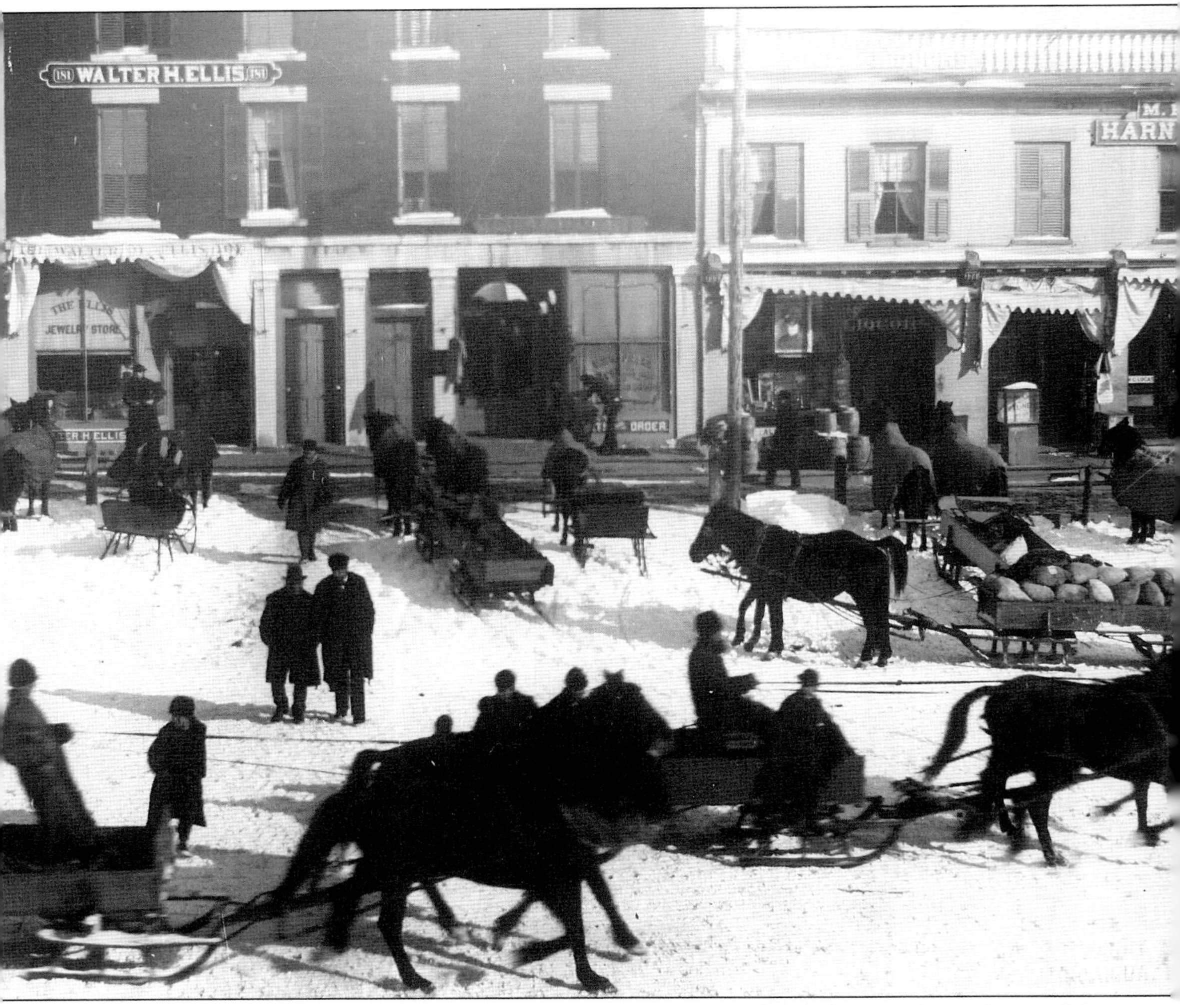

This busy scene from the winter of 1885 shows activities of daily life in Canandaigua. Many people have pulled their horse-drawn sleighs up to the hitching posts while they shop. Horses were vital to life in rural America. Notice how they are kept warm with blankets while waiting to pull the sleighs, and how one sleigh is loaded with grain.

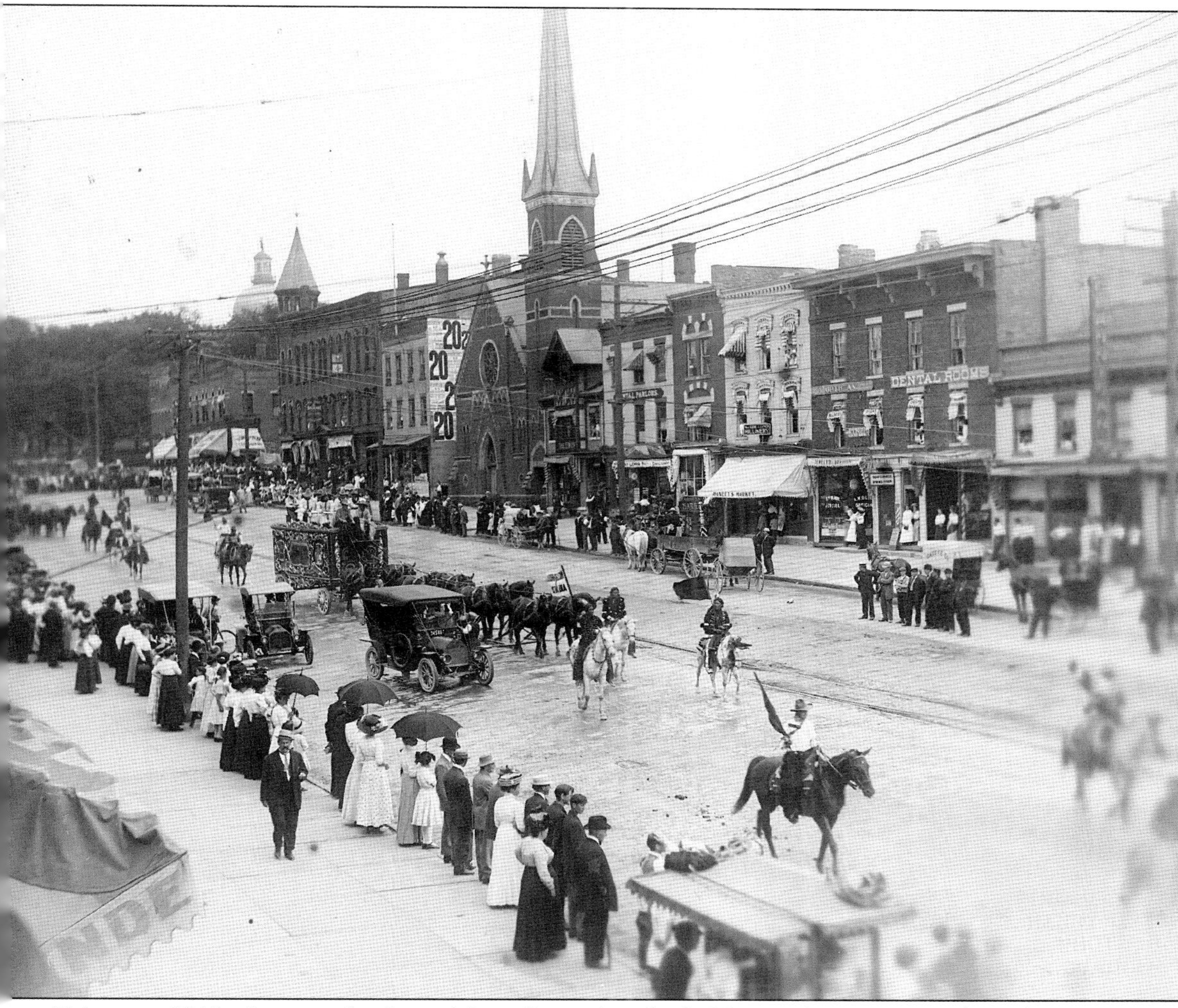

Taken *c.* 1915, this parade down Main Street has both Native Americans and cowboys riding in their finery. Notice how the ladies on the sidewalk keep the hot sun off themselves with parasols and bonnets. Gentlemen are dressed in suits and hats to observe the parade. Automobiles shared the bricked Main Street with the more common mode of transportation, horse-drawn carriages. A peanut vendor is set up in the lower-right corner of the photograph. Looking across Main Street you can see Flannigan's Restaurant, Dr. L.D. Sutherland's dental office, A.W. Gilbert Jeweler, Hanley's Market, Edward Kaufman Market, the *Ontario County Times* building, the First Baptist Church, F.W. Boswell Wines & Liquors, and Boswell & Egan Wines & Liquors. In the distance, Lady Justice sits atop the Court House dome.

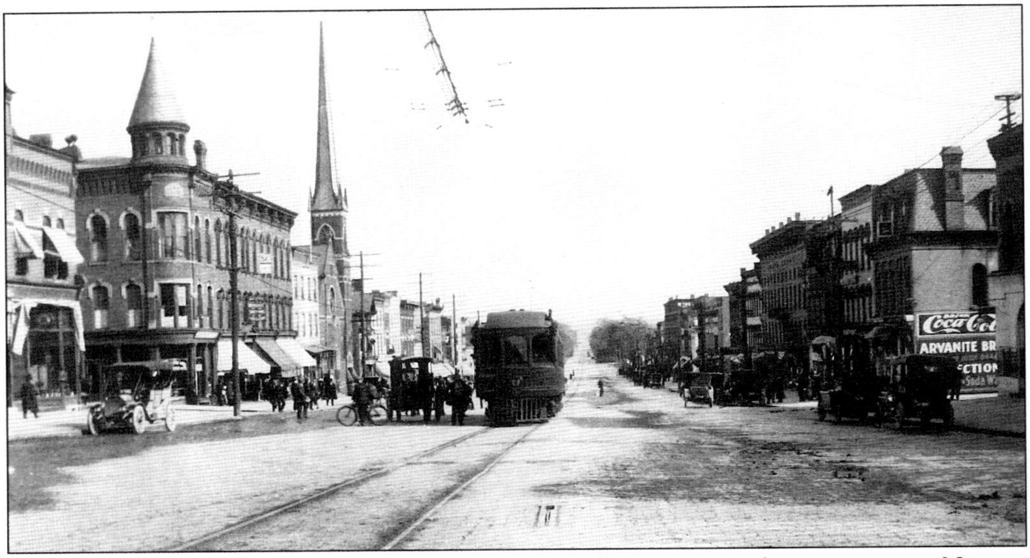

Looking south on Main Street c. 1915, we see the trolley as it stops for passengers at Niagara Street. Very few residents owned automobiles, so they relied on public transportation instead. The trolley depended on electricity for power; notice the cables above its tracks. On the right is Arvanite Brothers' Ice Cream and Confections, which is now the Renaissance Shoppe.

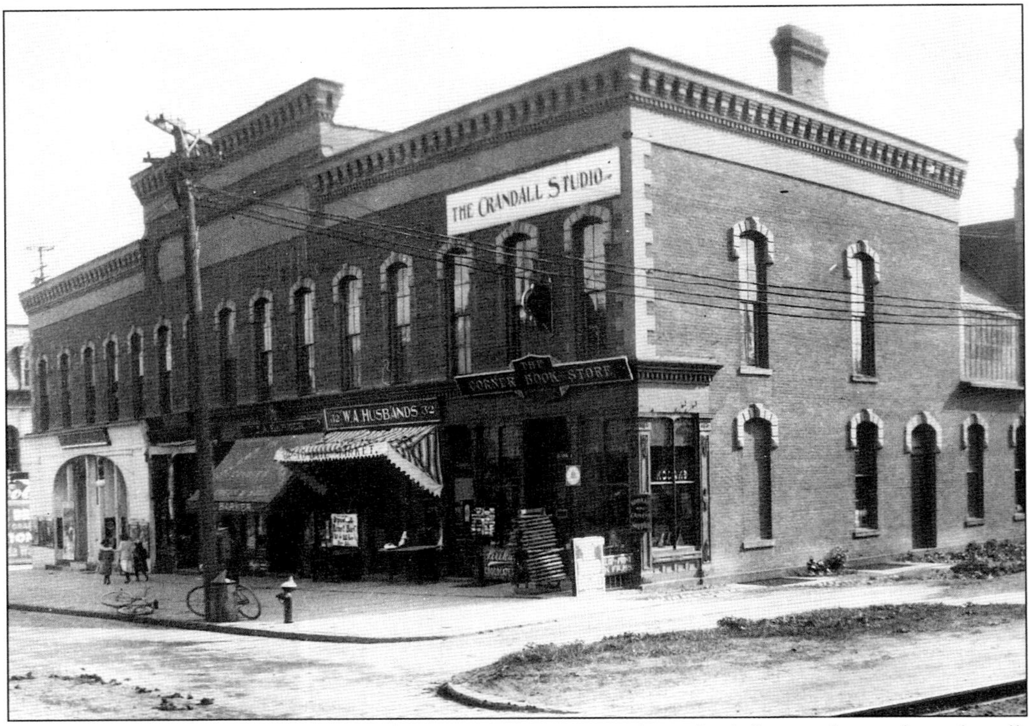

Some things never change. It is still a common site to see bicycles left outside on the sidewalk in front of these stores on Main Street. W.A. Husbands Meat Market provided a wide variety of meats for shoppers, often having elaborate displays of butchered animals hanging out front. The children in the picture may be on their way to Arvanite Brothers' for an ice cream treat.

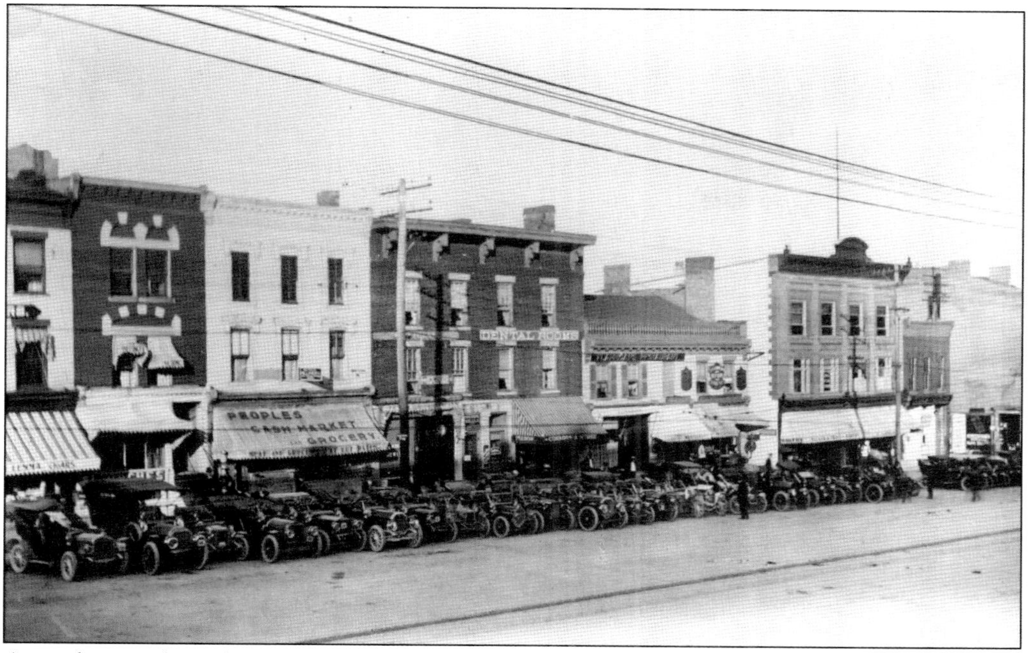

According to the unknown photographer, this photograph was taken at 6 pm on Monday July 8, 1908, before the days of parallel parking. Seventy-five road-weary drivers of the Geneva Automobile club have parked here after they "took supper," after driving from Geneva to Victor. Imagine the dust and insects these drivers contended with, driving the course without the modern convenience of air conditioning. The awnings on the building fronts add charm as well as protection from the scorching heat.

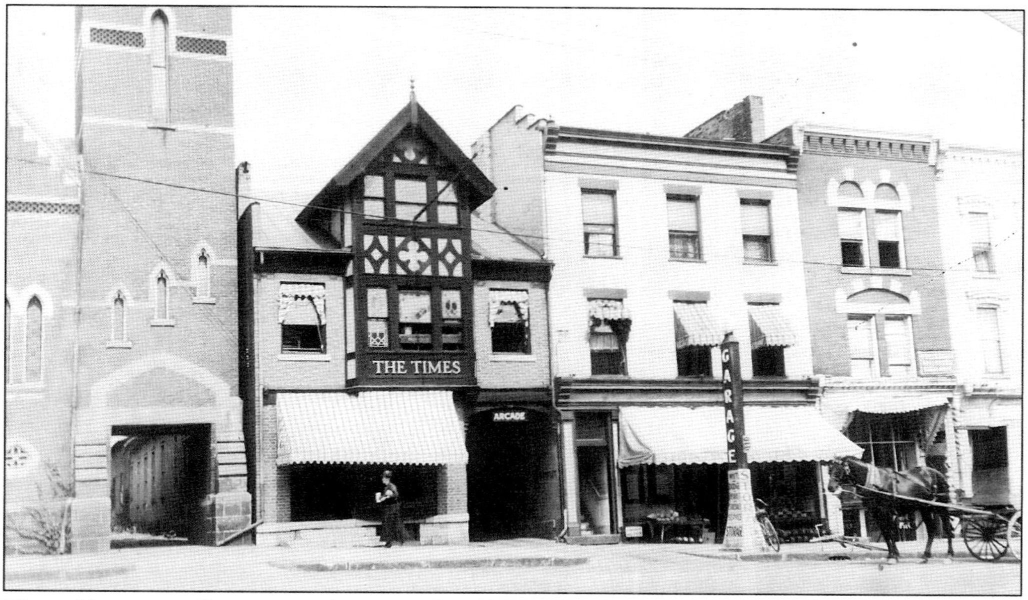

The still-present alleyway on the east side of Main Street was originally below the First Baptist Church's bell tower. Horses were led through the alley to the livery stable behind the block. In later years, the livery stable became a garage for taxis.

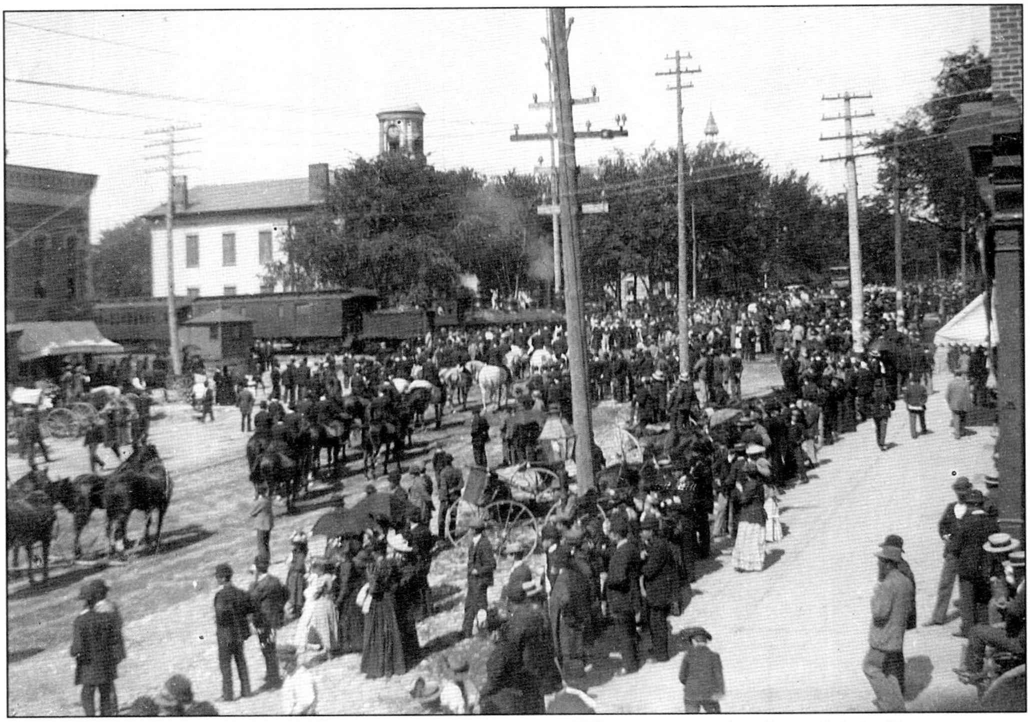

The circus unloads on Main Street during the 1890s. Imagine the excitement that the young and young at heart felt as they saw exotic animals, acrobats, and clowns unload from the train. People gathered to watch the activity in anticipation of the big event.

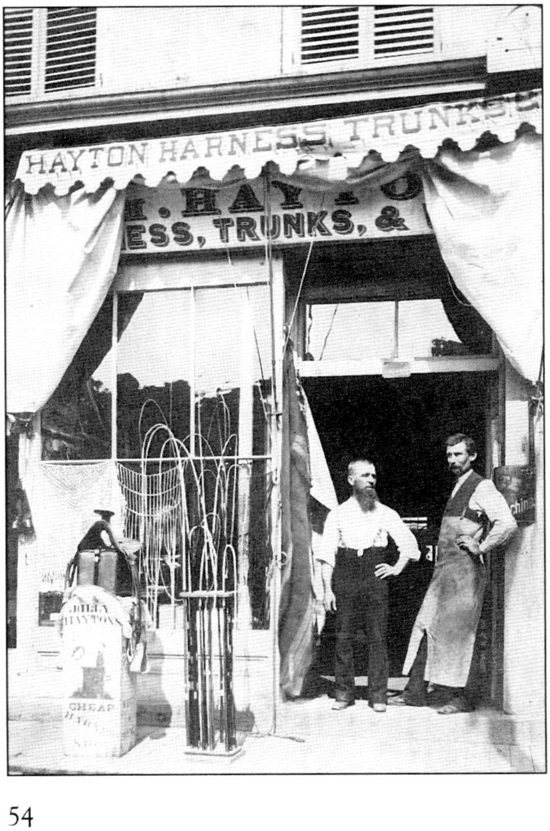

Hayton Harness and Trunks on Main Street was owned by William Blossom Hayton (1839–1920). Saddles and buggy whips are proudly displayed outside the store.

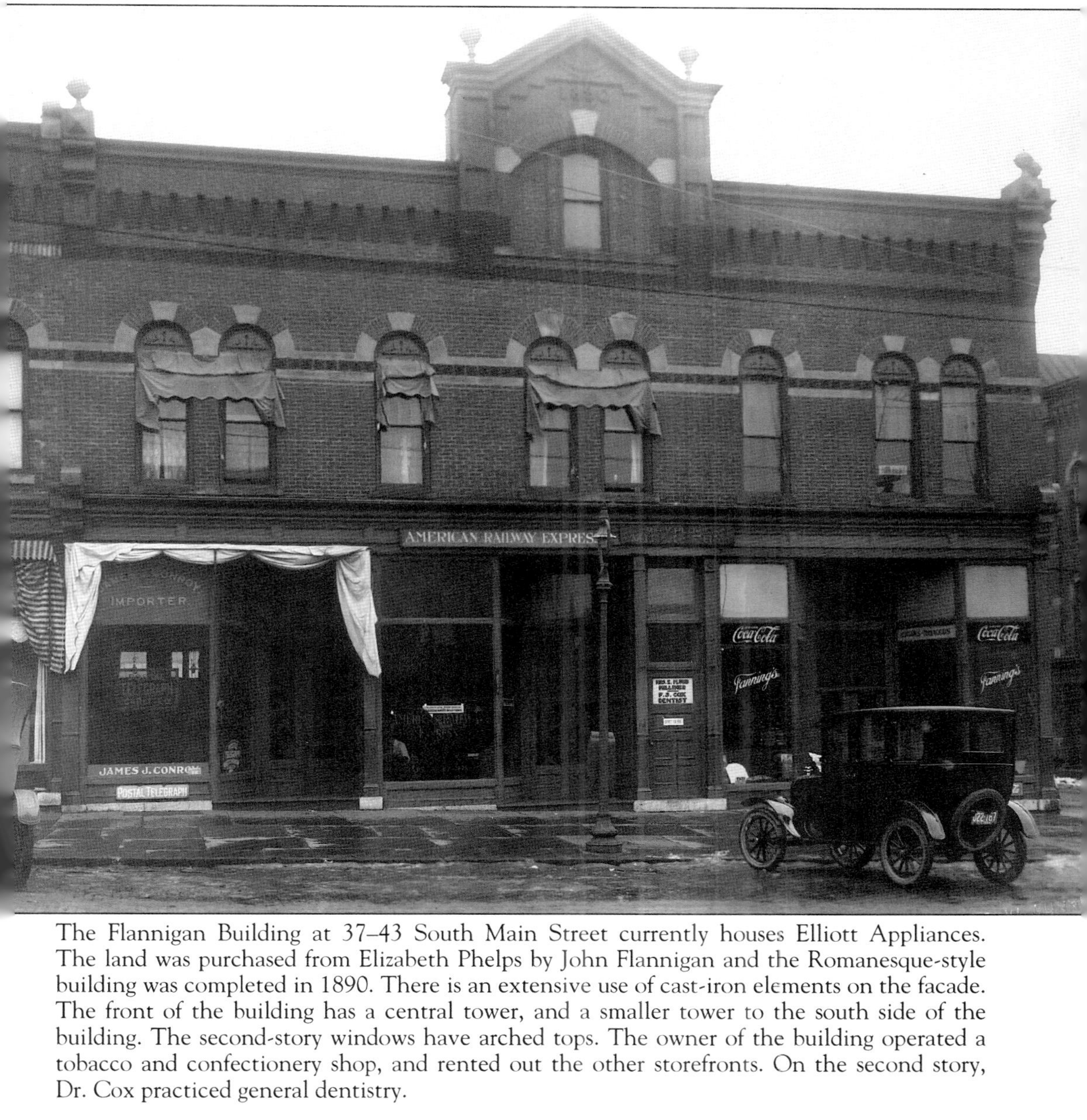

The Flannigan Building at 37–43 South Main Street currently houses Elliott Appliances. The land was purchased from Elizabeth Phelps by John Flannigan and the Romanesque-style building was completed in 1890. There is an extensive use of cast-iron elements on the facade. The front of the building has a central tower, and a smaller tower to the south side of the building. The second-story windows have arched tops. The owner of the building operated a tobacco and confectionery shop, and rented out the other storefronts. On the second story, Dr. Cox practiced general dentistry.

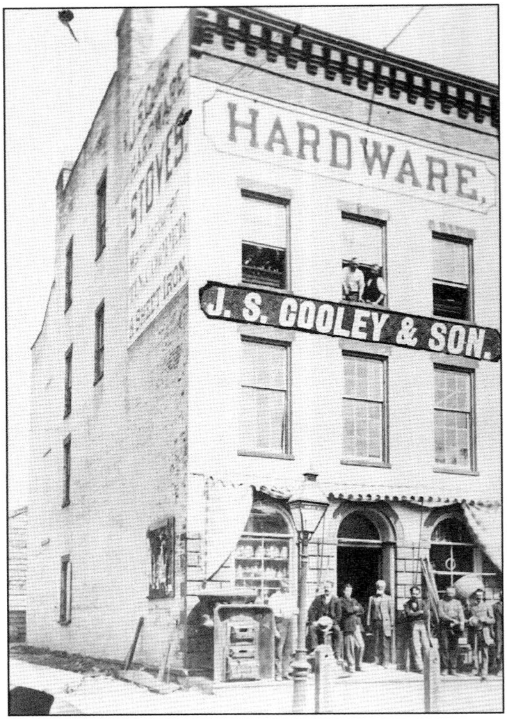

The Cooley Hardware Store at 129 South Main Street was built between 1823 and 1850 in what is known as the Phoenix Block. The simple Federal-style facade was later remodeled to the current bay-window appearance. A 16-foot wheel on the fourth floor of the building was used to hoist heavy materials into the upper floors. Notice the lovely gas lantern out in front as well as the hitching post for horses.

The facade has been altered in this later photograph of Cooley Hardware. The first tenant of the building in the 1850s was the M.H. Clark Hardware Company. Cooley Hardware followed in the 1880s. During the early 1900s, Panzarella Hardware occupied the building. The hardware occupation ended when Winship Pharmacy maintained its store at this location until the early 1970s. O'Neill's Florist now occupies this location.

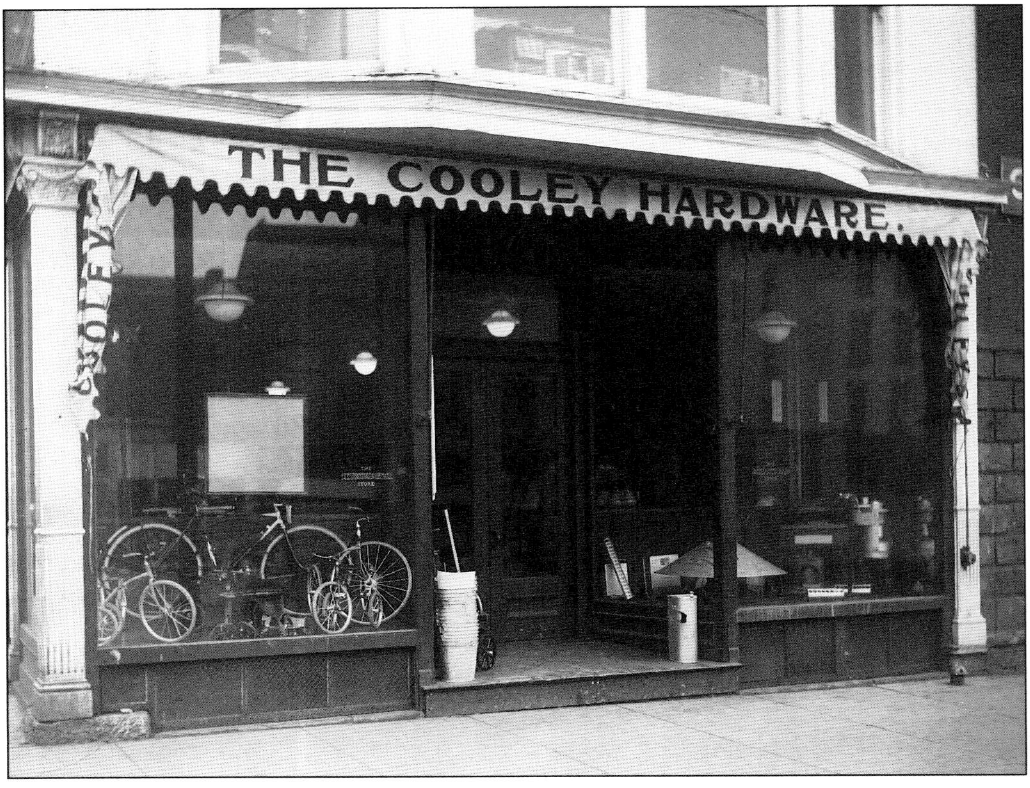

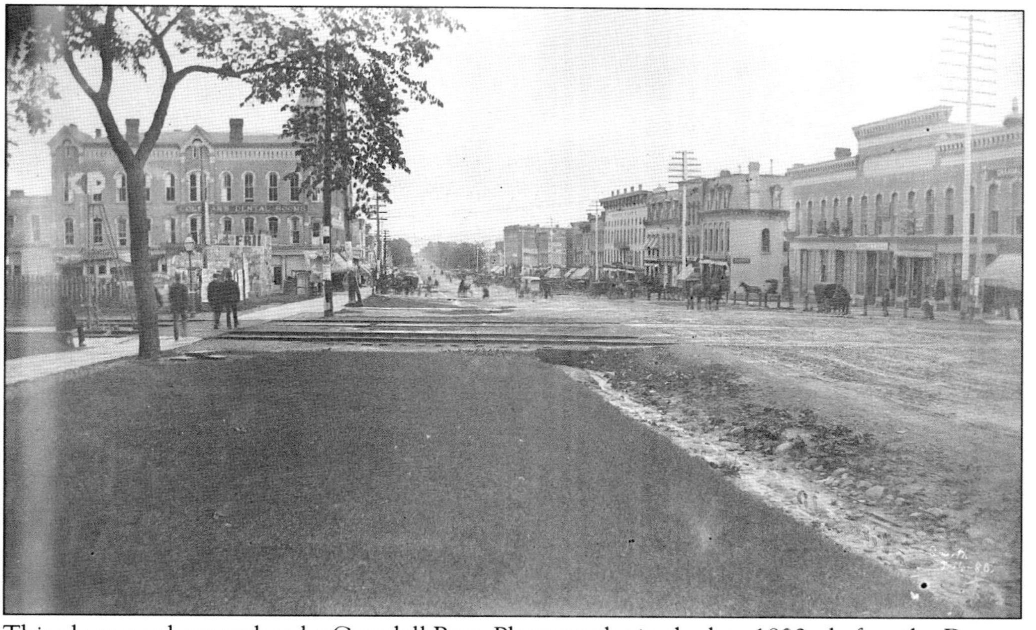

This photograph was taken by Crandall Bros. Photography in the late 1800s, before the Dwyer-Flannigan Block was constructed in 1890. Main Street has not yet paved with bricks, and a drainage ditch edges the street. Main Street must have been a much quieter place before automobiles came to Canandaigua.

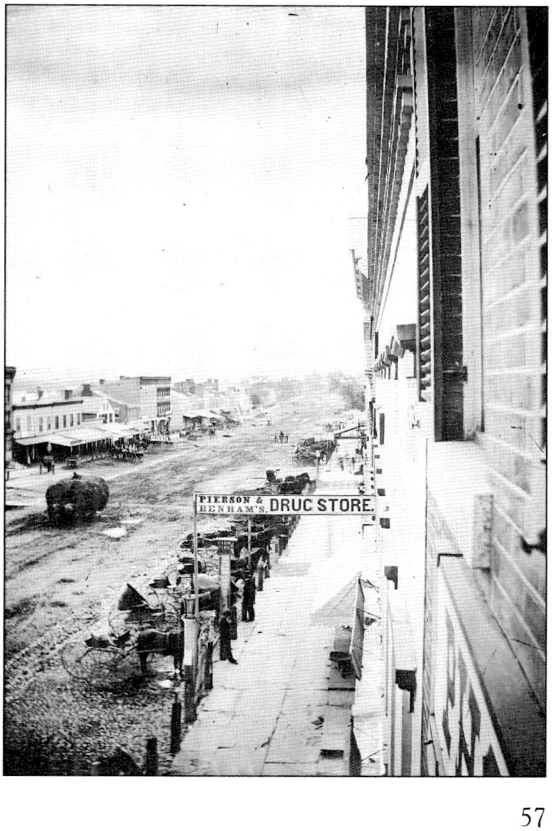

Here we have a chance to see Canandaigua in its infancy, as is evidenced by the muddy street and slate sidewalks. Note the hay wagon with its immense load traveling up the street. Horses wait patiently to carry supplies back home.

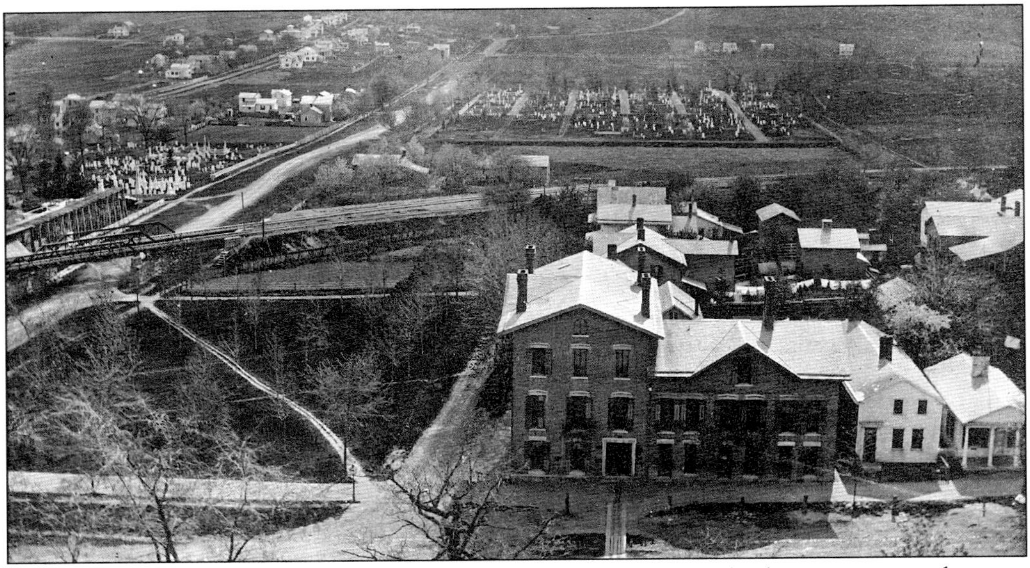

The Court House dome allowed a photographer to capture this bird's-eye view to the west of Canandaigua. The Atwater House (in the foreground) served as an office for Canandaigua attorneys from 1850 until 1910. The third floor had a large hall which was used for town meetings and entertainment. Mary Thompson purchased the property for the location of a new post office and had the building demolished. Notice the walkway that leads from the Atwater Building to the Court House—this was probably placed to keep mud off the shoes of the people coming back and forth between the buildings. The West Avenue cemeteries can be seen in the distance.

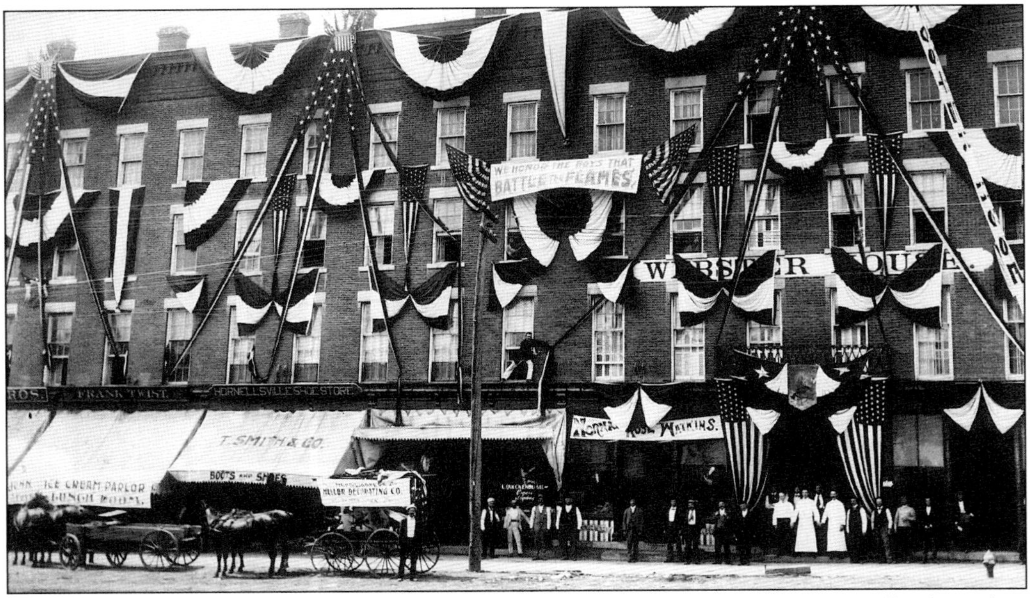

The Webster Hotel, located on the corner of Main and Coach Streets, is formally dressed to celebrate the work of the firefighters. Workers of the hotel are standing proudly outside the establishment. It is unfortunate that the hotel succumbed to fire in the mid-1960s when it was known as the Pickering Hotel.

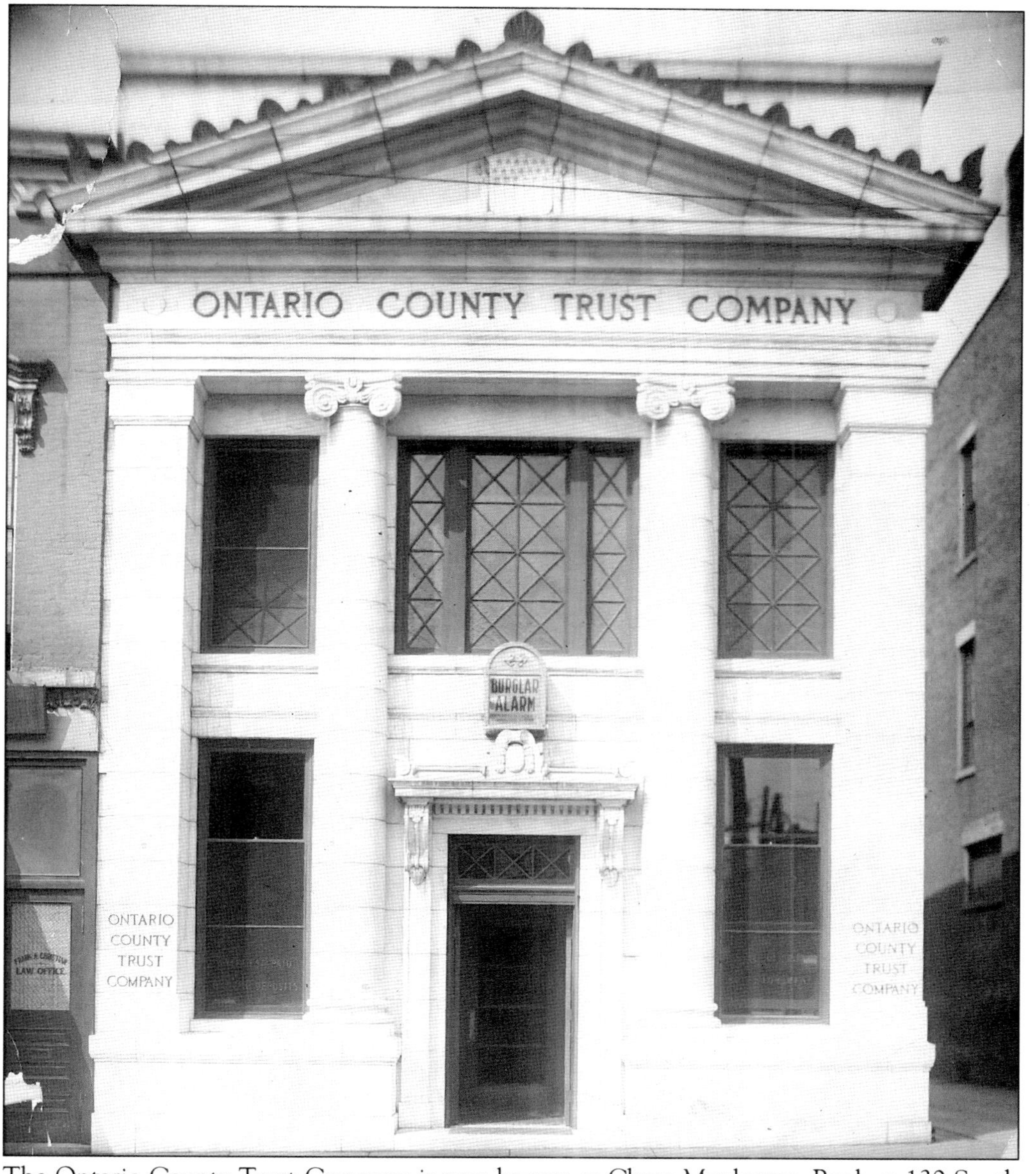

The Ontario County Trust Company is now known as Chase Manhattan Bank at 130 South Main Street. This bank began as the County National Bank on January 29, 1912. The County National Bank originated from the McKechnie Bank, once located on the east side of Main Street. A beautiful stained-glass window, hung in the west windows of the bank, depicts a woman representing "Abundance," bearing a cornucopia filled with the fruits of Ontario County. The window is now housed at the wine-tasting room of Sonnenberg Gardens. The beautiful white marble on the facade of the building was quarried from Vermont. The burglar alarm above the front door seems rather simple by today's standards. The clock that has for so many years told us if we were late to an appointment was dedicated in 1926. *The Daily Messenger* reported that, "Correct time is assured as the mechanism is regulated by a master clock, and all operations are controlled by electricity." An English chime from Westminster would strike each quarter-hour, and the hour would be announced by separate strikes.

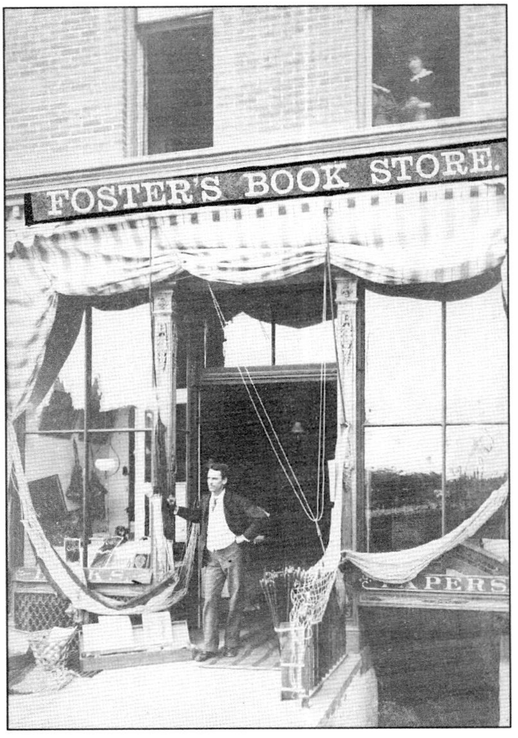

Fosters Book Store was located at 28 South Main Street, the first building below the railroad tracks. This building currently is the office of Edward Monaghan, Esq. The stairway leading to the basement is now gone.

Taken *c.* 1924, this photograph shows the truck of Walter Henry, a service station owner at 272 South Main Street, on the corner at Antis Street.

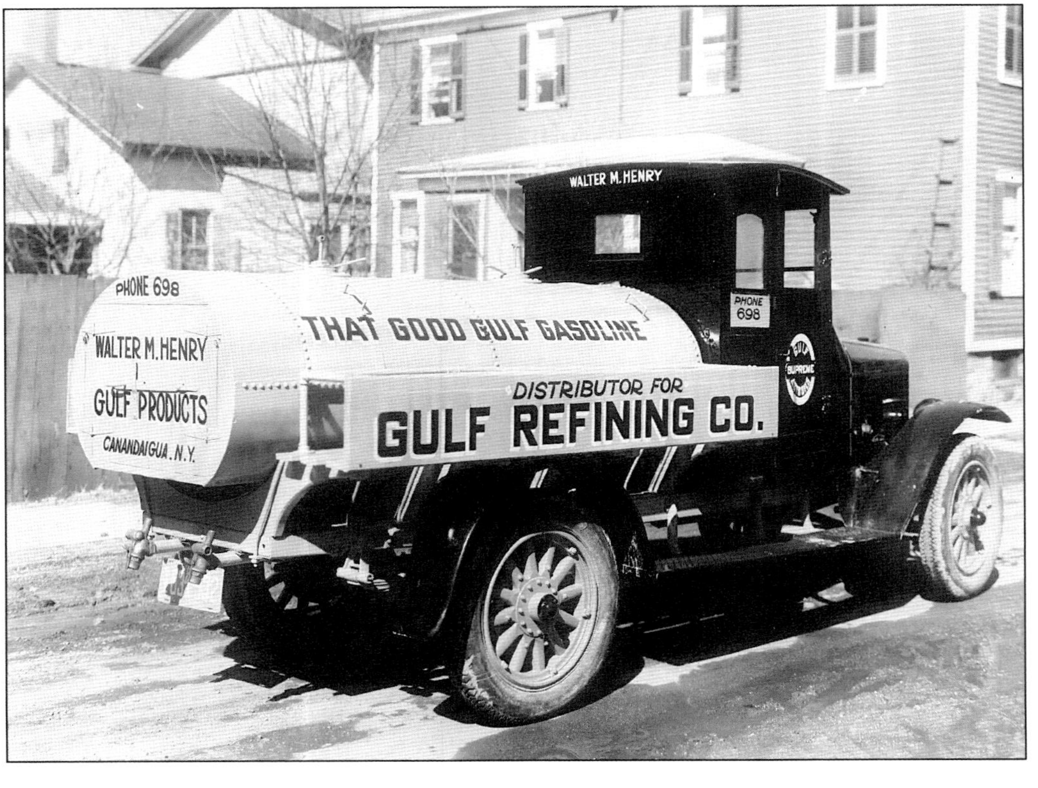

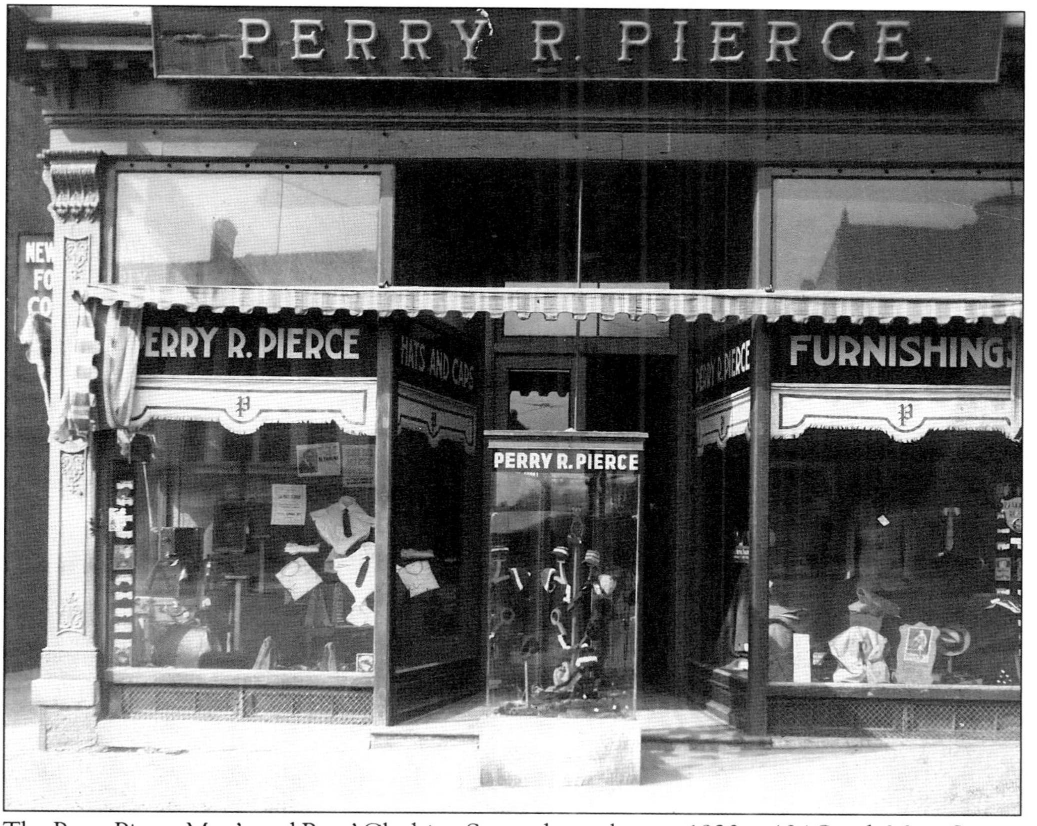

The Perry Pierce Men's and Boys' Clothing Store, shown here *c.* 1920 at 124 South Main Street, always claimed to have the newest clothing and furnishings for men, boys, and children. This store suffered during the Great Depression like so many others and ended up closing its doors.

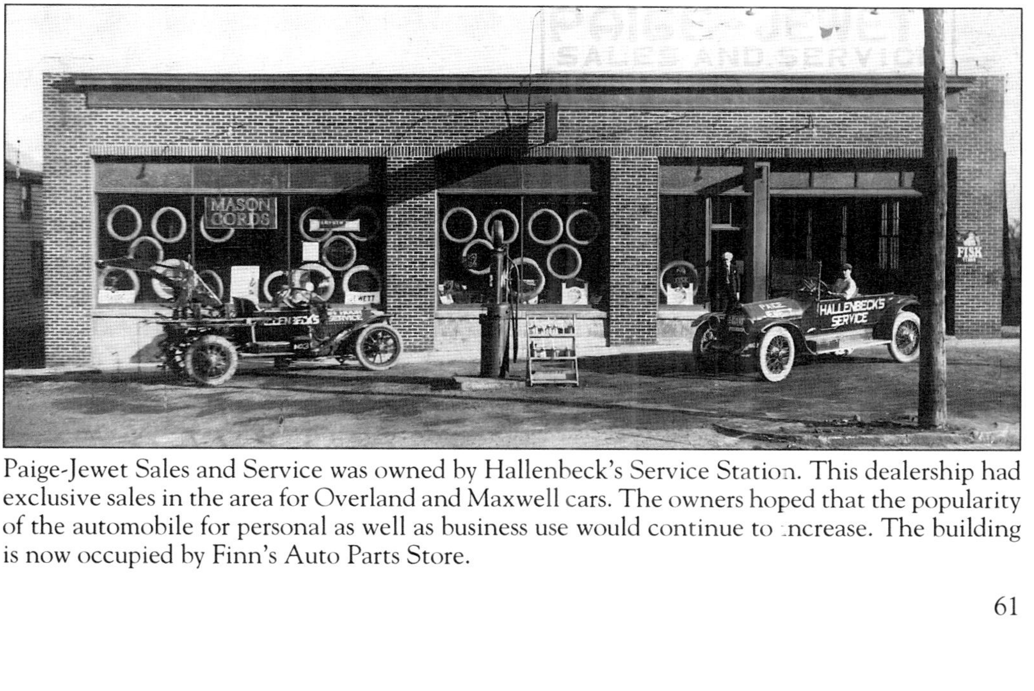

Paige-Jewet Sales and Service was owned by Hallenbeck's Service Station. This dealership had exclusive sales in the area for Overland and Maxwell cars. The owners hoped that the popularity of the automobile for personal as well as business use would continue to increase. The building is now occupied by Finn's Auto Parts Store.

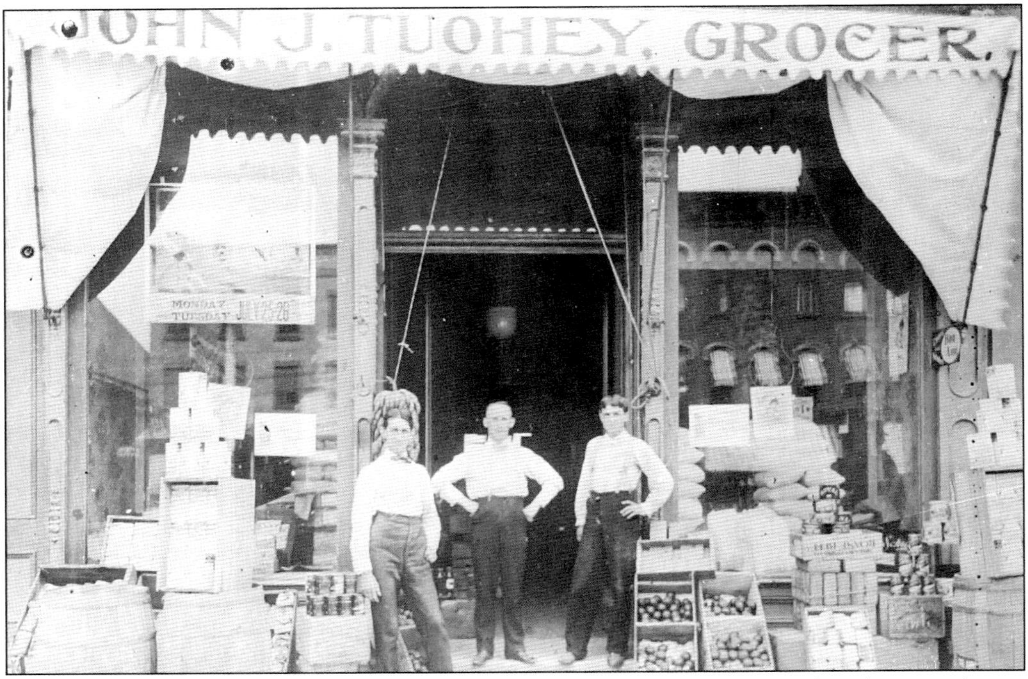

John J. Touhey operated this grocery store at 119 South Main Street. This photograph was taken *c.* 1900.

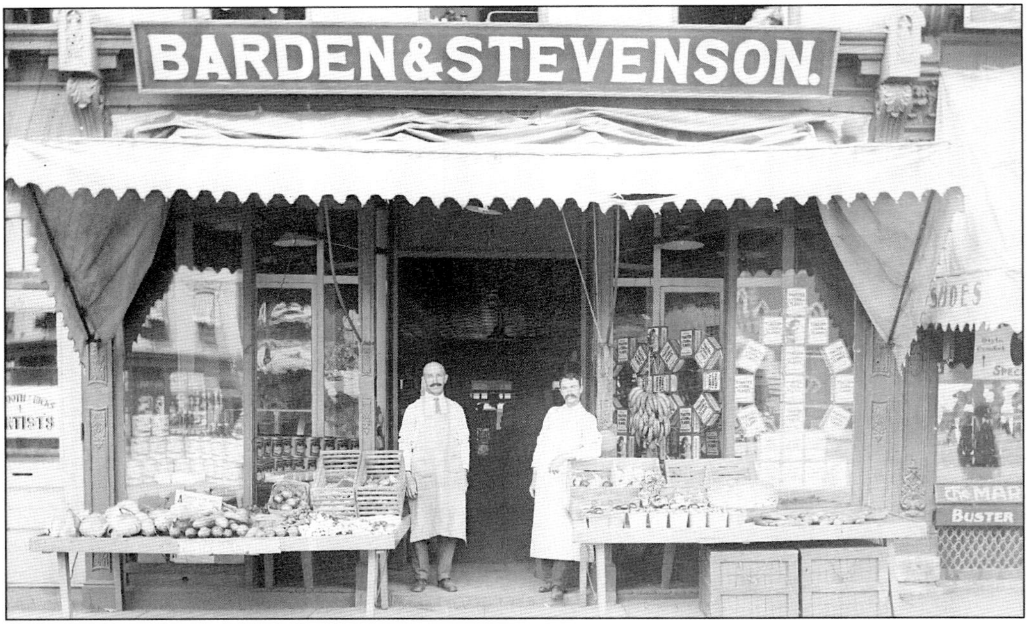

Taken in 1913, the owners of Barden and Stevens Grocery relax for a photograph. A unique display of corn flakes can be seen. The grocery store motto exclaimed,"Quality is always first." In an advertisement of 1913, the store wanted its customers to know that, "In grocery stores it will pay you to take the trouble to find out why this store is enjoying a constantly growing business. A trial order will give you the cue."

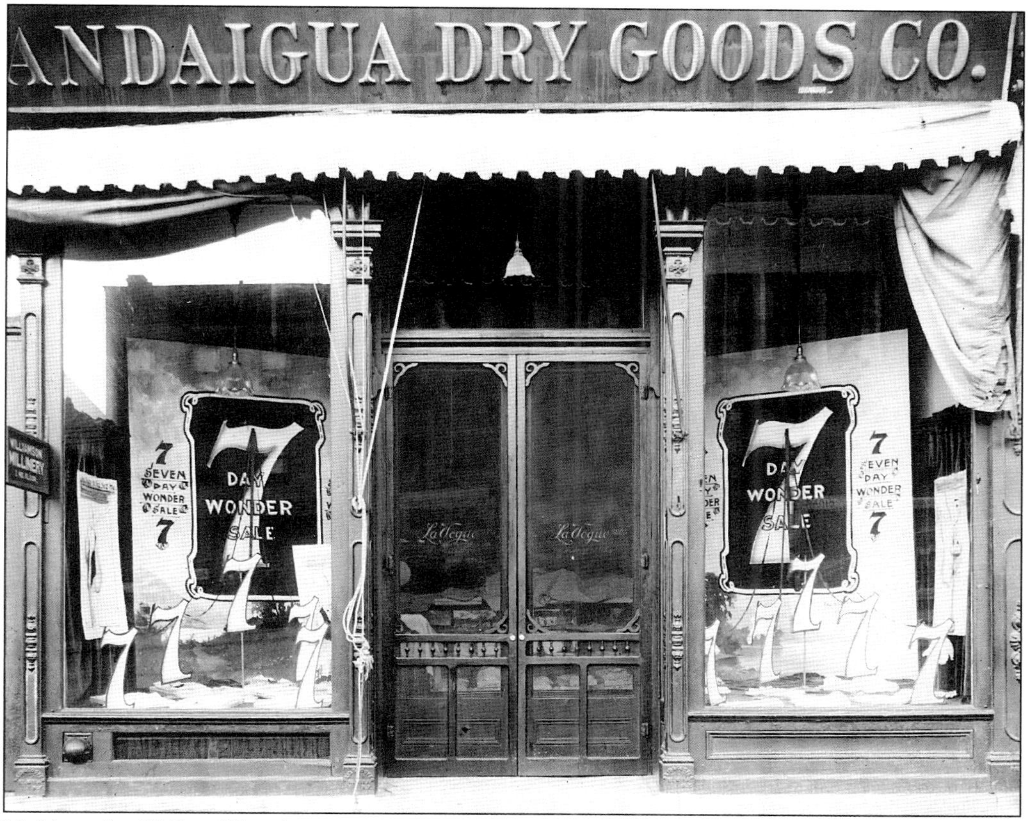

Holding the "7 Day Wonder Sale," Canandaigua Dry Goods was located at 100–102 South Main Street. The store proudly exclaimed, "where quality reigns." In later years this block housed the Endicott Johnson Shoe Store.

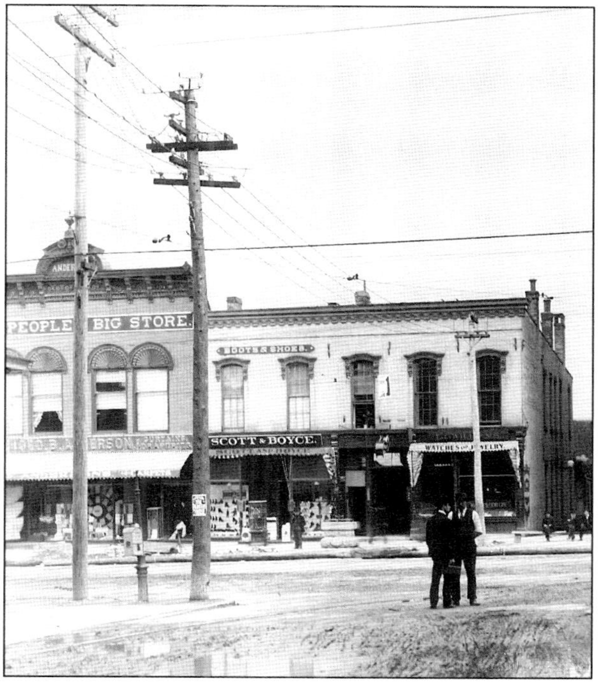

The E.C. Williams Jewelry Store was located at the present location of the Chase Bank on Main Street. Williams Jewelry was the oldest jewelry house in the county, and was the only member of the security alliance in the vicinity. Notice the stone fountain in front of Scott and Boyce Shoe Store. This fountain is now placed in Atwater Park for thirsty pedestrians.

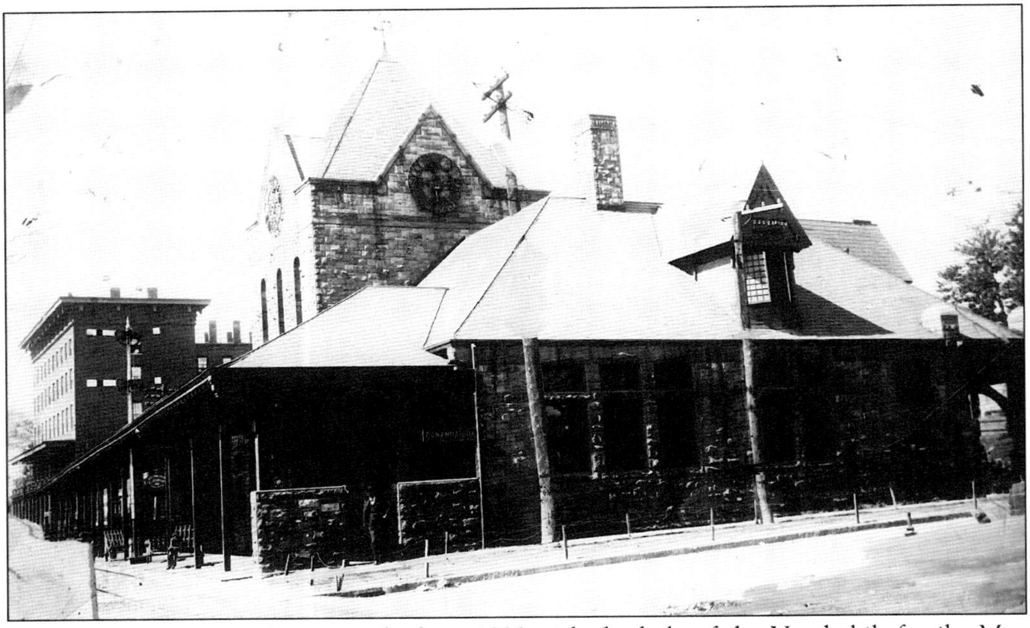

The depot on Niagara Street was built in 1890 with the help of the Vanderbilt family. Mrs. Thompson, however, made the building elegant with a donation of foliage and landscaping. The rail system claimed that this station was the best in the whole system. Before its construction, passengers departed from the Canandaigua Hotel, but Mrs. Thompson felt this was not an adequate place for her out-of-town guests and therefore set about to make a new station.

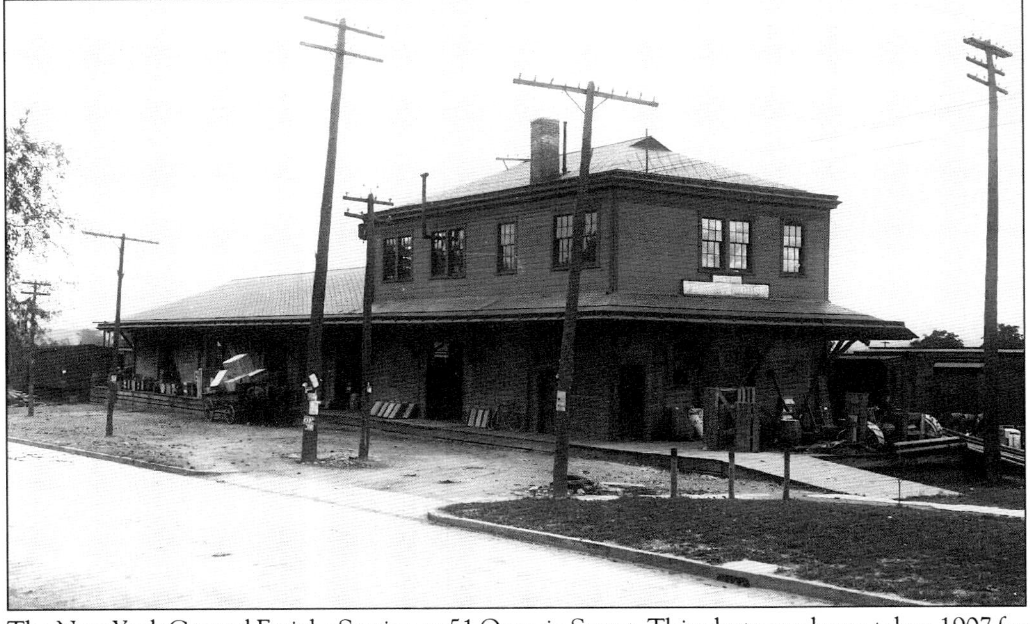

The New York Central Freight Station at 51 Ontario Street. This photograph was taken 1907 for the Canandaigua Board of Trade, the fore runner of the Canandaigua Chamber of Commerce. The building is now occupied by Outhouse Feed.

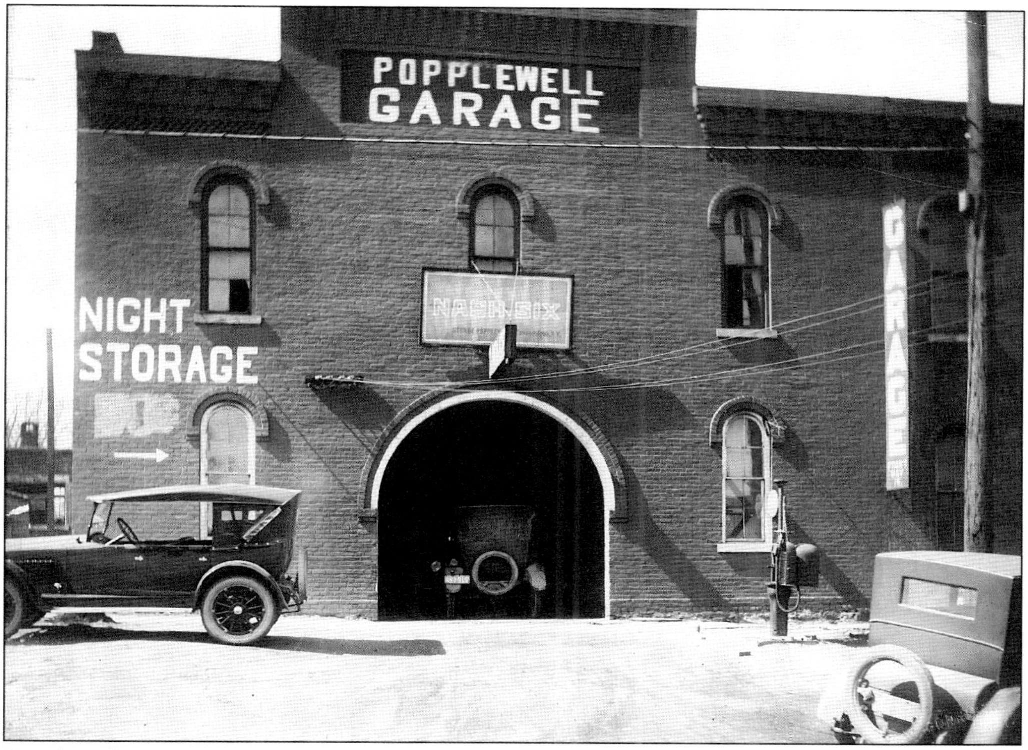

Popplewell Garage was located at 36 Ontario Street. The owner, George Popplewell, claimed that "skill and equipment gives my garage its reputation." The garage sold Studebaker cars, but serviced other types of cars as well. The business operated during the early part of this century.

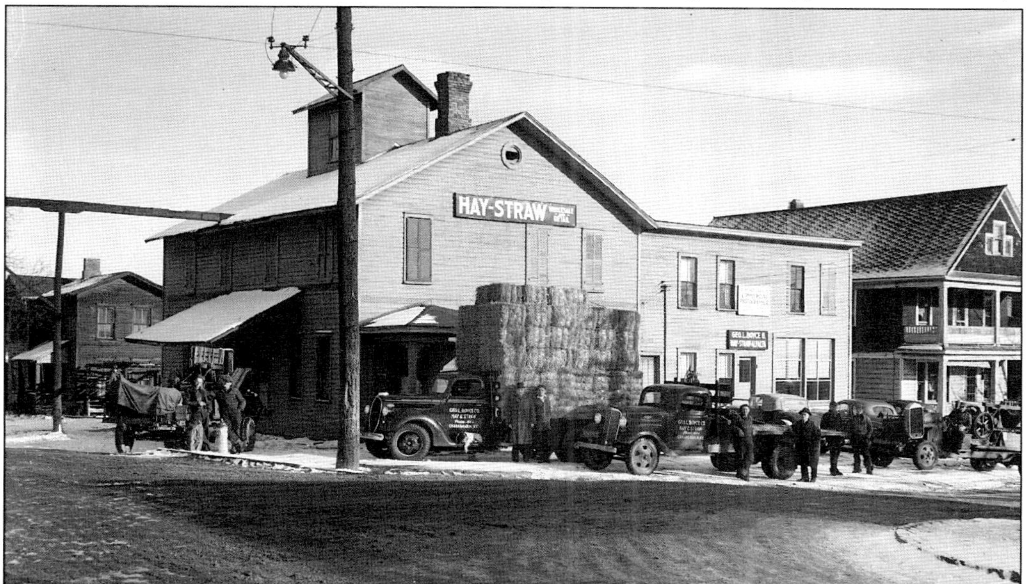

This photograph was taken on the corners of Niagara and Pleasant Streets in the 1930s. The Boyce brothers operated a feed store here. The large house next door still stands.

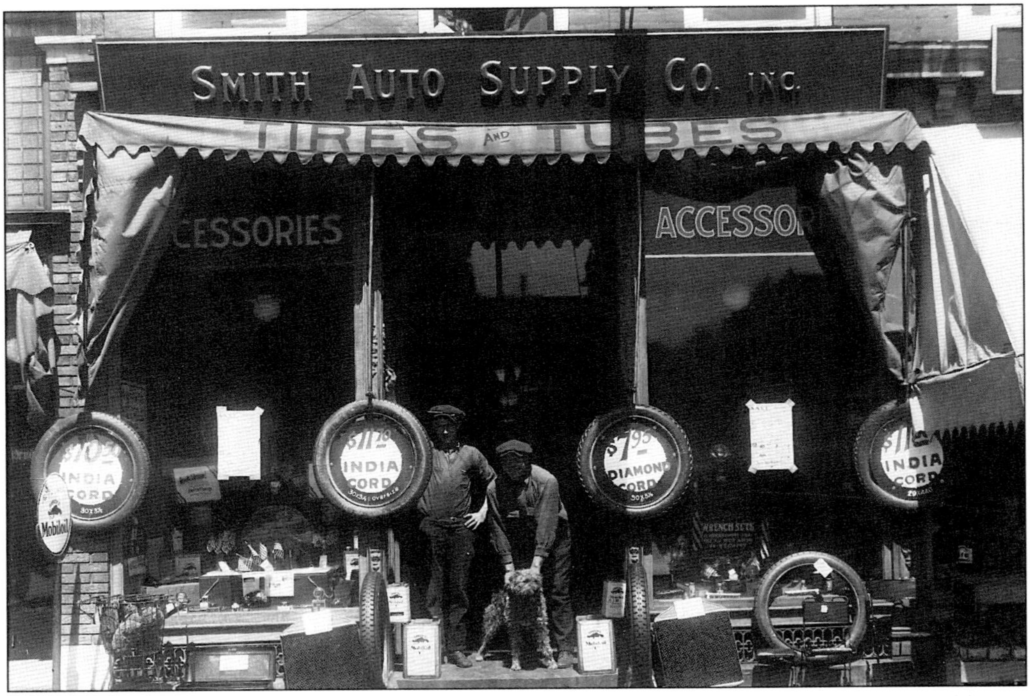

This is a view of Smith Auto Supply, at 183 South Main Street, taken on June 2, 1927. Notice the Mobil Oil cans on the front steps. The tires hanging on the front windows are relatively inexpensive compared with today's prices.

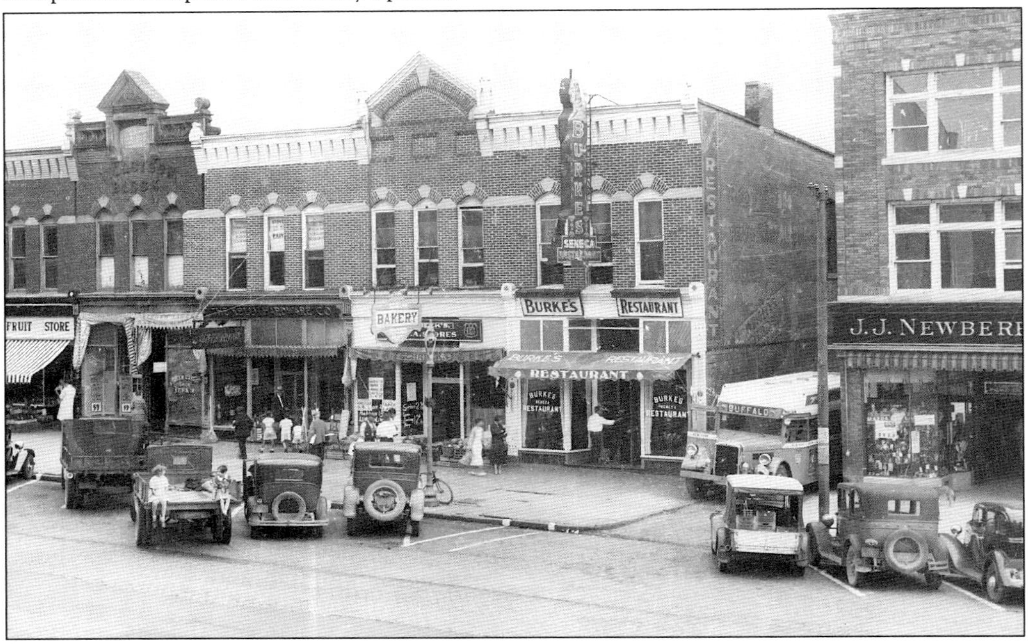

A Greyhound bus pulls out from the alley between Burkes Restaurant and J.J. Newberry's, c. 1930. Main Street is busy with shoppers. Three children head into Ellis hardware with an elder gentleman in tow. The street is paved with bricks.

The Smith & Co Steam Bakery was once located at 113 South Main Street. This 1890 photograph shows the hardworking employees. Advertisement for the bakery claimed that, "We make saltines fresh every day."

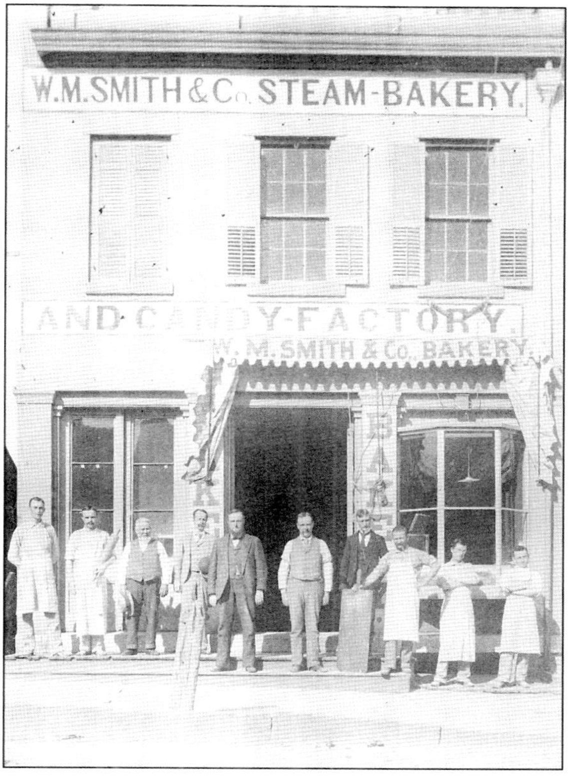

This photograph, taken *c.* 1960s, shows the Cole & Raes Sports Center, before its move to the Parkway Plaza. Crown Jewelers later occupied this storefront. M.H. Fishmans survived until the mid-1960s, selling household goods and sundries. L.M. Campbell Jeweler moved across the street in 1961, giving the bank room to expand.

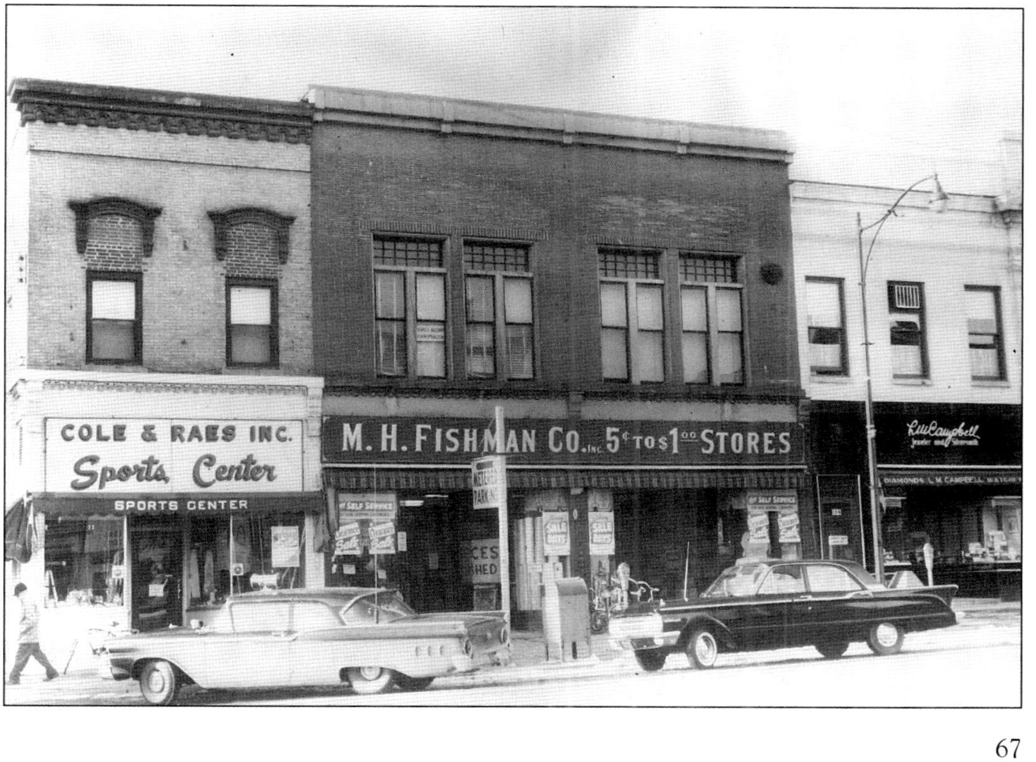

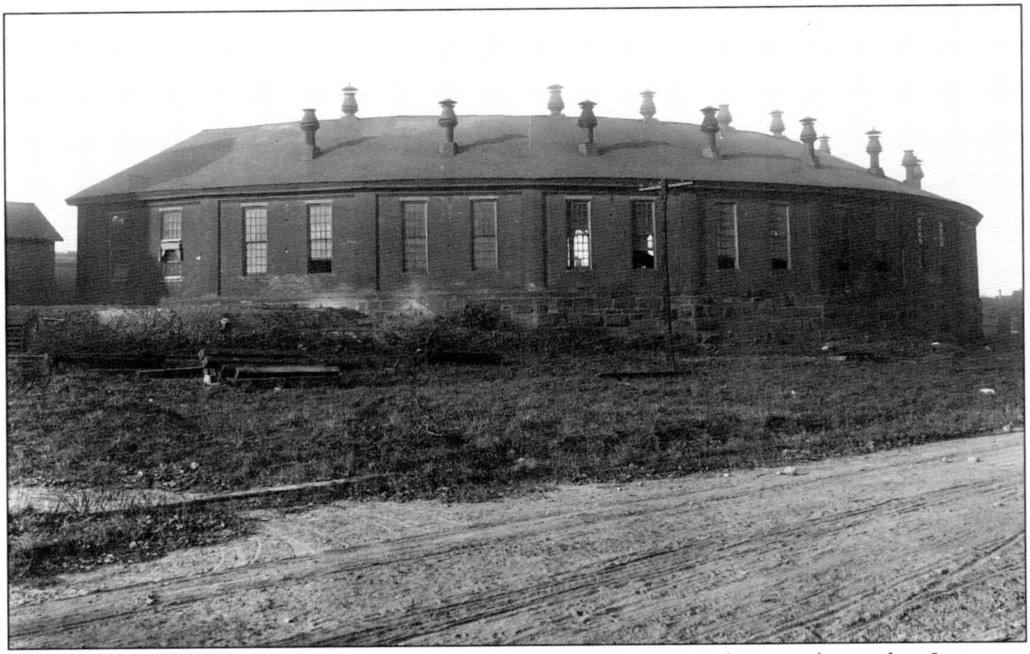

This turn-of-the-century view shows the Northern Central Round House located at Leicester and Ontario Streets.

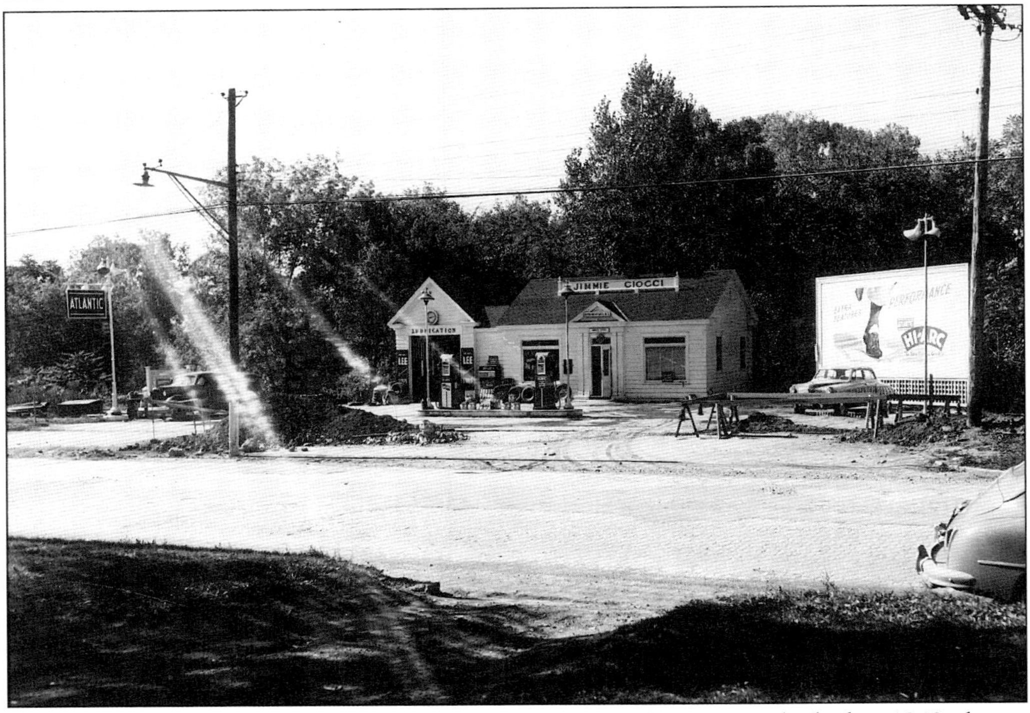

Jim Park took this photograph of Jimmie Ciocci's Service Station as it looked in 1949, during the initiation of the Million Dollar Main Street Project, which widened and improved Main Street. The service station was located on the lower end of South Main Street.

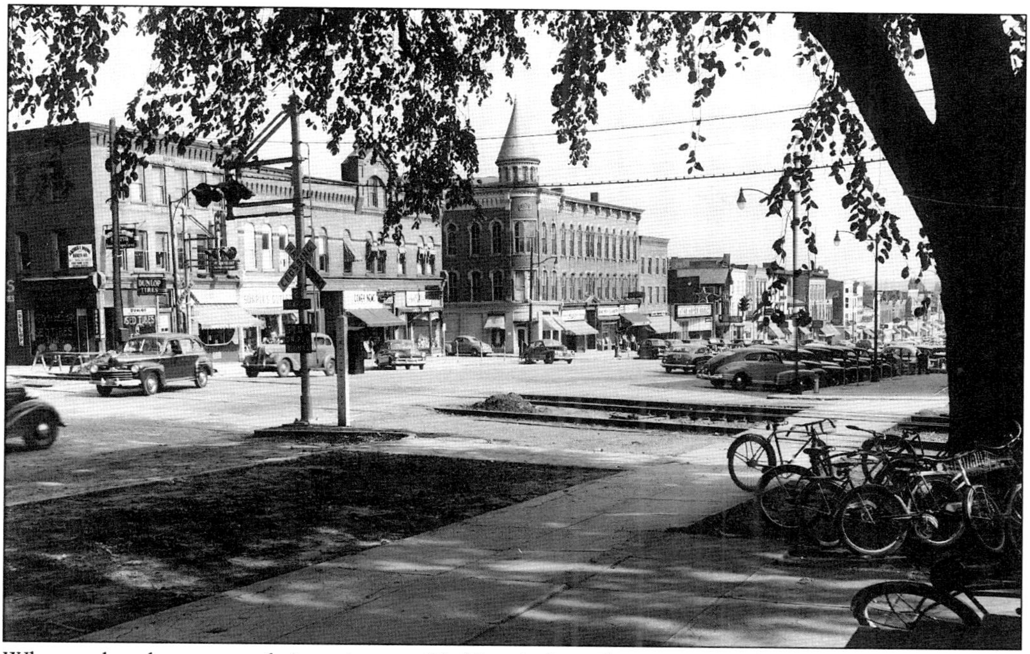

What a lovely scene of Americana. Children's bicycles rest outside City Hall, shaded by giant elm trees. Parked cars give an indication that businesses are doing well despite the construction of the new Main Street. Notice the McKechnie Building on the corner of Main and Niagara Streets.

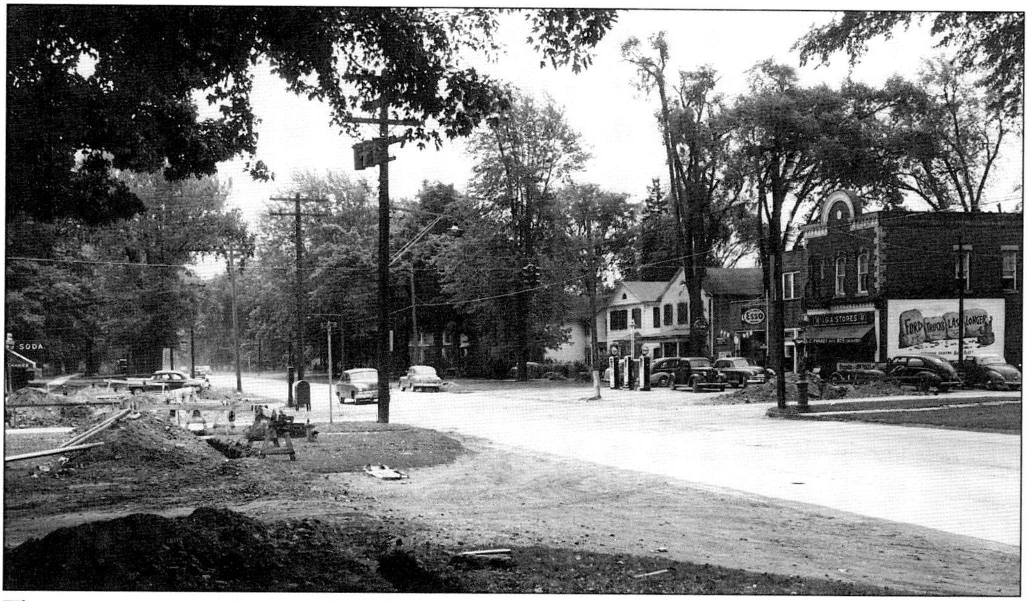

The intersection at Main and Buffalo Streets seems very quiet compared with today. The IGA on the corner was Vecchi's IGA at one point. The building was once owned by the Frarey family and is currently McMillan Realty. A Gold Medal Flour advertisement still evident on the side of the building gives passersby a clue to the building's past uses. The service station gave travelers a place to fuel up before heading out of town.

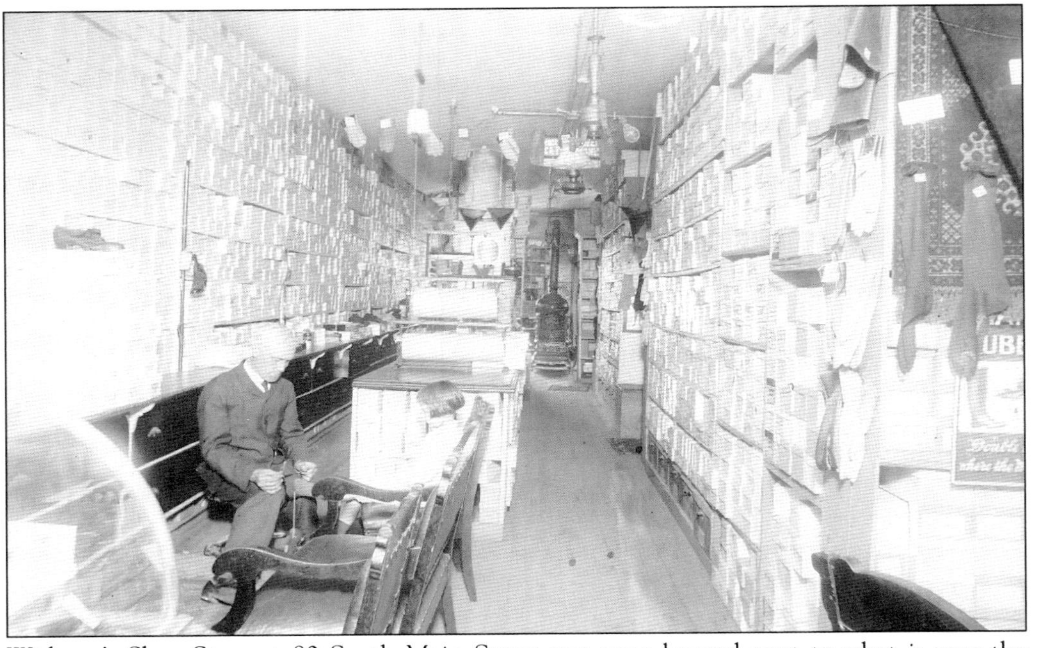

Widman's Shoe Store at 80 South Main Street was once located next to what is now the Renaissance Shoppe. A Widman's advertisement in the Canandaigua City Directory of 1916 claimed that buyers should try Widman's Gun Metal Shoes for $2–$4. In later years, the storefront became a fabric store.

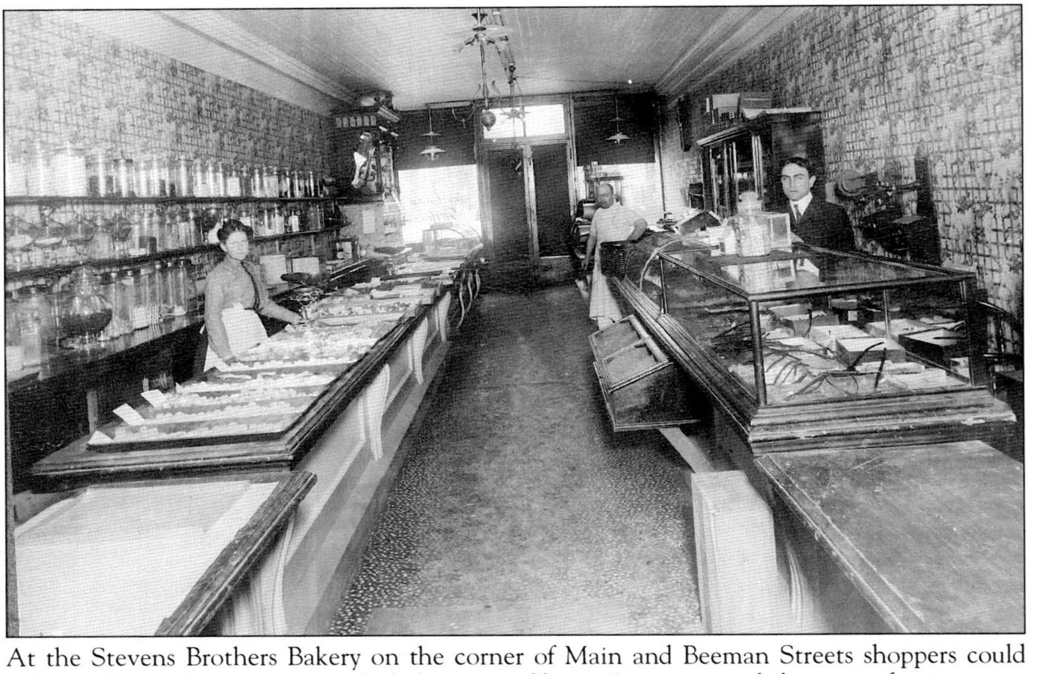

At the Stevens Brothers Bakery on the corner of Main and Beeman Streets shoppers could order wedding cakes, macaroons, lady fingers, and kisses. Ice cream and choice confections were always on hand. What child would not like a visit to this shop? The offices of *Valvano Central News* now occupies this storefront.

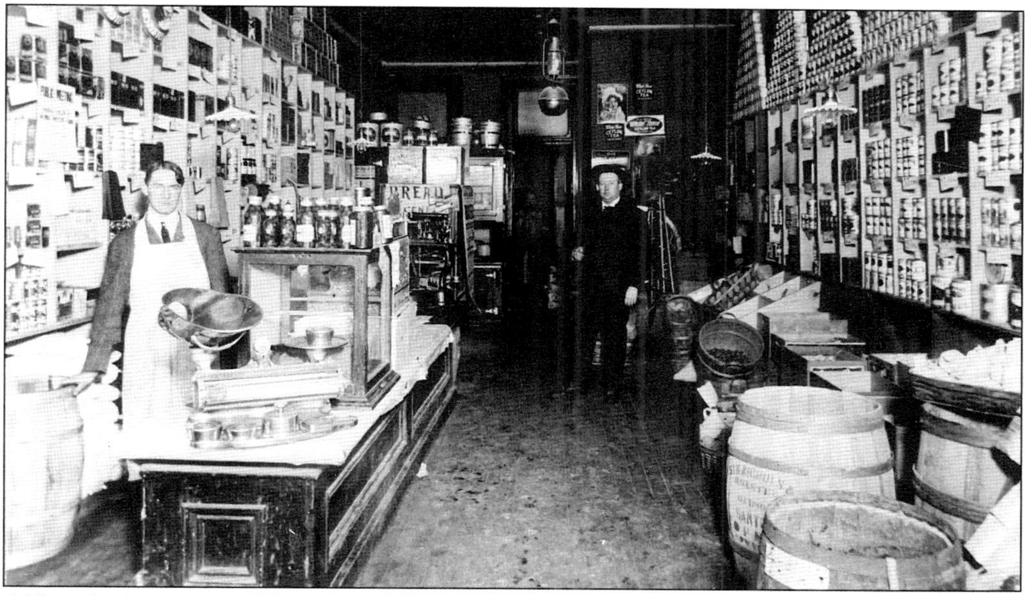

Although the name and location of this grocery store is unknown, it is an interesting image of yesteryear. The barrels in the foreground hold fruit and pickles. The produce would be measured on the elaborate scale on the counter. The cans are neatly arranged on the shelves and would have to be expertly removed by the grocer to avoid an avalanche.

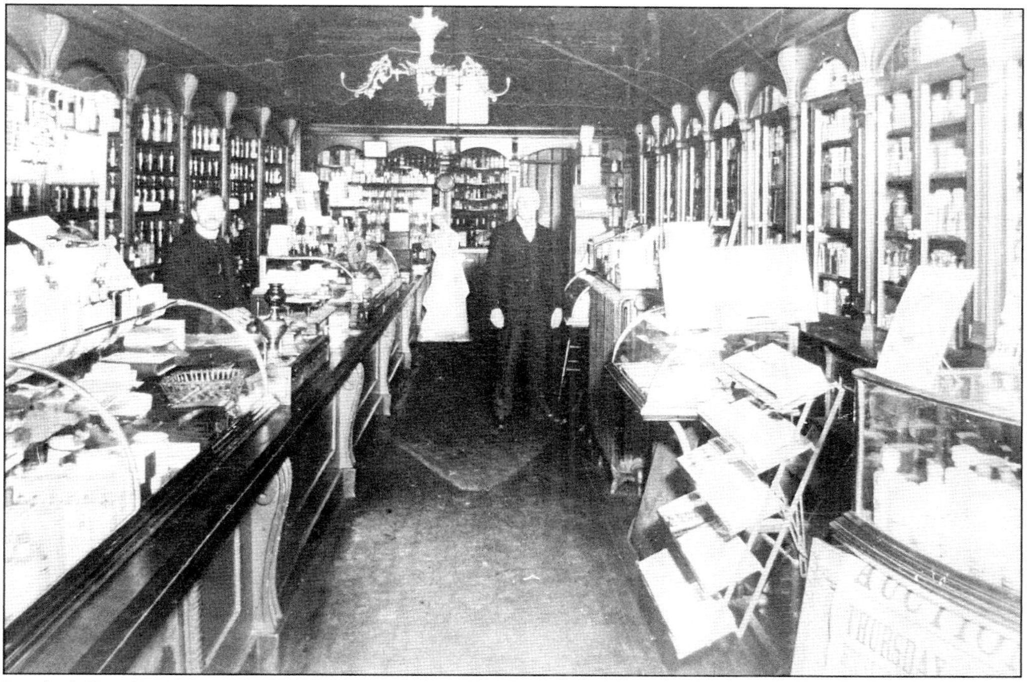

Paul A.D. & Company Druggist at 142 South Main Street is now the location of Crown Jewelers. In this photograph, Mr. Alexander Paul is in the center of the store, while Mr. Alfred Pearce is on the left. The building was owned by Mary Paul from 1869 until 1923. Notice the apothecary jars on the left wall.

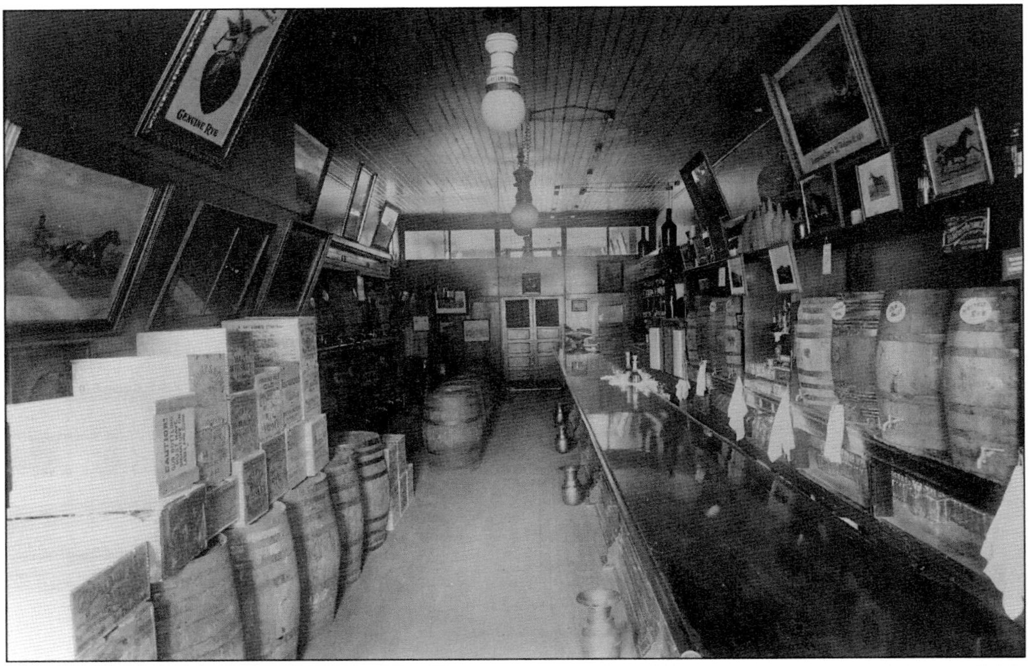

Coyle's Saloon at 155 South Main Street on the east side sold cigars, tobacco, and liquor. This tavern was owned by Charles and Thomas Coyle. The gentleman in the background is Aaron Dorsey. Today's equivalent to a micro-brewery, this tavern was in existence during the 1880s.

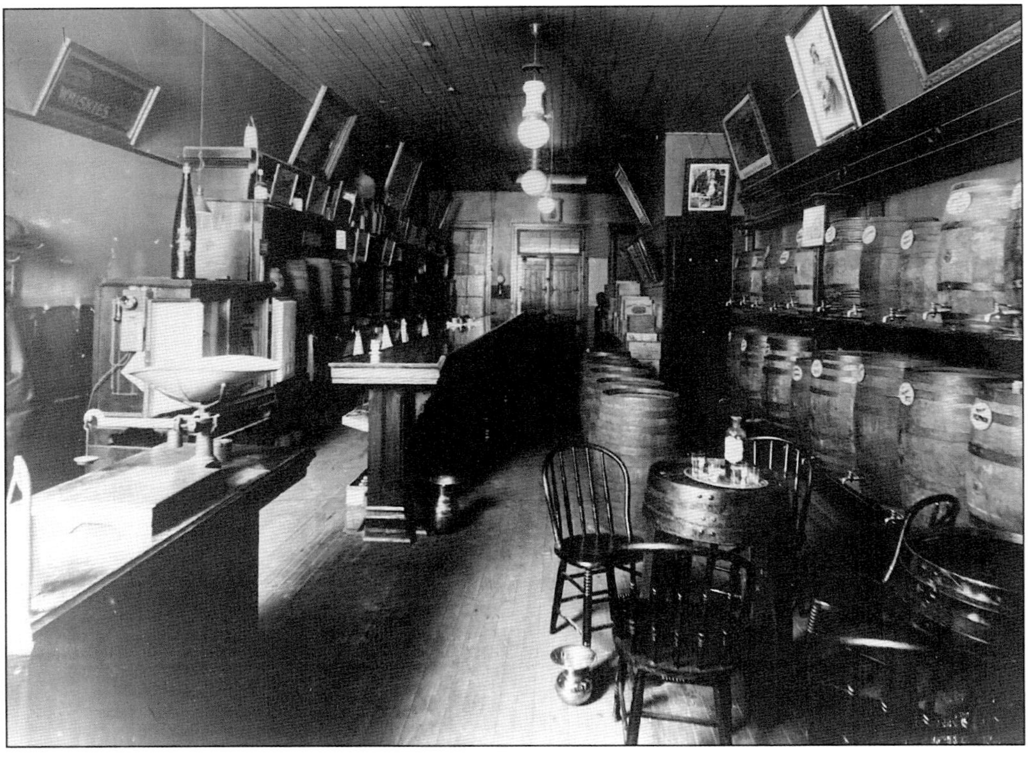

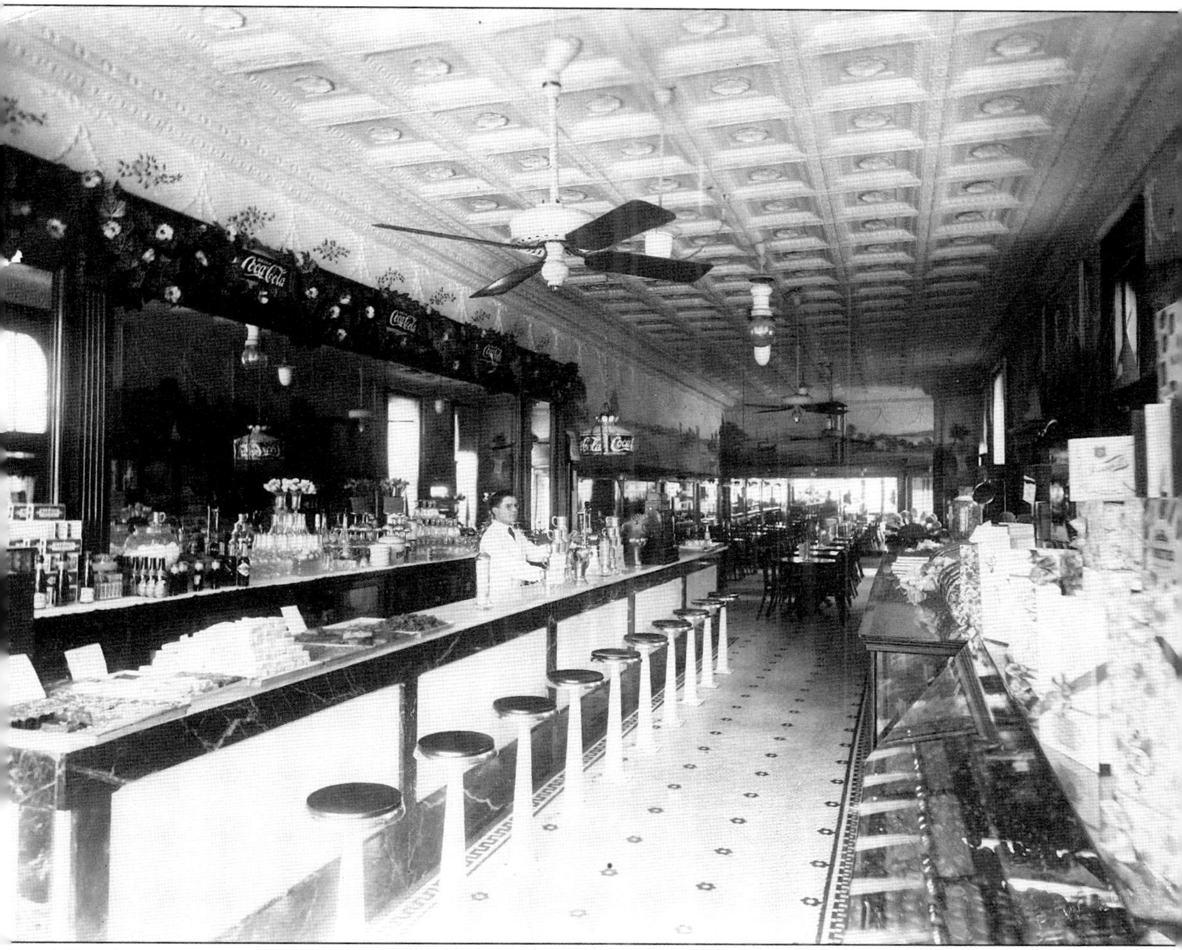

The Arvanite Brothers Store at 56 South Main Street, (now the Renaissance Shoppe) opened May 4, 1907. Brothers George, Steven, and Peter promised the purest of ingredients and the most beautiful of surroundings with mirrors and potted plants. This was the second store for the brothers in Canandaigua, and it provided a soda fountain counter for patrons. The brothers' other store, located at 184 South Main Street, sold candies in fancy packages. Who wouldn't want to step into the past, sit down at the counter, and enjoy a treat here? A cool sweet treat on a hot summer's day makes everyone smile.

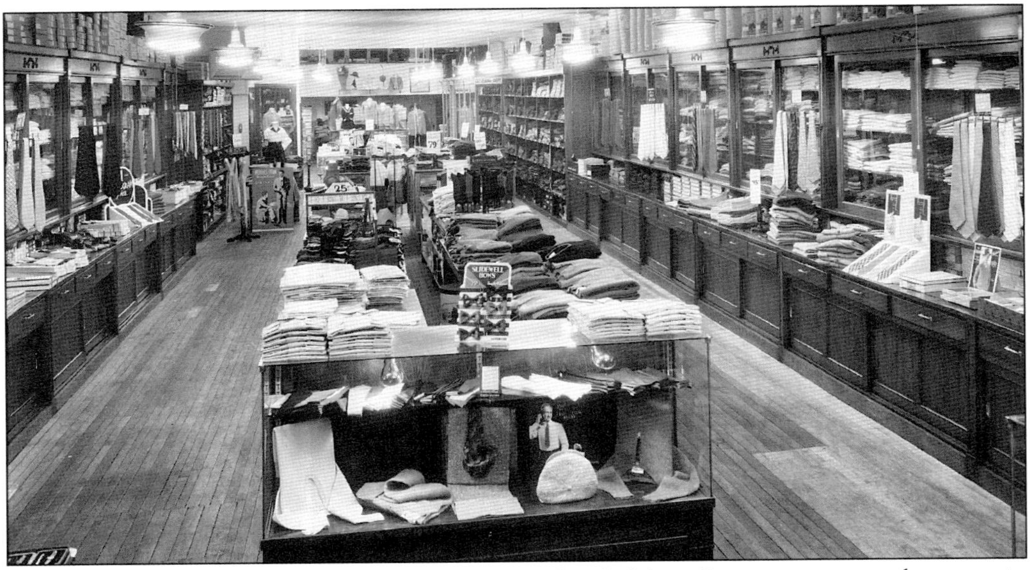

Shenkman's Clothing for men and boys at 139 South Main Street was a popular store in Canandaigua for over fifty years. The business was started by Louis Shenkman c. 1915. He had immigrated to Canandaigua from Russia and opened his family business. His son, Bernard Shenkman, ran the business with his brother-in-law, Victor Aronson, until 1975, when they sold the store to Marshall Seager and Harold and Ken Unger. Gentlemen could find the latest in formal and sportswear here. The basement of the store was also utilized, selling jeans and tee shirts. The Davidson Shoe Store was also owned by the Shenkmans until the 1970s, when they sold it to Edward Hogan.

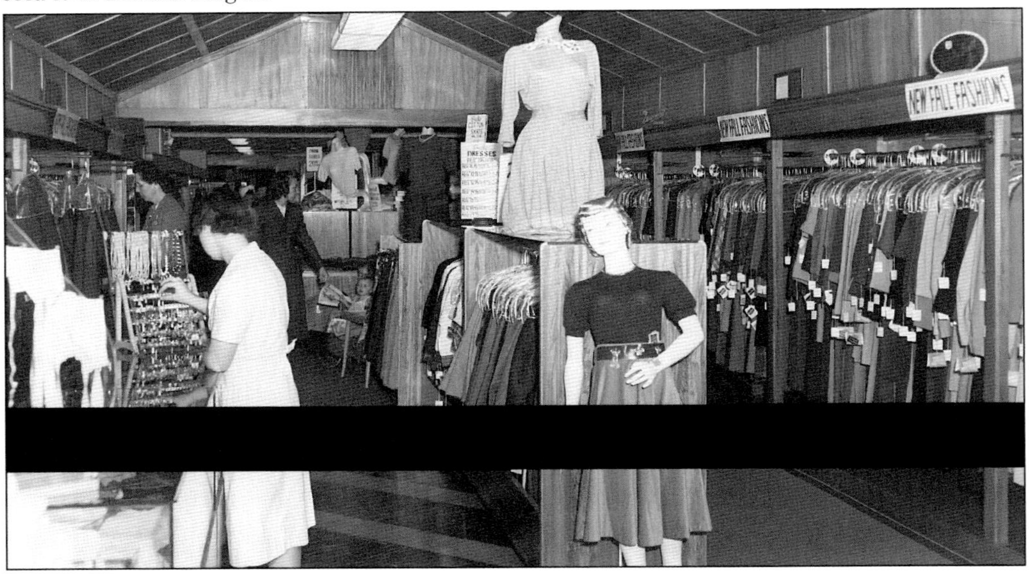

The Norma Shop, located next door to Shenkman's, gave ladies in Canandaigua the finest selection in women's fashions. The shop was named for Norma Aronson, Louis Shenkman's daughter. Victor Aronson managed The Norma Shop, which sold foundations, costume jewelry, dresses, and overcoats. If your purchase came from The Norma Shop you could be assured quality.

Six

City Buildings

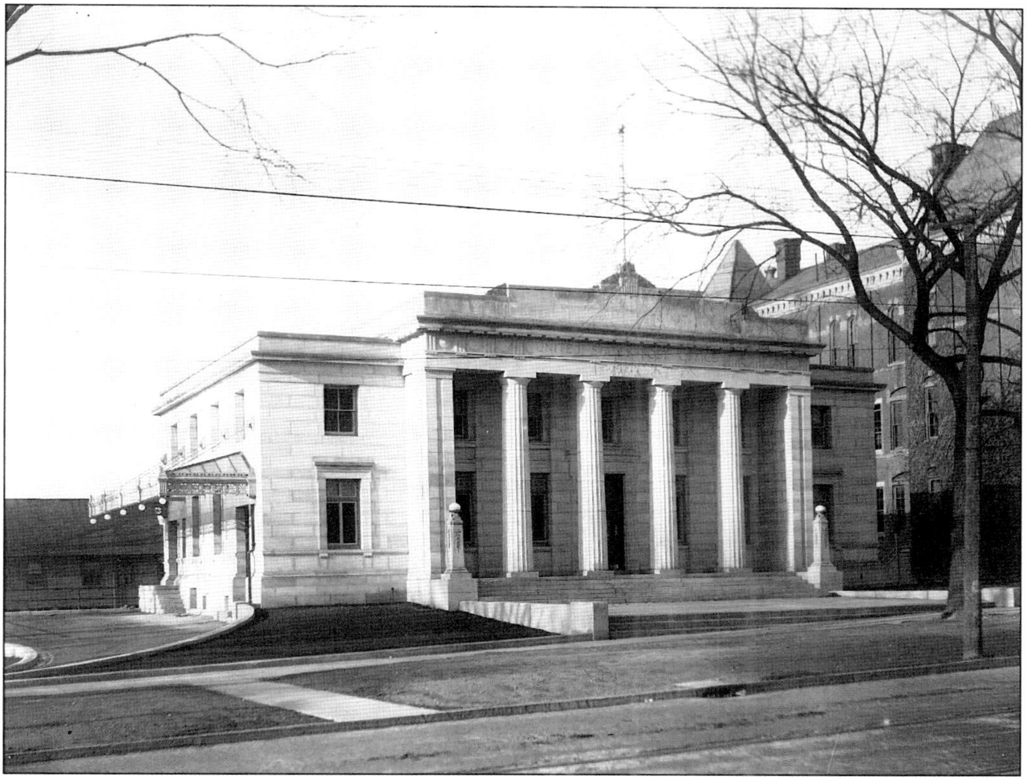

The U.S. Post Office, located at 28 North Main Street next to Atwater Park, operated at that location from 1911 until October of 1991. The site originally housed the Atwater Building, which was razed for the post office's construction. Mary Thompson hired architects Arthur and Collens of Boston to design the building. She felt Canandaigua deserved a more stately building than what the government could provide, so she supplemented the monies given by the government for the beautiful building. The third-story courtroom was added to the building for family court needs.

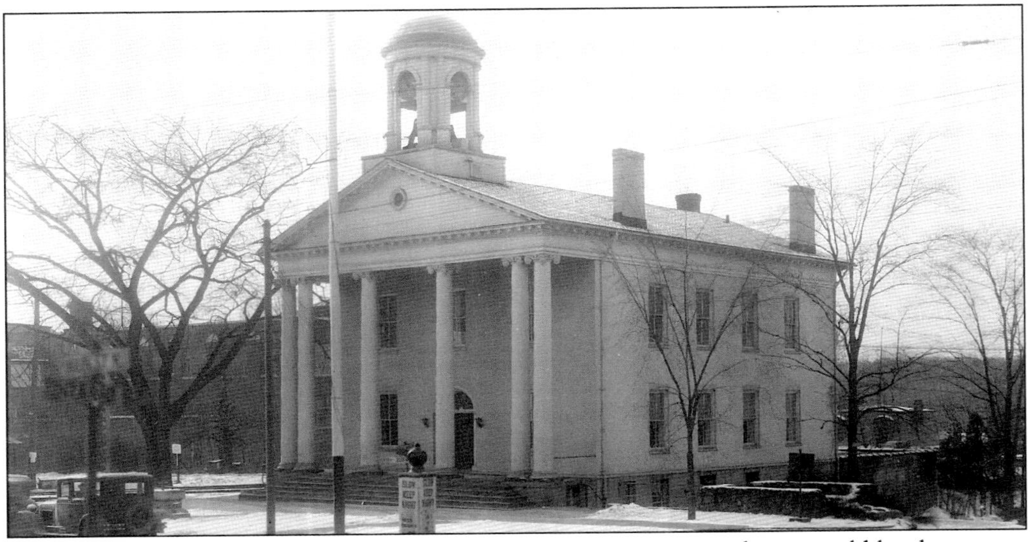

Canandaigua City Hall was the courthouse for Ontario County, and it was sold by the county to the village and town of Canandaigua in 1859. It is believed that the architect of the 1824 structure was Abner Bunnel, although Francis Granger was certainly influential in its design. The famous Mason trial was held here in 1826. Outraged Masons had William Morgan arrested on false charges when it was discovered that Morgan planned on exposing the secrets of free masonry. While in jail, Morgan was kidnapped from his cell, never to be found. Nicholas Chesebro, Edward Sawyer, Loton Lawson, and John Sheldon were tried for conspiracy to kidnap Morgan; only Sheldon was acquitted. The building underwent renovations in 1878, 1916, and 1991—when it was returned to its original appearance.

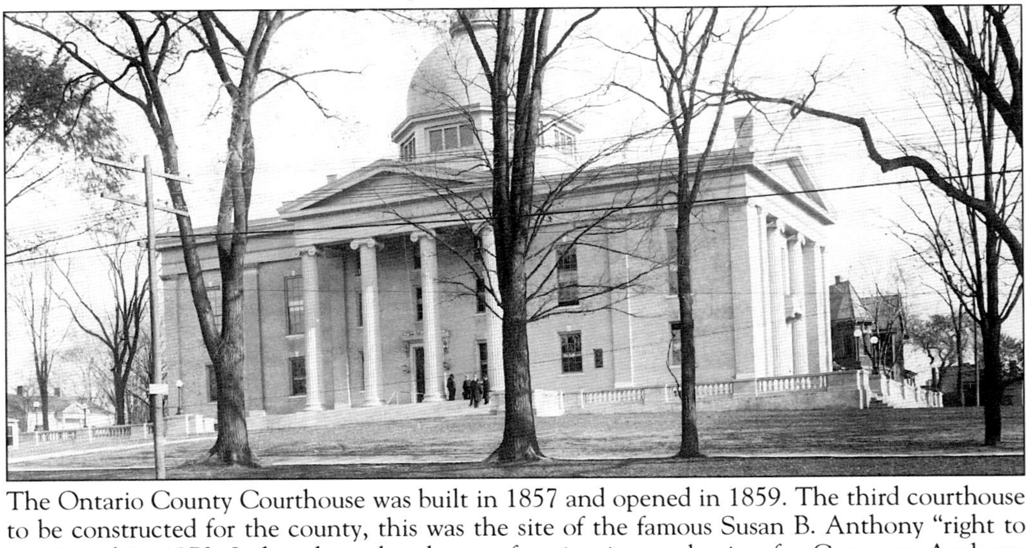

The Ontario County Courthouse was built in 1857 and opened in 1859. The third courthouse to be constructed for the county, this was the site of the famous Susan B. Anthony "right to vote" trial in 1873. Indicted on the charge of voting in an election for Congress, Anthony was found guilty and ordered to pay a $100 fine. She refused to pay, preferring to go to jail, but her attorney paid the fine. Anthony was quoted, "May it please your honor I shall never pay a dollar of your unjust penalty . . . I shall earnestly and persistently continue to urge all women to the practical recognition of the old revolutionary maxim, that resistance to tyranny is obedience to God."

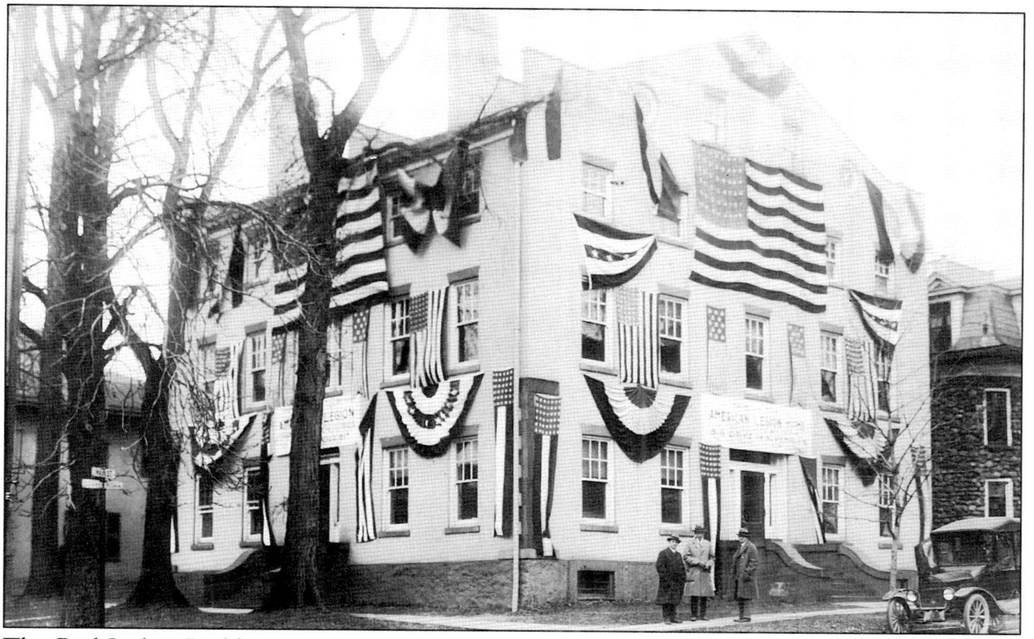

The Red Jacket Building on the corner of Main and Gorham Streets was built in the 1850s by Nathaniel Gorham Jr. During the 1870s it was briefly owned by Amos Burdick. A meeting of three prominent citizens—McKechnie, Williams H. Adams, and M.D. Munger—during December of 1888 focused on the possibility of formulating a social club here. The club lasted until 1910, after which the American Legion occupied the building. The American Legion held events here until 1945, when it relocated to the McKechnie House on North Main Street.

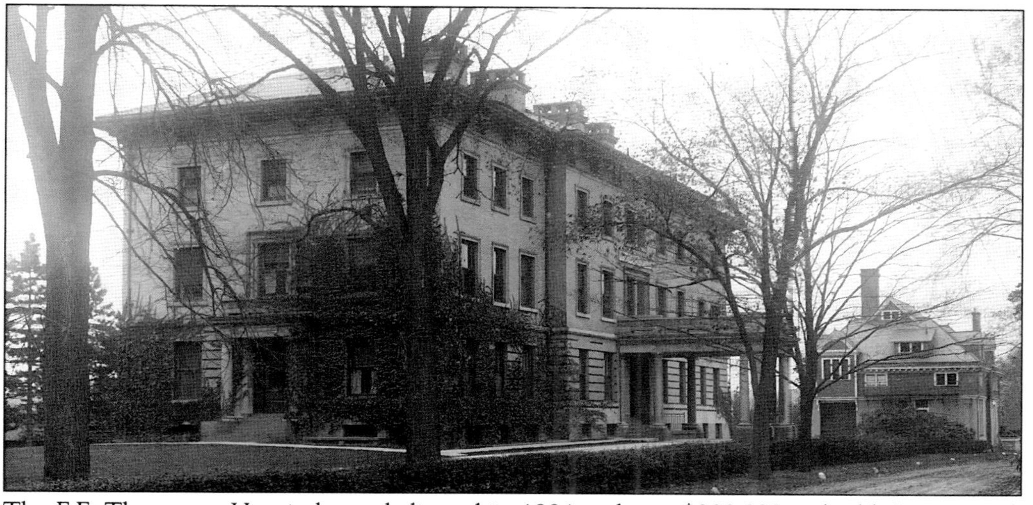

The F.F. Thompson Hospital was dedicated in 1904 and cost $200,000 to build. It was a gift to the city of Canandaigua from Mary Thompson in memory of her husband. Francis Allen of Boston was the architect. According to the *Ontario County Chronicle*, the hospital's first patient was Herman Hatchins of Chapin Street. The original hospital had 50 rooms and a staff of 34. By 1959, there were 142 beds and a staff of 200. A 1959 addition provided home to surgical units. A new 6-million-dollar building was constructed on Parrish Street, and in 1971 the hospital moved to its present location. The building on Main Street is now used as senior housing.

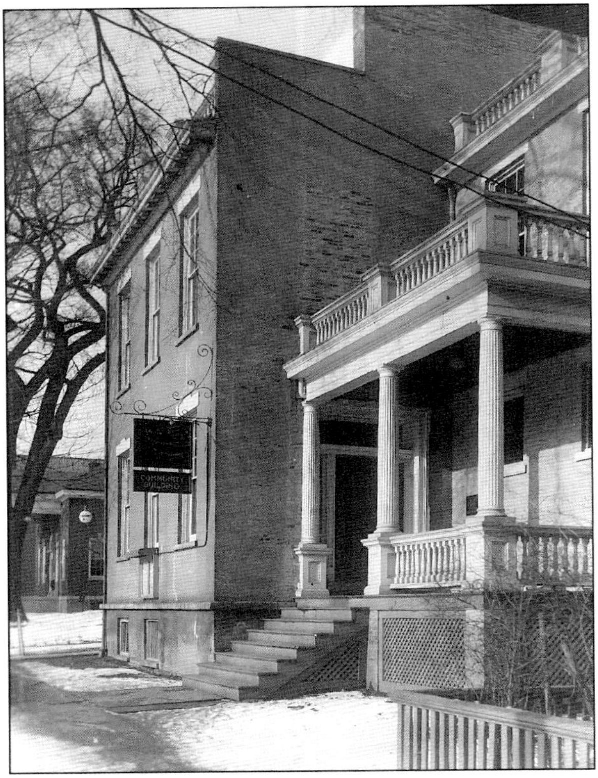

The YMCA Community Building was once located at 45 North Main Street. This building served the youth of Canandaigua before the present YMCA was built across the street. It was first used by the Utica Branch Bank and was later known as the Crosby House.

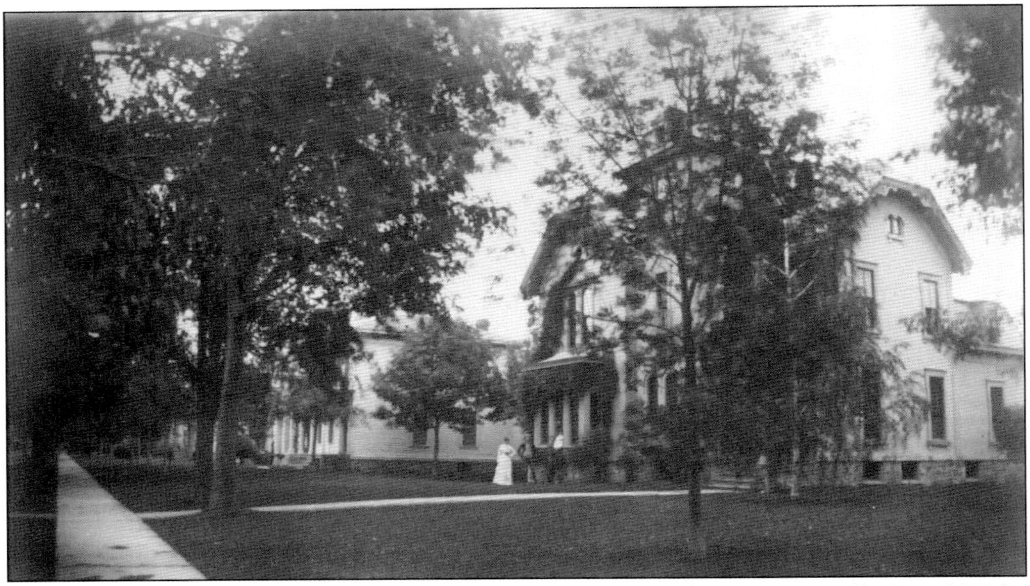

This beautiful Victorian home at 129 Howell Street is a Canandaigua treasure. Built in 1871 by Hugh King in Italianate villa style, the house is known as the Adams House after the original owner, Judge Willam H. Adams. The Know family purchased the home at the turn of the century, making several changes to the first floor. The home has several stained-glass windows and fireplaces. At one time, servants were summoned with a whistle button and speaking tube.

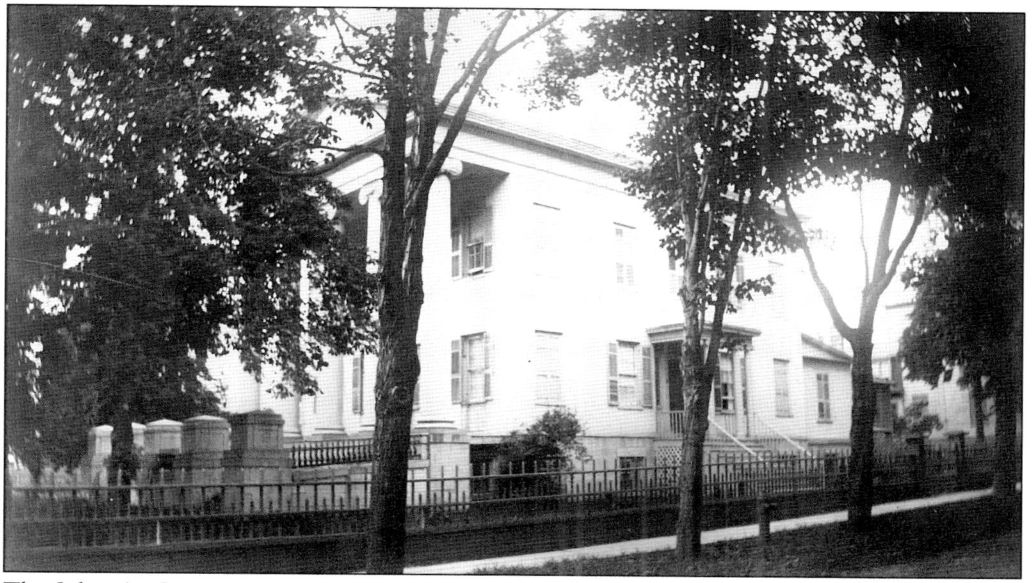

The John A. Granger House is located at 16 Gibson Street, next to St. Mary's Church. The home was built in 1834 by Canandaigua businessman John Granger, the son of Gideon Granger, postmaster general under Thomas Jefferson. The large front porch was used for entertaining friends in the summer. The grounds included an enchanting sunken garden between the house and Main Street. In 1873, Father Dennis English purchased the property and converted the house into a convent for the nuns of St. Mary's. The building now serves administrative needs of the church.

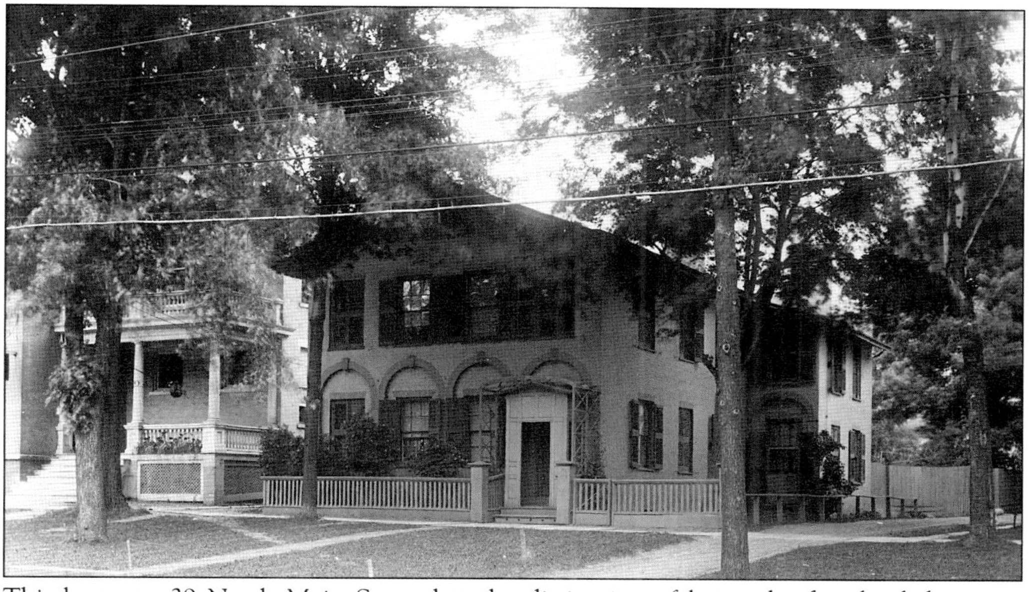

This house at 39 North Main Street has the distinction of being the first brick house in Canandaigua, built in 1809. It was used as a Masonic Temple from 1809 to 1819. Druggist C.R. Paul and his sisters lived in the home during the early 1900s. For many years, the home was occupied by Canandaigua dentist Howard Coons and his wife Corona. The fence no longer remains at this charming residence.

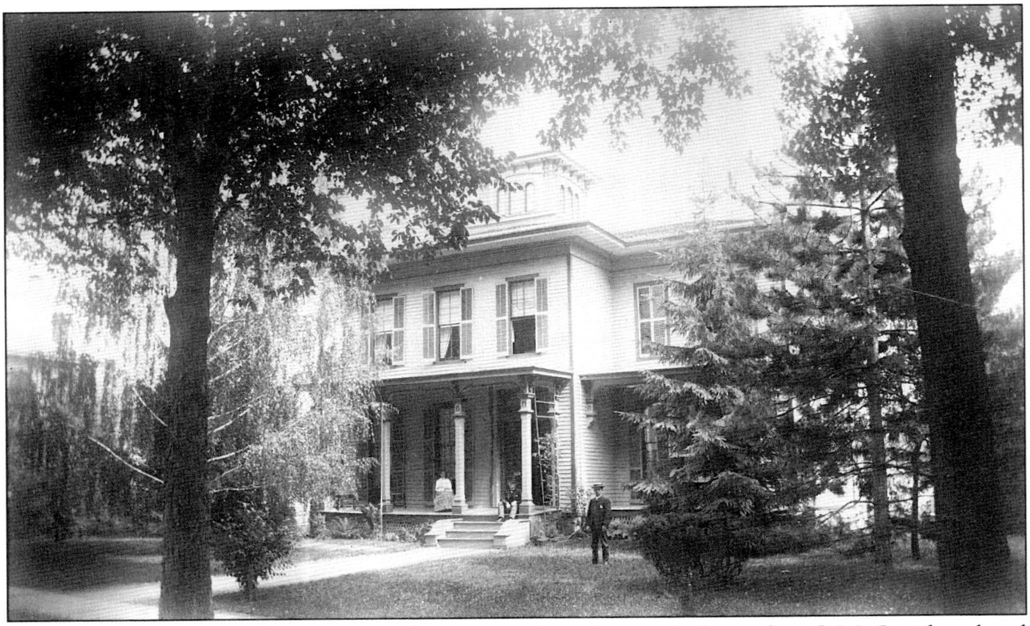

This home at 69 Howell Street is no longer standing. It once belonged to O.M. Smith, a local accountant, and it resembled a home further down the street at 107 Howell Street.

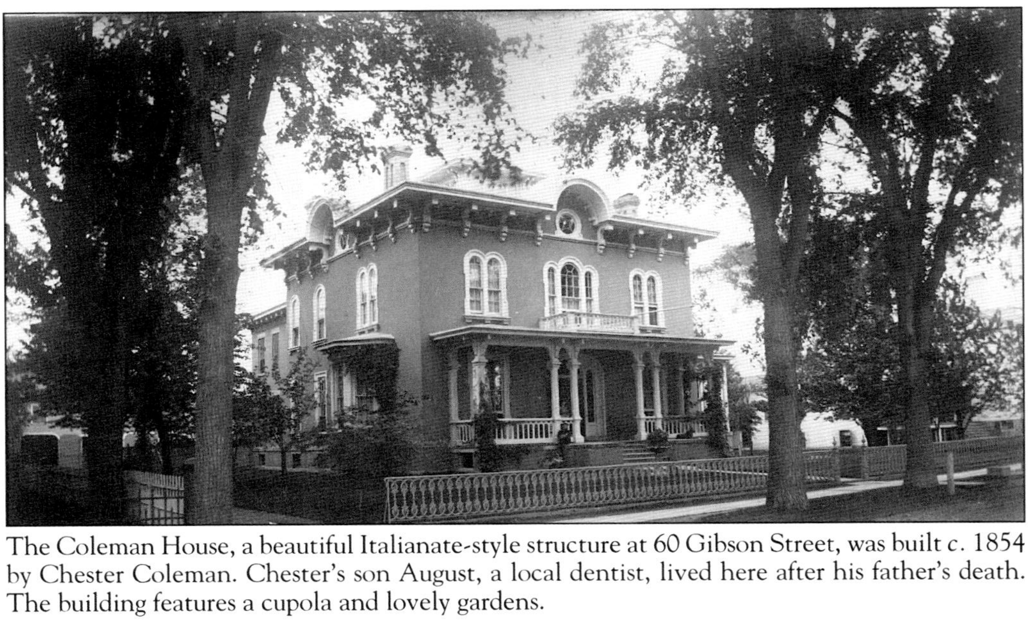

The Coleman House, a beautiful Italianate-style structure at 60 Gibson Street, was built *c.* 1854 by Chester Coleman. Chester's son August, a local dentist, lived here after his father's death. The building features a cupola and lovely gardens.

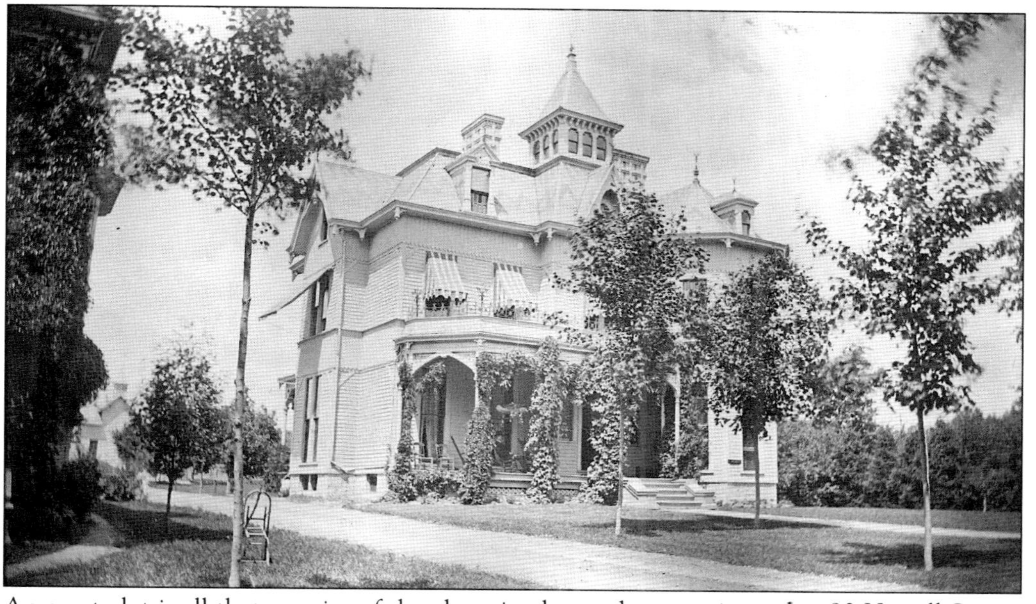

An empty lot is all that remains of the charming home that was situated at 90 Howell Street. The house was built by J. Albert Granger, the grandson of Gideon Granger. Granger later sold the home and moved to New York City. At the time of the photograph, the home was owned by Dr. Wolmsley, a local physician. Later converted to apartments, the home was damaged beyond repair in 1966 and was leveled.

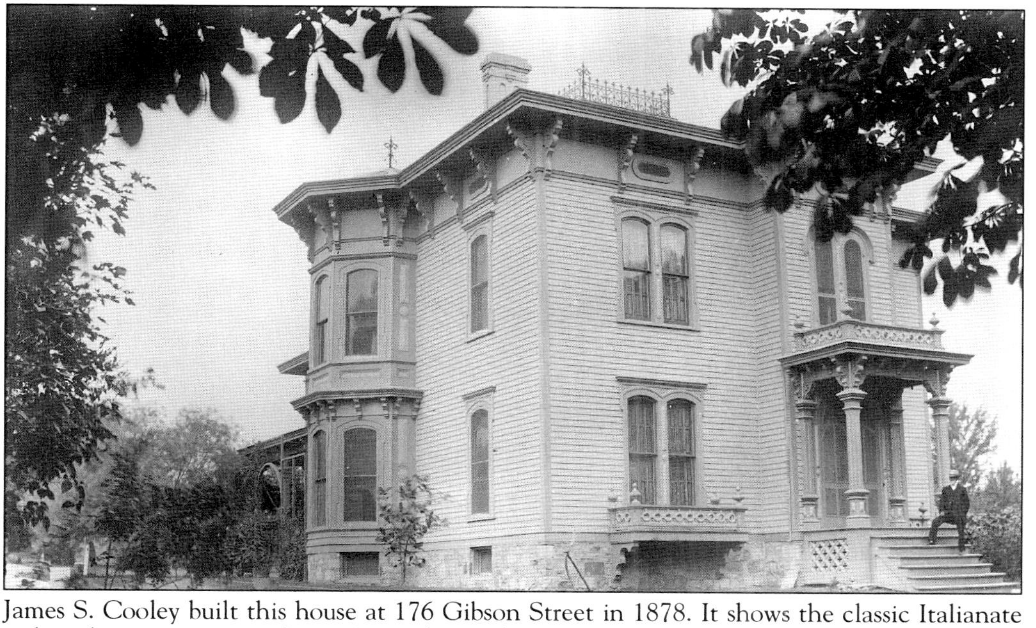

James S. Cooley built this house at 176 Gibson Street in 1878. It shows the classic Italianate styling that was very popular in Canandaigua during the 1880s. It was remodeled in April 1892 by Saunders and Mead. The home now has several apartments within its walls.

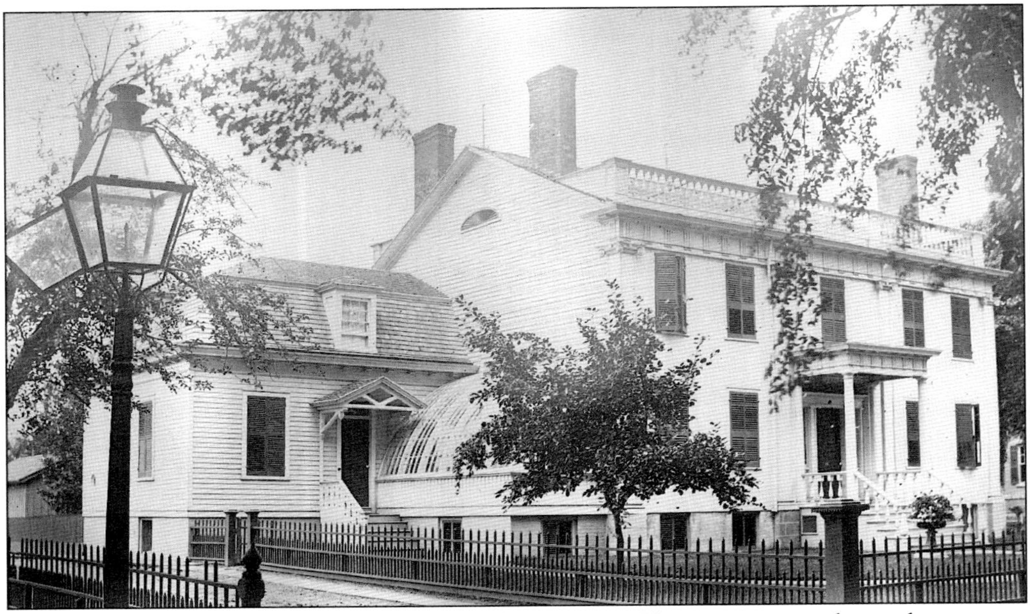

The E. Carr House was built in 1824 at 50 Gibson Street. The west wing and greenhouse were removed prior to 1936. The land for the home was purchased from H.B. Gibson just after the street was opened. Dr. Carr was described as the best-loved physician that Canandaigua ever knew. The home is now divided into four apartments.

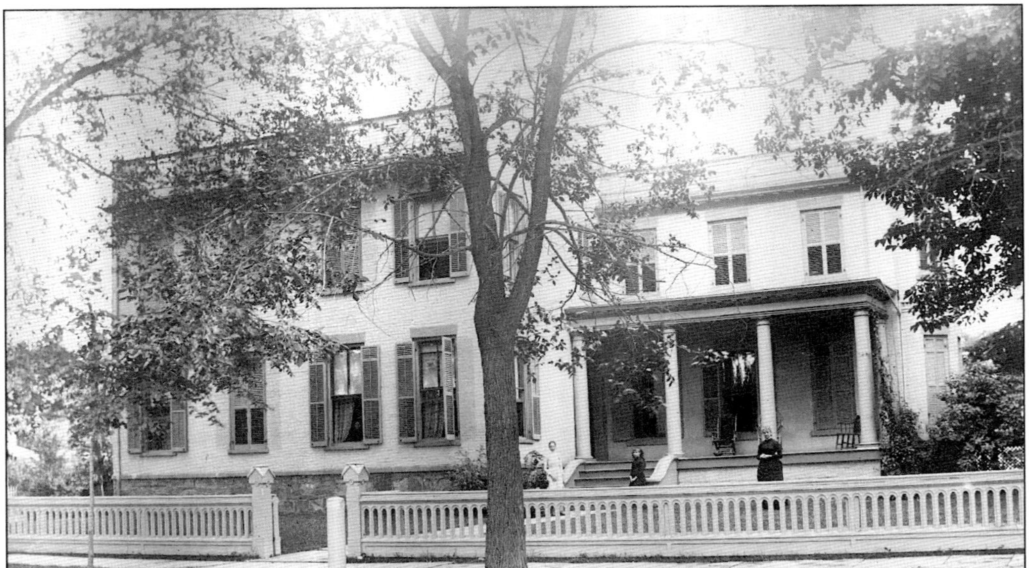

This home was built by Judge Taylor and was known for many years as the Hoekelman House, located at 37 Gibson Street. It has an attractive curved stairway and several fireplaces.

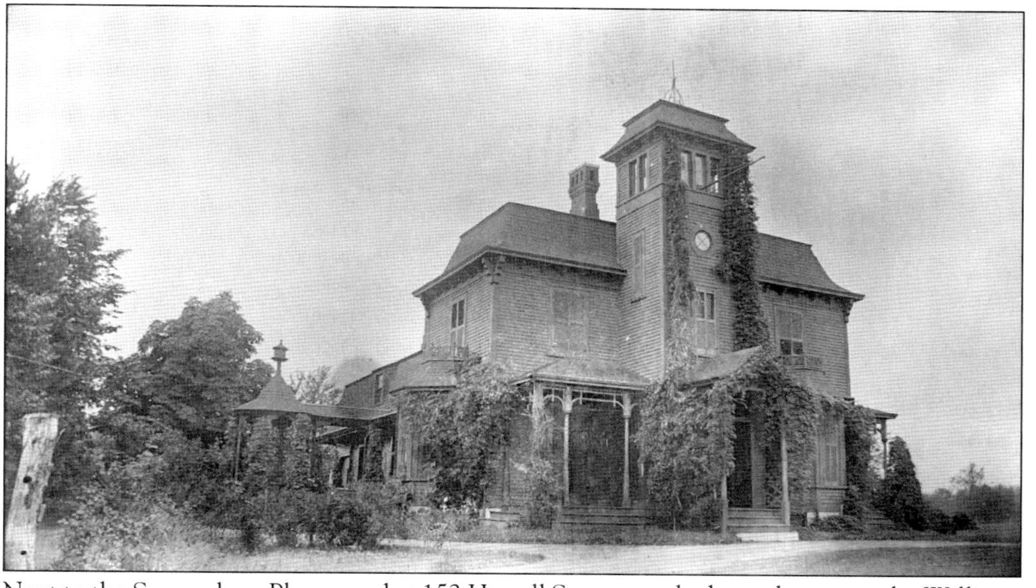

Next to the Sonnenberg Playground at 152 Howell Street was the house known as the Williams House. Williams was a relative of Mary Thompson. The home was built *c.* 1870 with a carriage house at the rear of the property. A lovely copper beech tree graces the front lawn. The tall tower on the front of the house, known as a clock tower, gives the home a church-like appearance.

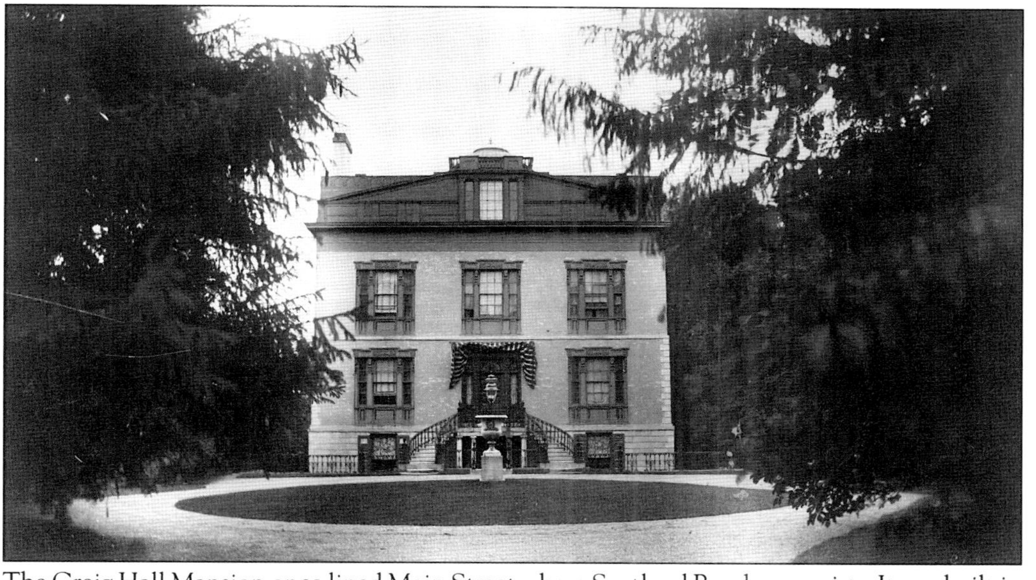

The Greig Hall Mansion once lined Main Street where Scotland Road now exists. It was built in 1832 by Mr. John Greig, a native of Moffat, Scotland. He came to the U.S. with Mr. Johnston, an agent for Sir William Poultney, who held extensive lands in New York. Greig studied law here and entered into a partnership with Judge Howell. According to *A Leaf From the Past* , by M.H. Hamilton, in 1896 the home that initially sat upon this property was donated to the Episcopal Church for a parsonage and was removed to Gibson Street.

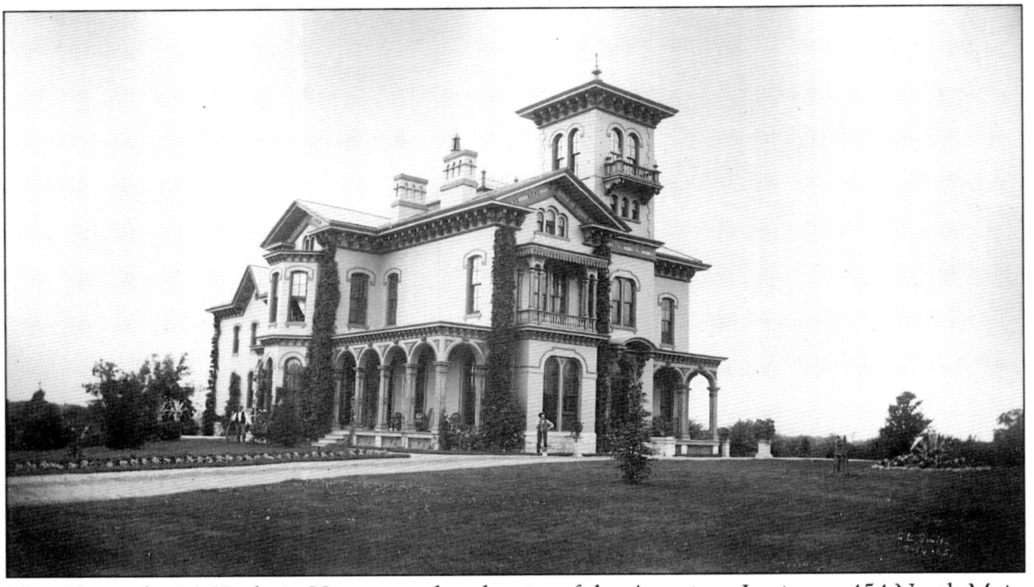

The Alexander McKechnie House stood at the site of the American Legion at 454 North Main Street. This home was built in 1870 following an Italianate design. It was purchased by the American Legion in 1944 but was destroyed by fire in the 1960s. The brick carriage house remained until the early 1980s.

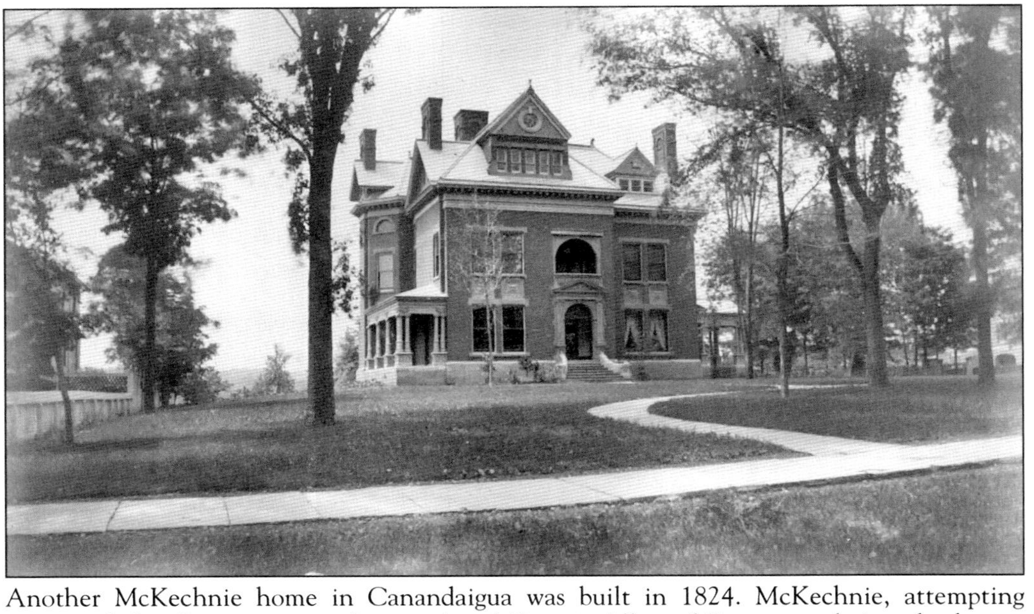

Another McKechnie home in Canandaigua was built in 1824. McKechnie, attempting to exceed the Greig estate in beauty, hired Francis Allen of Boston to design the house. The property once housed the Canandaigua Female Seminary. The home and land were purchased by Mary Thompson and demolished around 1902 to make way for the first F.F. Thompson Hospital.

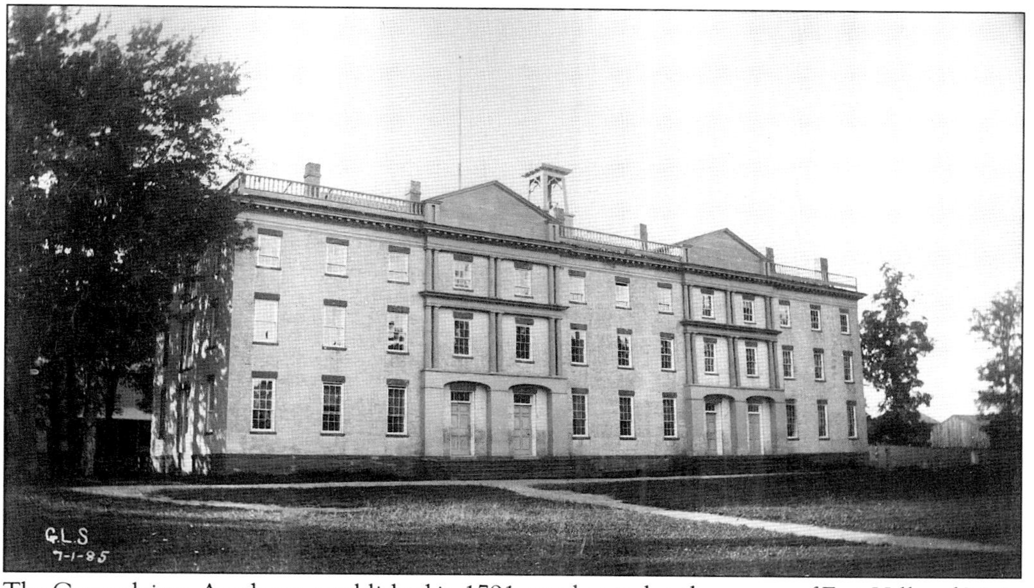

The Canandaigua Academy, established in 1791, was located at the corner of Fort Hill and Main Street. The school is noted for being the first educational institute in western New York. It was built in 1804 on land donated by Phelps and Gorham. The building pictured was demolished in 1904, when the institution changed to a public school, and was replaced with the present structure. That building has now been converted into apartments.

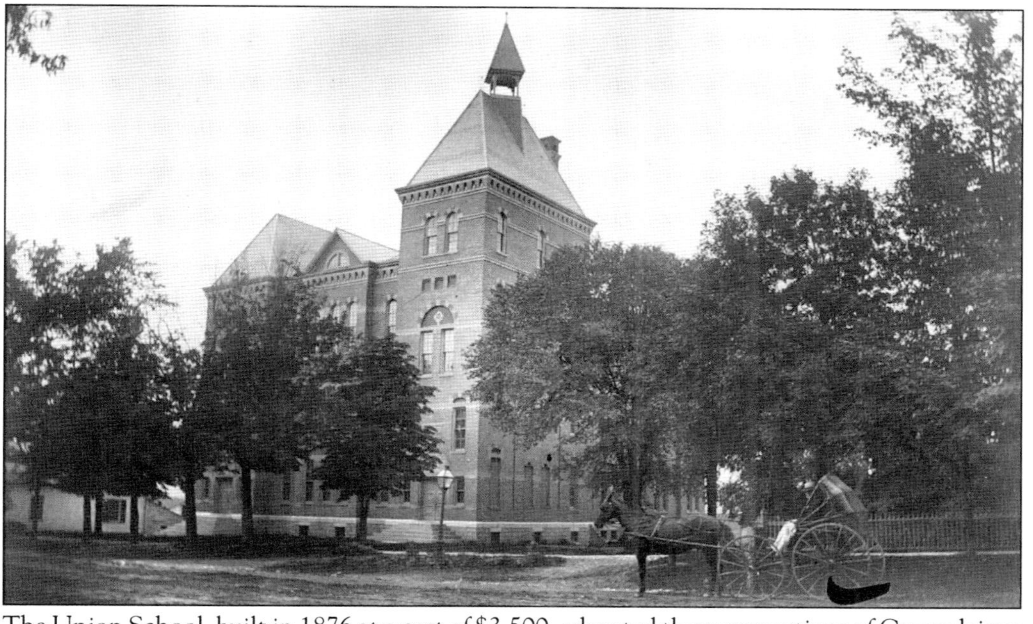

The Union School, built in 1876 at a cost of $3,500, educated three generations of Canandaigua children. Its construction consolidated the education system in Canandaigua, bringing together children from all areas of the town. Initially all grades were housed here, but later the building became an elementary school when the academy opened its doors to the public in 1900. This building remained at the corner of Greig Terrace and Main until the early 1950s, when a growing population made a new school necessary.

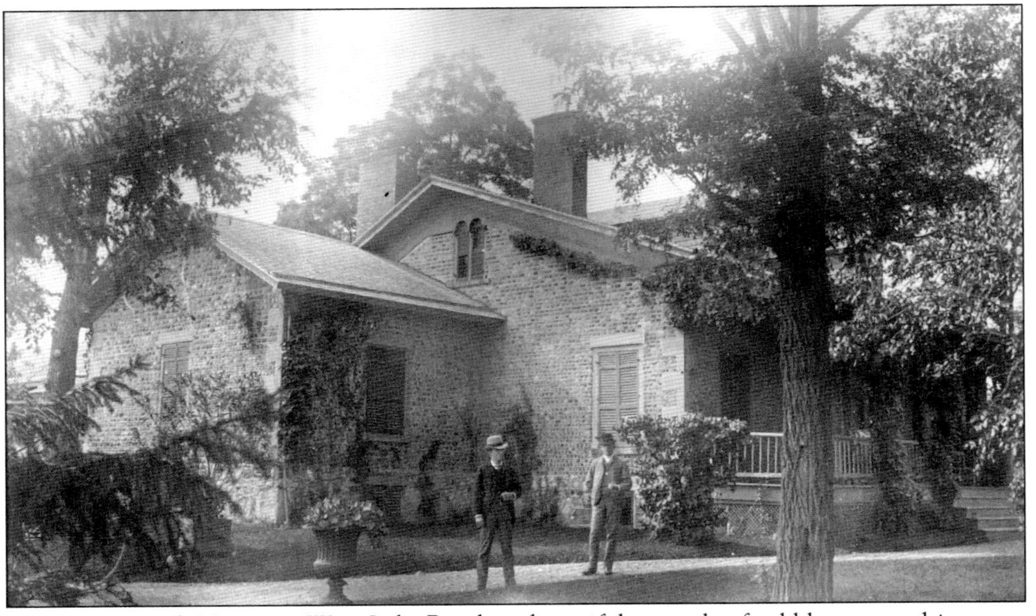

The Isaac Parrish House on West Lake Road is a beautiful example of cobblestone architecture. A fireplace marks the possible date of construction as 1837. A secret room, once entered from a downstairs closet, is now only accessible through the attic. The drive is lined with stone pillars and topped with mill stones.

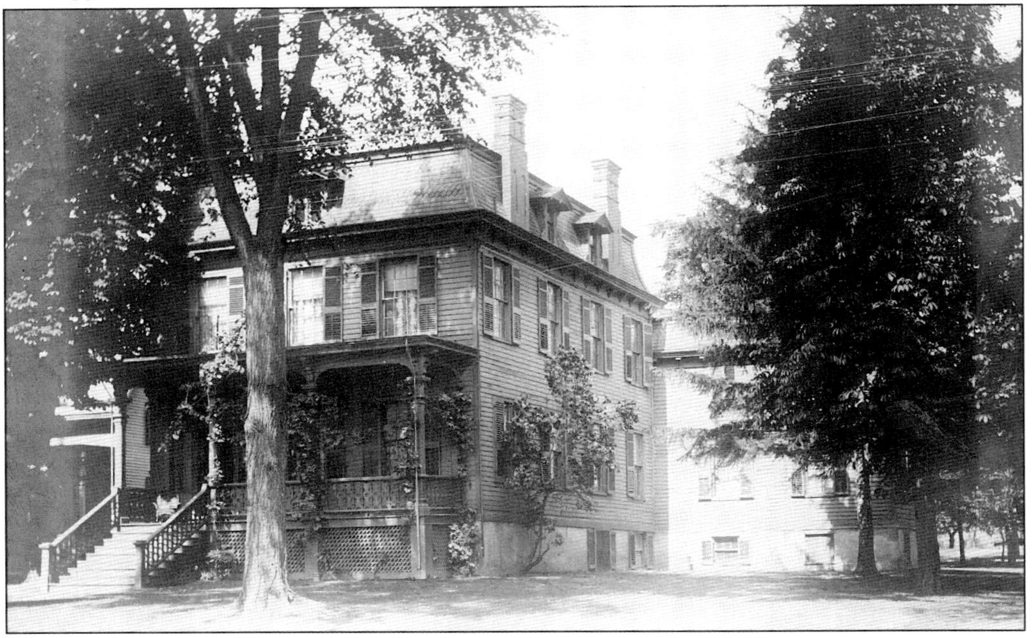

This home, constructed in the 1830s, is believed to have been a safe house for escaping slaves on the Underground Railroad. A trap door leading to the basement exists in a back room. The home contains four fireplaces, two of which are marble. A patio in the backyard is paved with bricks that once covered Gibson Street. Through writings on a bedroom wall, it was also discovered that Maria Seymour Tyler occupied the home for twenty-three years.

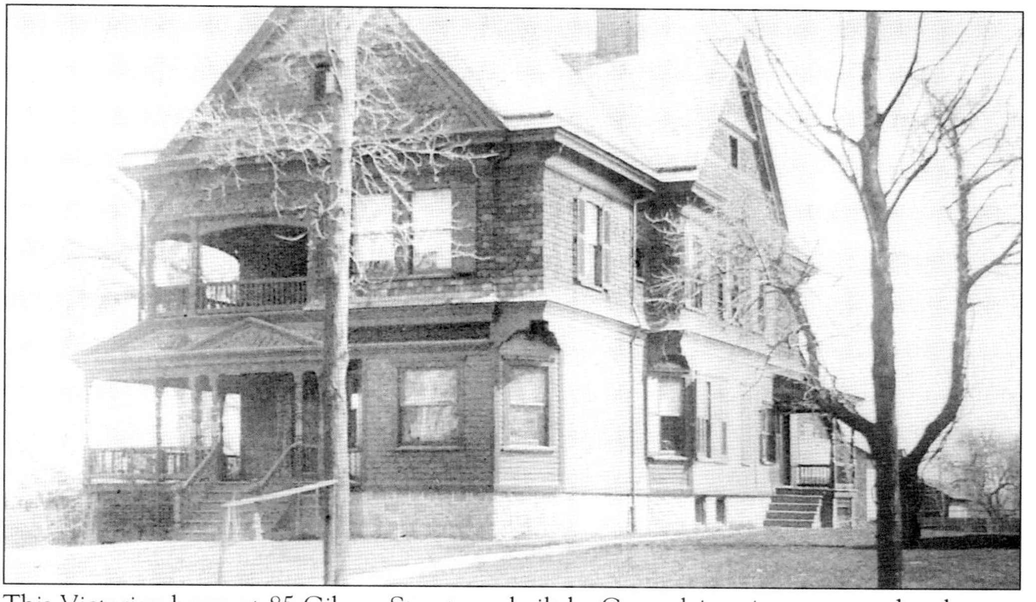

This Victorian home at 85 Gibson Street was built by Canandaigua insurance and real estate agent E.C. Church in 1886. Church also served as county treasurer. Orlando K. Foote, a Rochester architect, designed the building, which was constructed by Charles Robertson. The home had numerous owners and was used as apartments until its restoration in 1991. Note the cedar-shake shingles cut into patterns on the second and third stories.

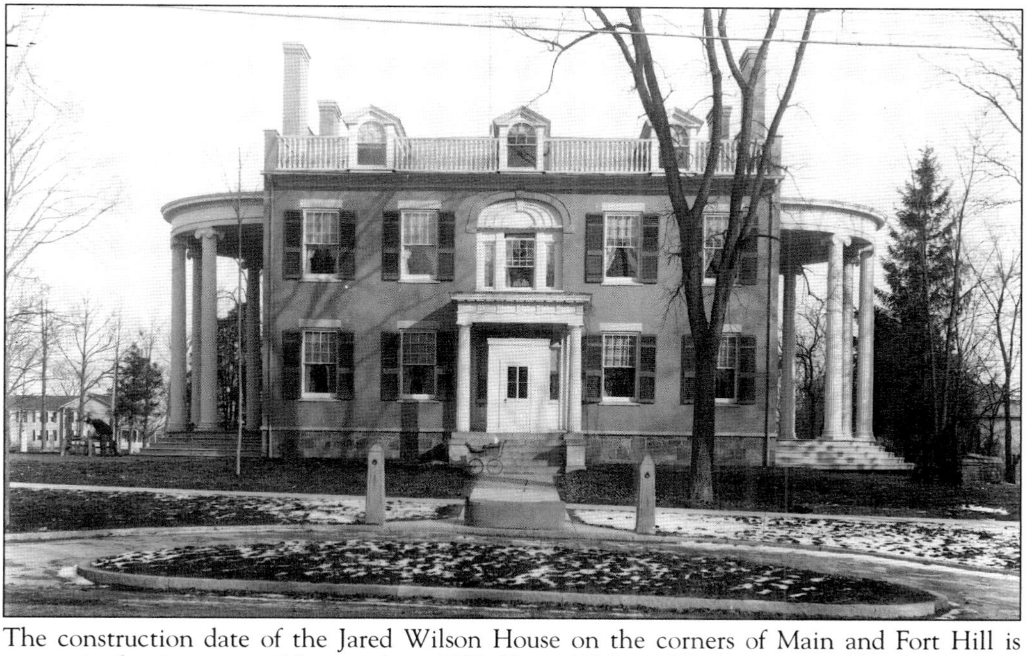

The construction date of the Jared Wilson House on the corners of Main and Fort Hill is uncertain, but it was possibly as early as 1829. From 1927 to 1960 it was owned by the Garlock family, who spent $250,000 refurbishing the home. The house is known for a light which continually shines in the front window in memory of a son lost in World War I. The stately circular drive was sacrificed for the widening of Main Street in 1949.

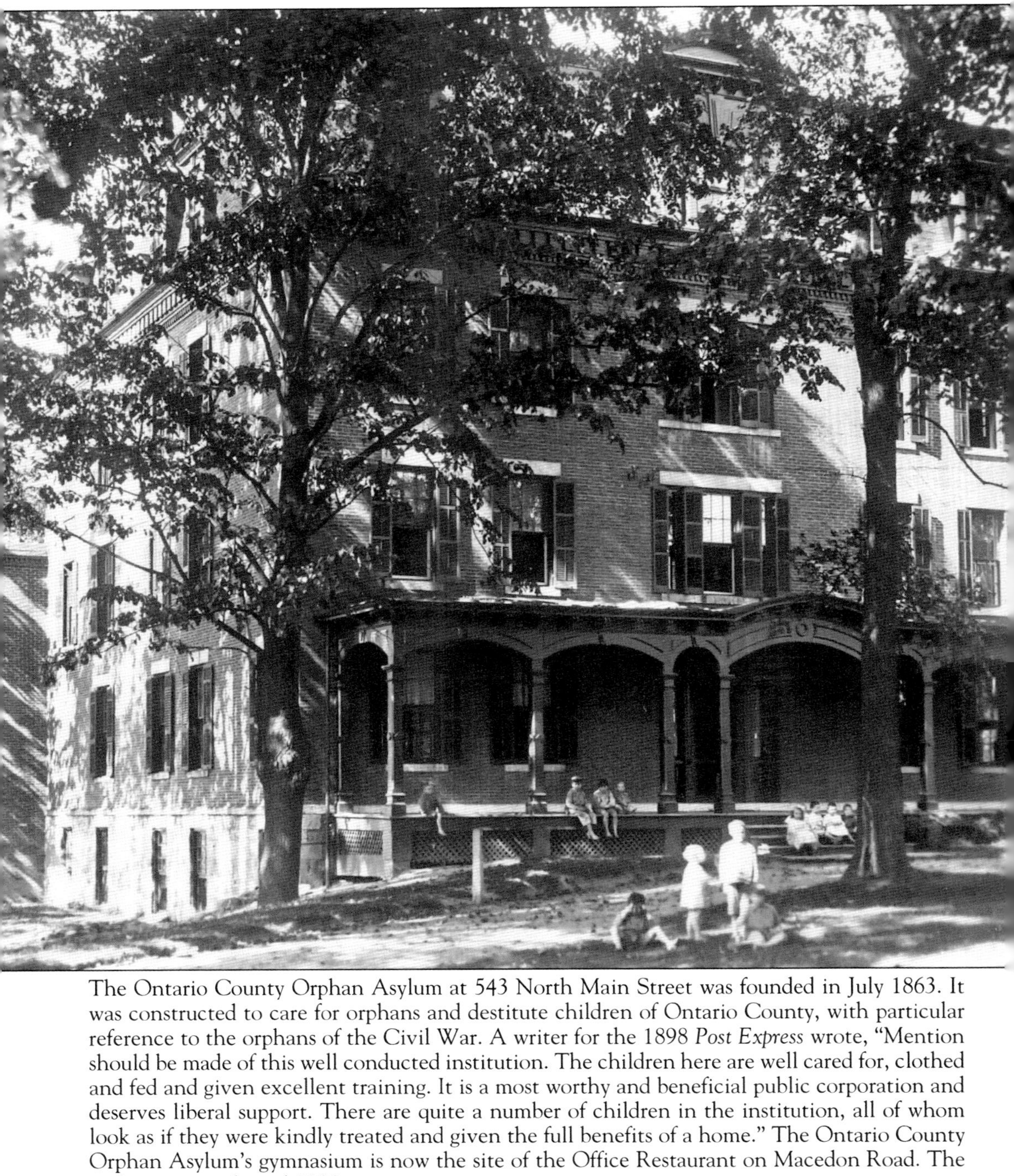

The Ontario County Orphan Asylum at 543 North Main Street was founded in July 1863. It was constructed to care for orphans and destitute children of Ontario County, with particular reference to the orphans of the Civil War. A writer for the 1898 *Post Express* wrote, "Mention should be made of this well conducted institution. The children here are well cared for, clothed and fed and given excellent training. It is a most worthy and beneficial public corporation and deserves liberal support. There are quite a number of children in the institution, all of whom look as if they were kindly treated and given the full benefits of a home." The Ontario County Orphan Asylum's gymnasium is now the site of the Office Restaurant on Macedon Road. The asylum operated until 1933.

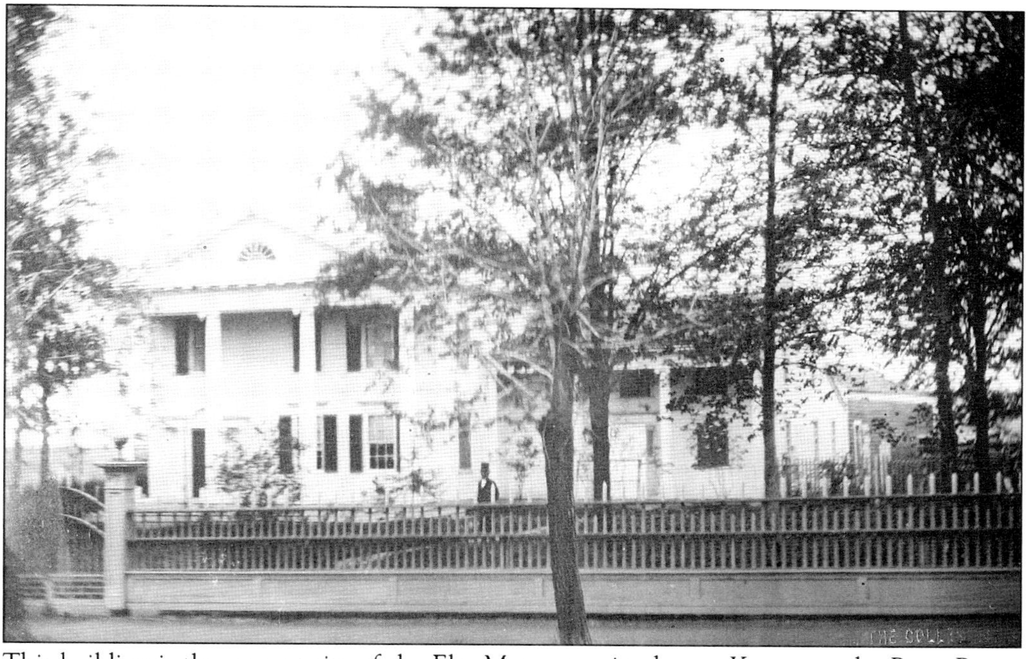

This building is the current site of the Elm Manor nursing home. Known as the Peter Porter House, the structure at 210 North Main was built by General Peter Porter in 1797. Porter was secretary of war in John Quincy Adams' cabinet. During its history, the house was later owned by John Spencer, who was secretary of war to President John Tyler. Another well-known owner was Elbridge Lapham, a U.S. Senator in the 1880s. John McKechnie purchased the property in 1895 and it was held by his family until the 1950s.

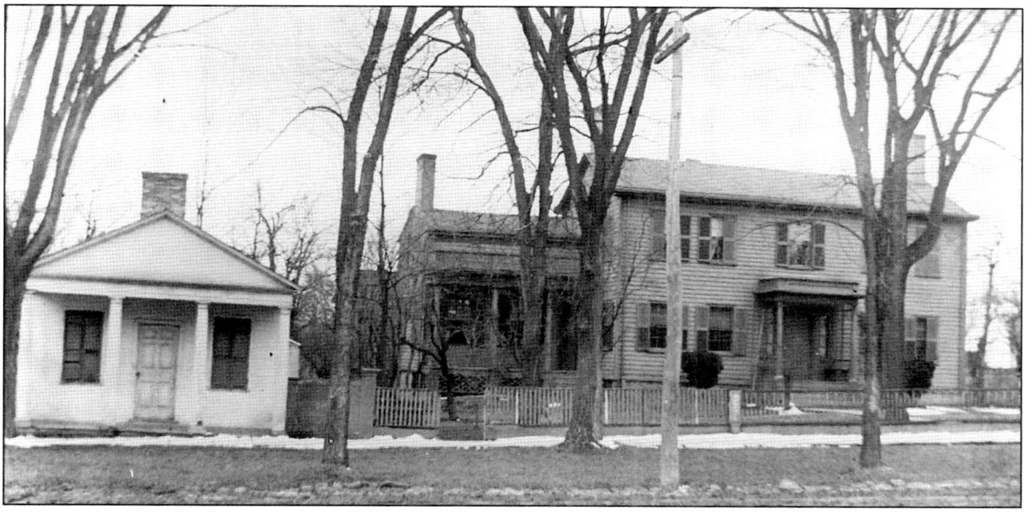

This Federal-style home was built in 1822 by Walter S. Hubbell at 164 North Main Street. Mr. Hubbell was a lawyer in the early 1800s. The small building at the left served as his law office. Hubbell was described as a brilliant Christian man who cared little for public life, and who aided the less fortunate people in Canandaigua. Steven Douglas, who ran against Abraham Lincoln for president, studied law here with Hubbell. The law office now resides on the grounds of the Granger Homestead.

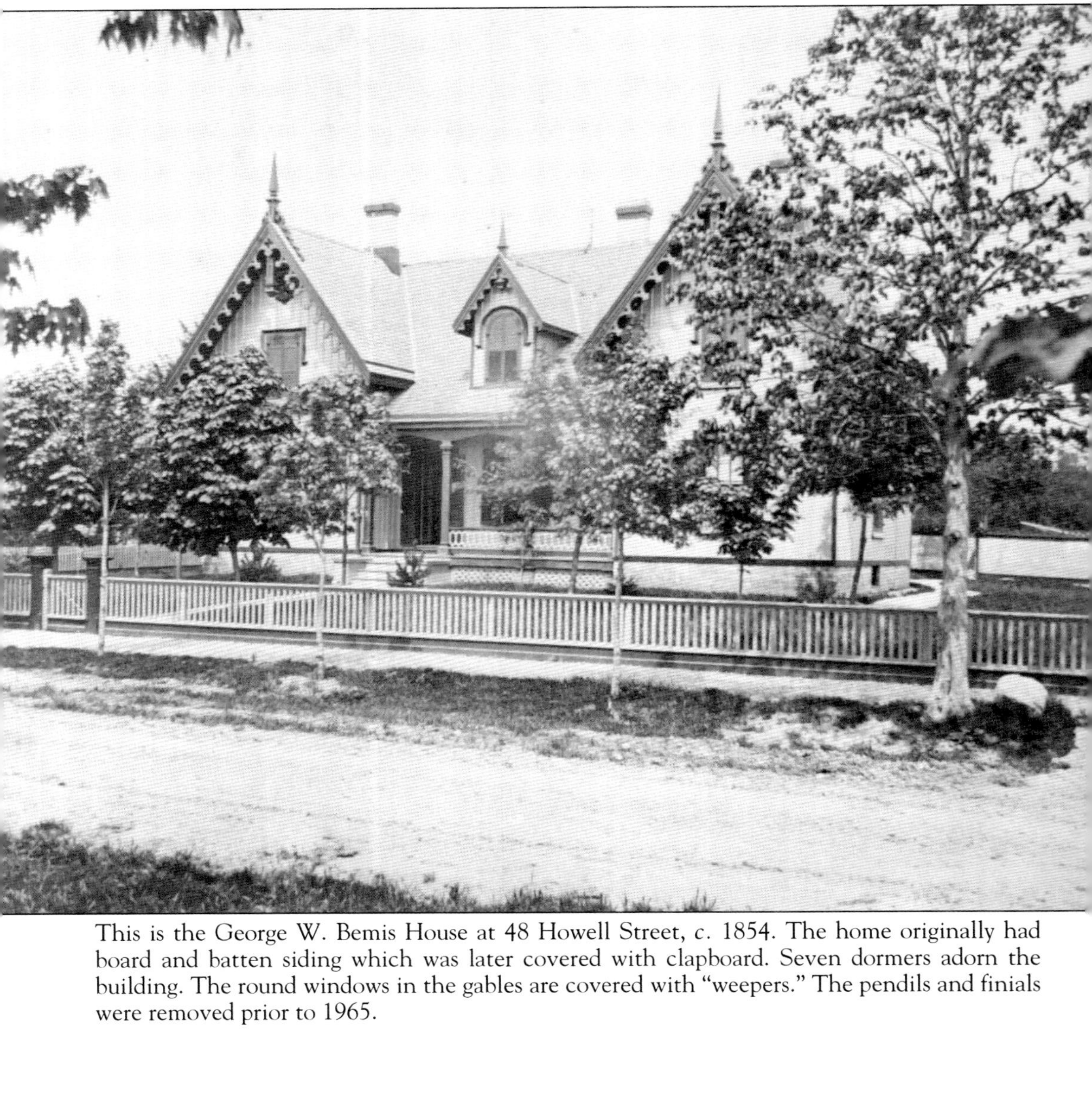

This is the George W. Bemis House at 48 Howell Street, *c.* 1854. The home originally had board and batten siding which was later covered with clapboard. Seven dormers adorn the building. The round windows in the gables are covered with "weepers." The pendils and finials were removed prior to 1965.

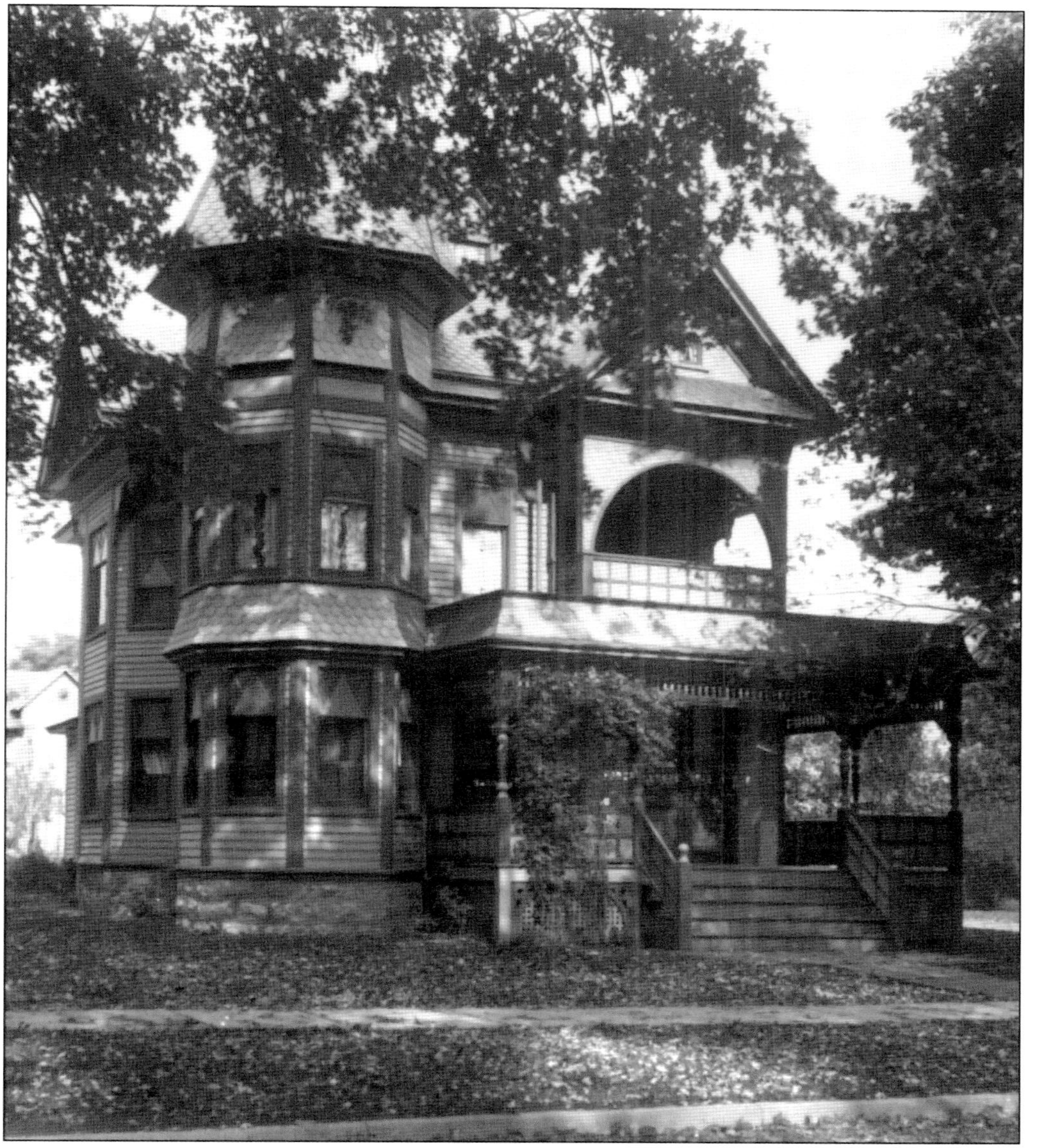

This Victorian home was built in 1889 at 20 Howell Street for Herman Van Vechten by Child and Field. It was originally designed with clapboard siding and scalloped cedar shingles. The beautiful turret is unique to homes of this period.

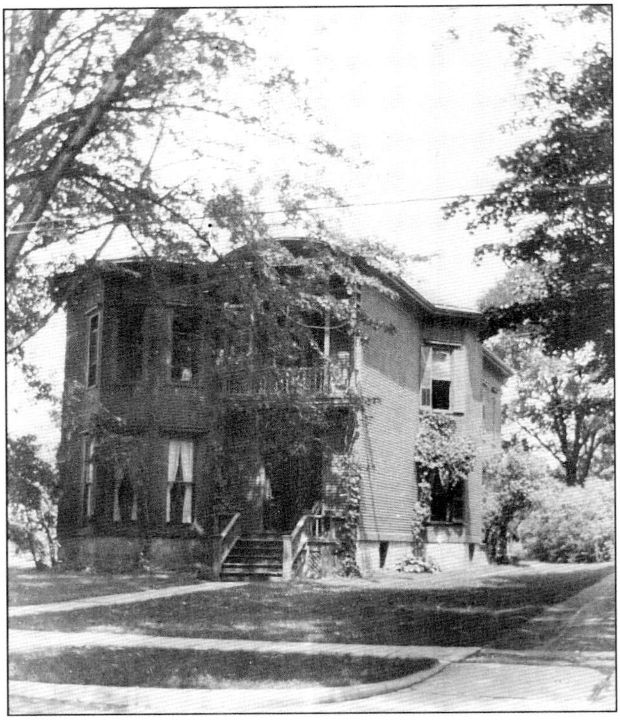

This home at 86 Howell Street was constructed in 1878 and is known as the Bristol House. It features a two-story bay window at the front and a shed-roofed dormer on the attic roof. A balcony sits atop the front porch.

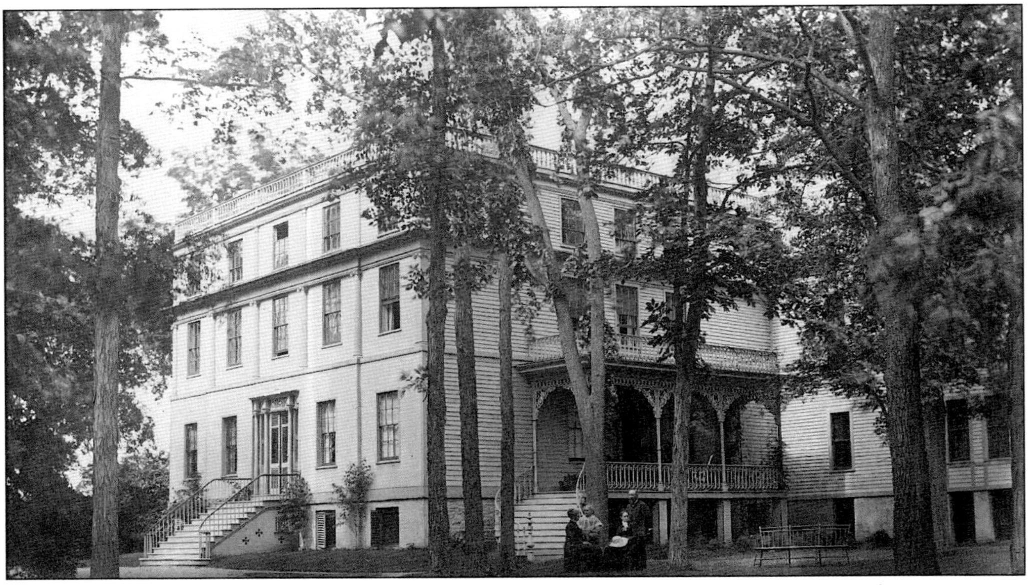

The Granger Homestead at 295 North Main Street was built in 1814 by Mr. Gideon Granger. The original structure had four rooms on both the first and second floors, each with a fireplace. During Francis Granger's occupancy, several changes to the home were made, including a large addition to the north side of the building. The building operated as the Granger Place School from 1876 to 1906. It was later purchased by a group of concerned citizens, who established the Granger Homestead Society for the purpose of maintaining the historic home. Tours of the home and carriage house are available.

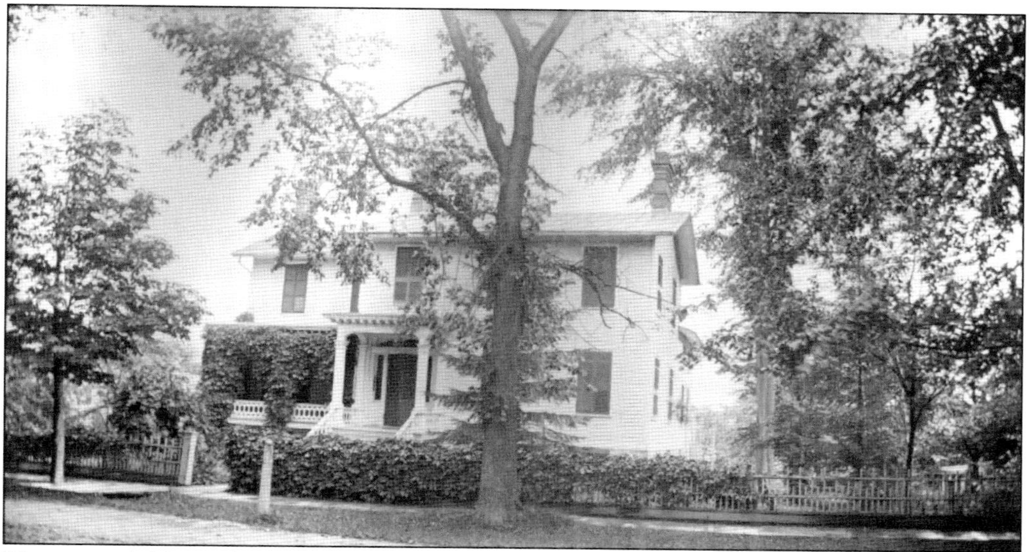

The original Alexander H. Howell House at 101 Gibson Street was constructed in 1829 in the classic Federal style. The thin clapboard siding was covered with ripple-edged asbestos and an east wing was added in later years. The home has been converted into a multiple-family residence.

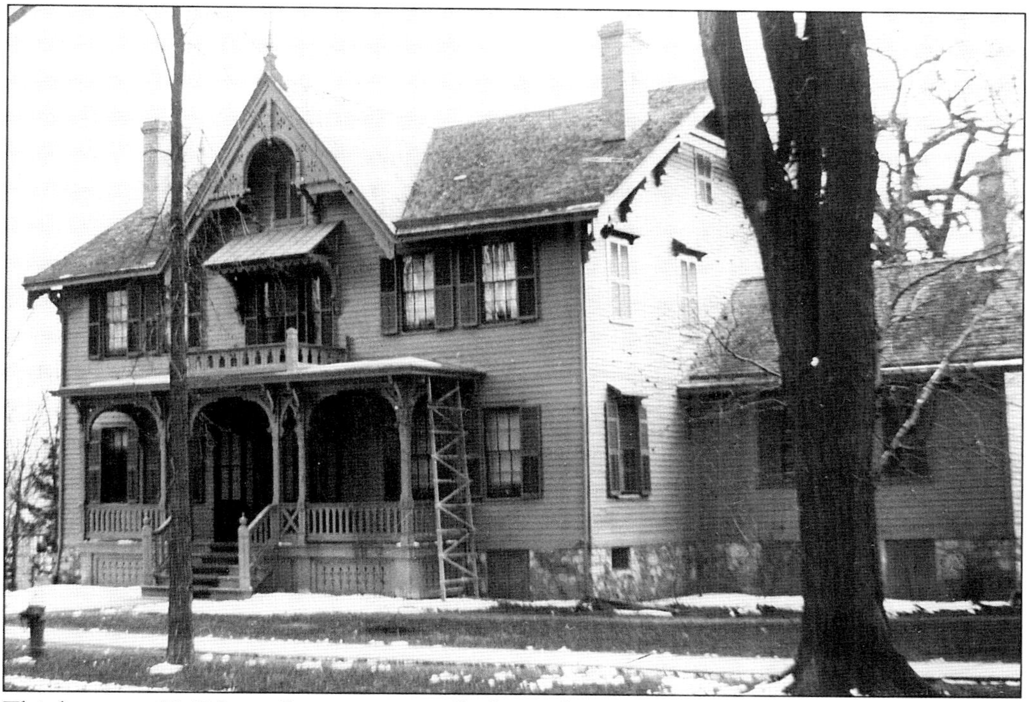

This home at 91 Gibson Street was initially located on North Main Street at Scotland Road. It was built c. 1800 by Augustus Porter and moved to its current location about 1830. The Federal-style home was altered with Victorian-era decorations, such as the center gable and brackets over the windows. The building was expertly restored in 1991 after a devastating fire on the second and third stories.

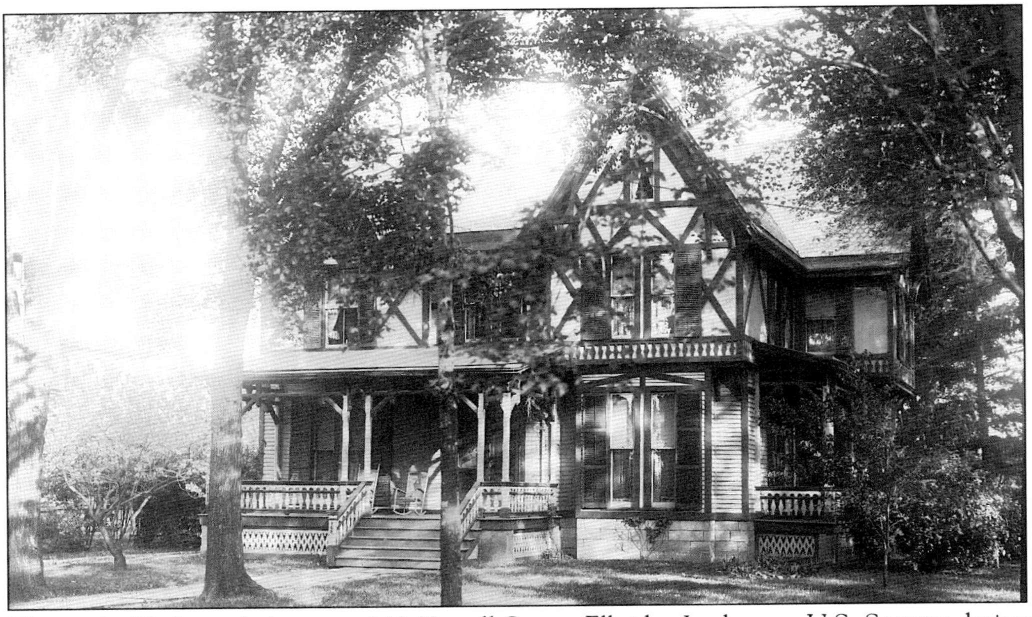

This is the Tudor-style home at 143 Howell Street. Elbridge Lapham, a U.S. Senator during the 1880s, owned this property between 1868 and 1870. It was then owned by Charlotte Adams, who may have been the wife of Lapham's law partner. The home has been divided into several apartments.

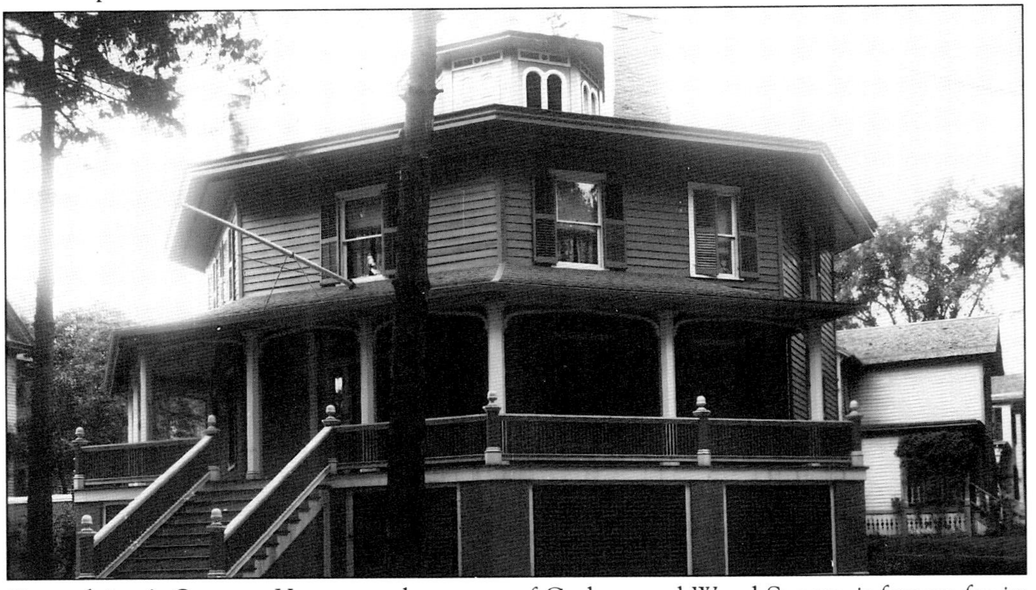

Canandaigua's Octagon House, on the corner of Gorham and Wood Streets, is famous for its style and one-time occupant, Senator John Raines. The home was built by Solon Van Burkirk, c. 1860. Senator Raines bought the house in 1872. The design was formulated by Orson Fowler, a Cohocton native who practiced phrenology, the art of studying the bumps on the head. This style gained popularity during the mid-1800s. Fowler claimed through mathematical processes that this form provided more interior space in proportion to wall area than the regular rectangular form.

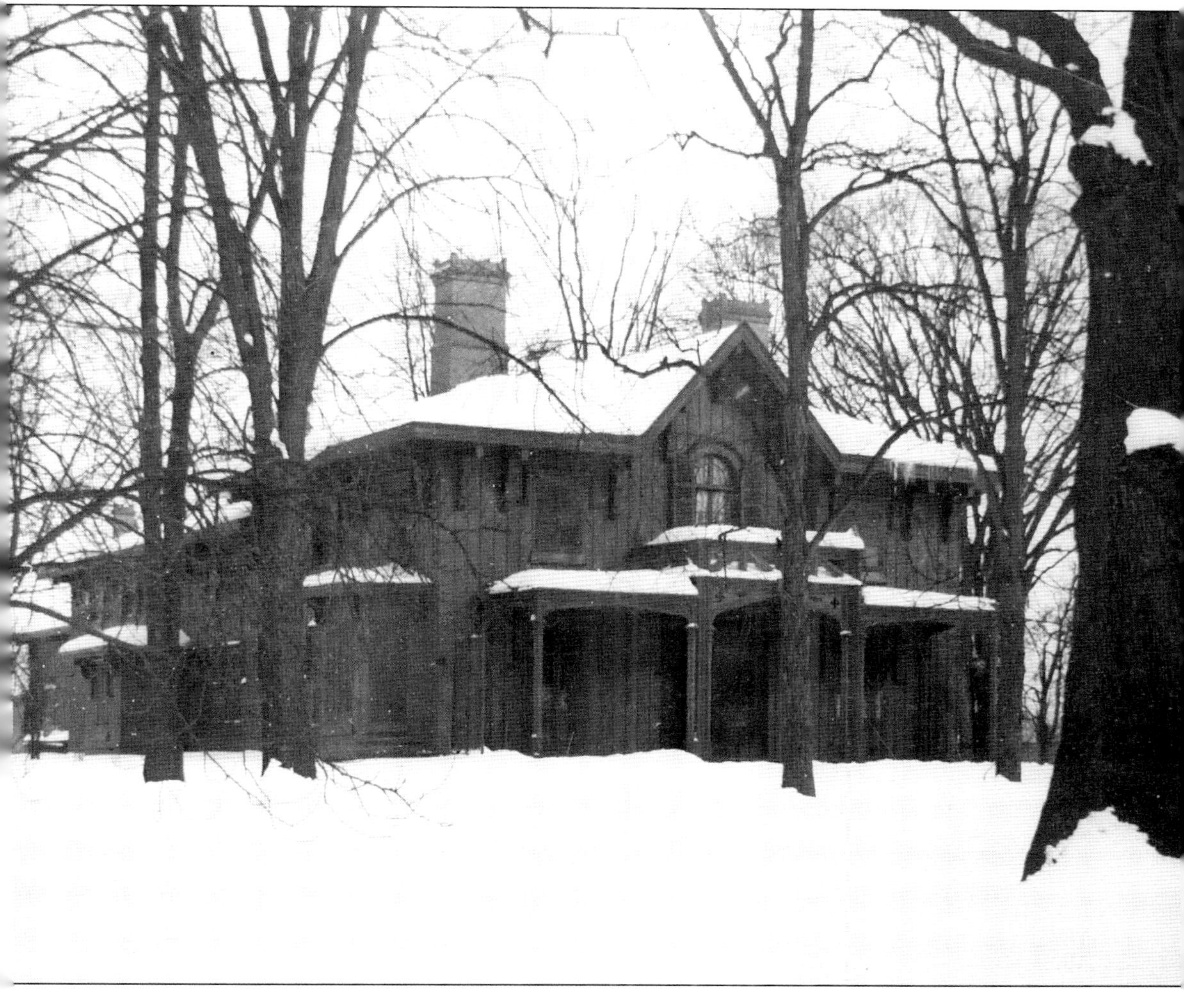

This home was once known as the Granger Cottage. It was built in the 1840s and stood at the corner of Main and Granger Streets. The structure is covered in board and batten siding, familiar to Gothic Revival architecture. Francis Granger built the house for his son Gideon II, and used it as a winter residence. In 1860, Gideon II returned with his family to the homestead to keep his father company. Both Gideon II and his father died within six days of each other in 1868, prompting the family to leave the homestead for the cottage. When the homestead ceased serving as the location of the Granger Place School, the family again returned to it, and sold the cottage to James McLaughlin, president of Lisk Manufacturing. McLaughlin had the cottage moved to its present location on Granger Street.

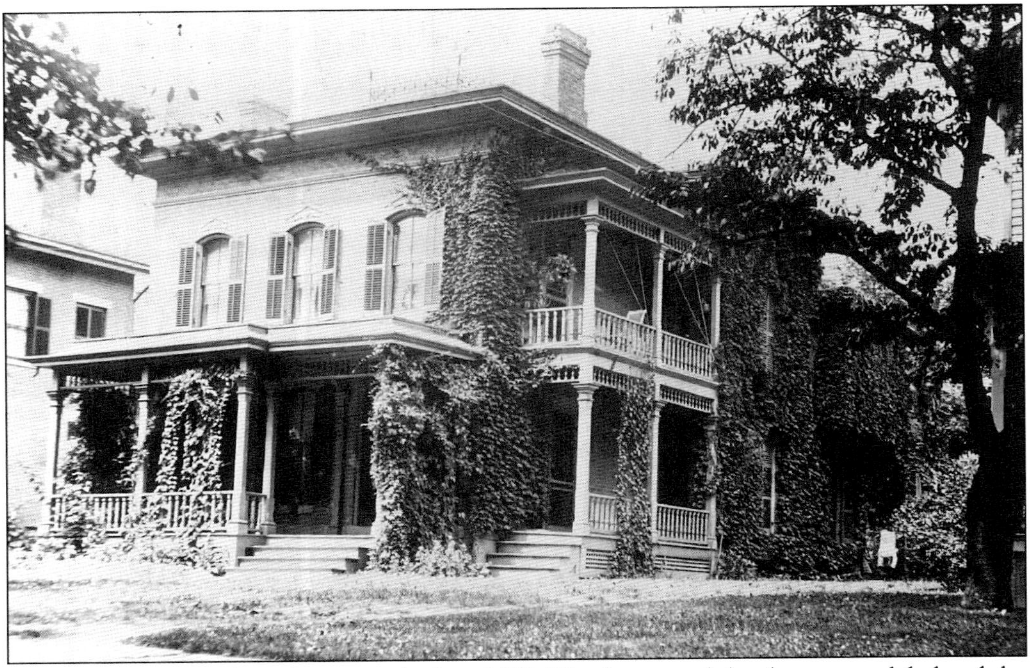

This home at 70 Gorham Street was built *c.* 1853. The front porch has been remodeled and the side porch and balcony have been removed, leaving a smaller porch. The beauty of this brick Italianate still remains, despite the alterations.

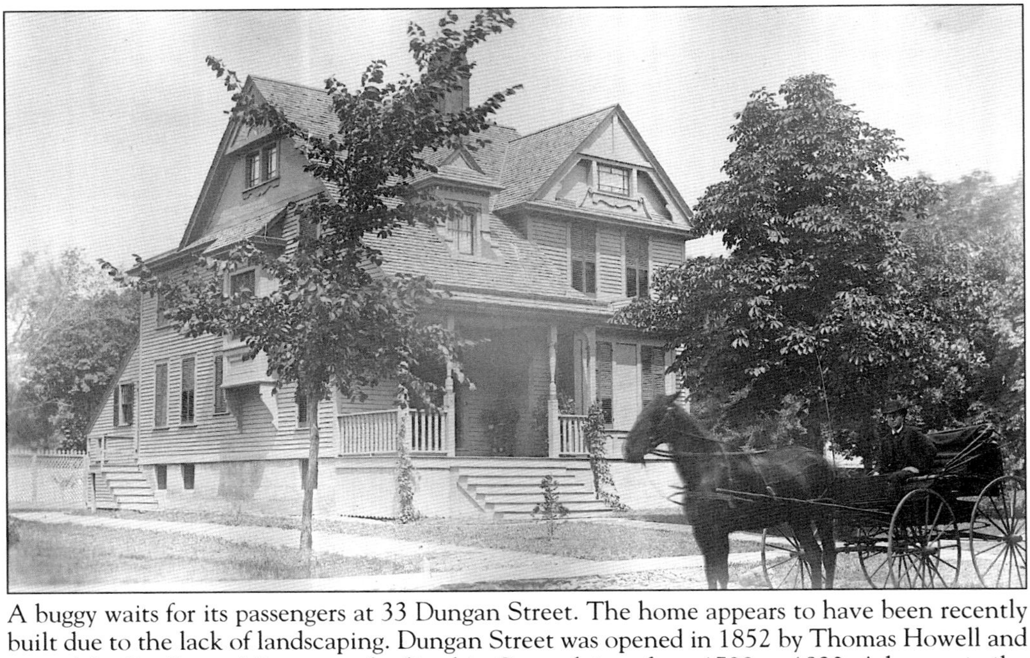

A buggy waits for its passengers at 33 Dungan Street. The home appears to have been recently built due to the lack of landscaping. Dungan Street was opened in 1852 by Thomas Howell and named for Dr. Samuel Dungan, who lived in Canandaigua from 1799 to 1820. A house similar to this one also exists on Dungan Street.

Seven

PLACES OF WORSHIP

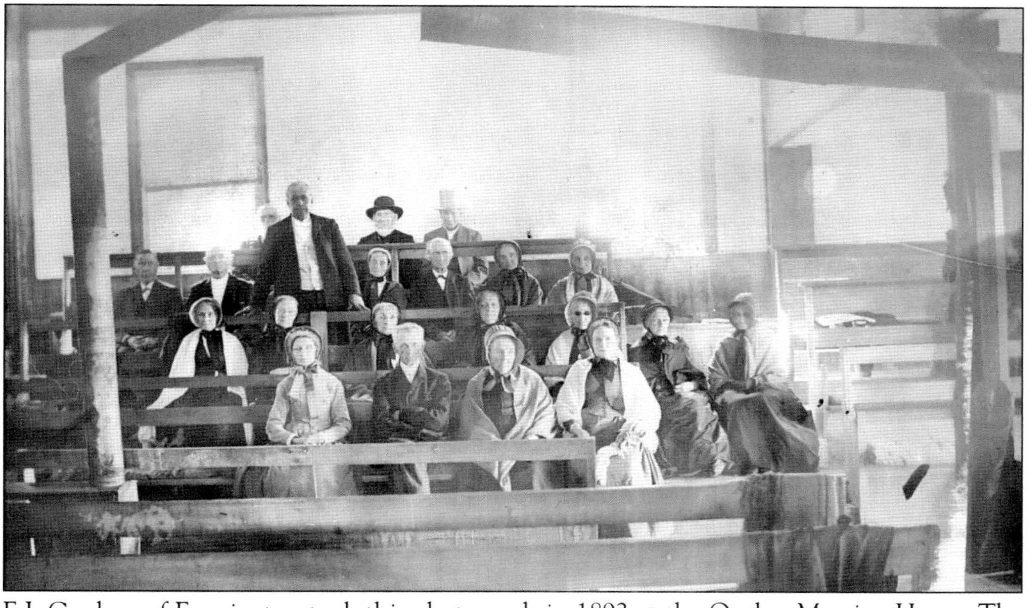

E.J. Gardner of Farmington took this photograph in 1892 at the Quaker Meeting House. The church was constructed in 1804 after a fire destroyed the initial building on the northeast corner of County Road 8 and Allen Padgham Road. It is important to recall that a group of Pennsylvania Quakers came to Canandaigua to assist the Native Americans in negotiating the Pickering Treaty.

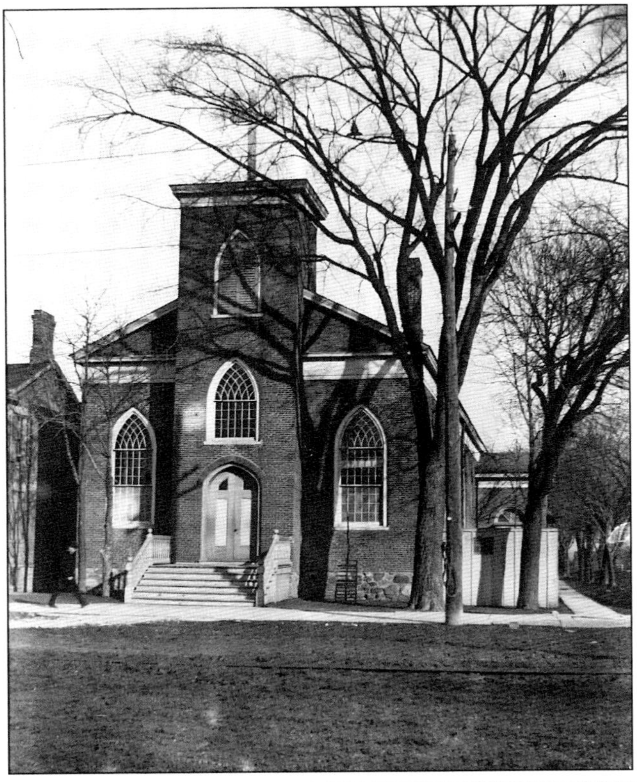

The original Saint Mary's Catholic Church stood at the corner of South Main and Saltonstall Streets. It was constructed in 1848, enlarged in 1852 and 1861, and used until the present church was erected in 1903. The building was later converted to the Temple Theater.

This photograph shows the sanctuary of the original St. Mary's Church on South Main Street. Note the use of the banners and flags inside. Gas lights are suspended from the ceilings. The church's design appears much more austere when compared with the current church.

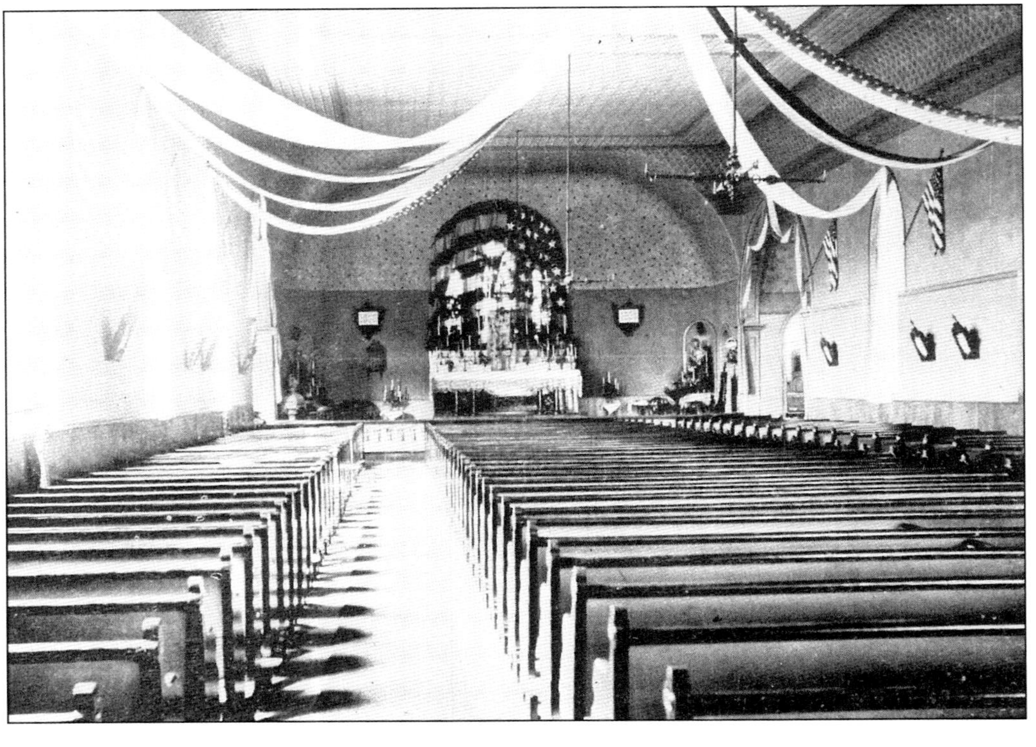

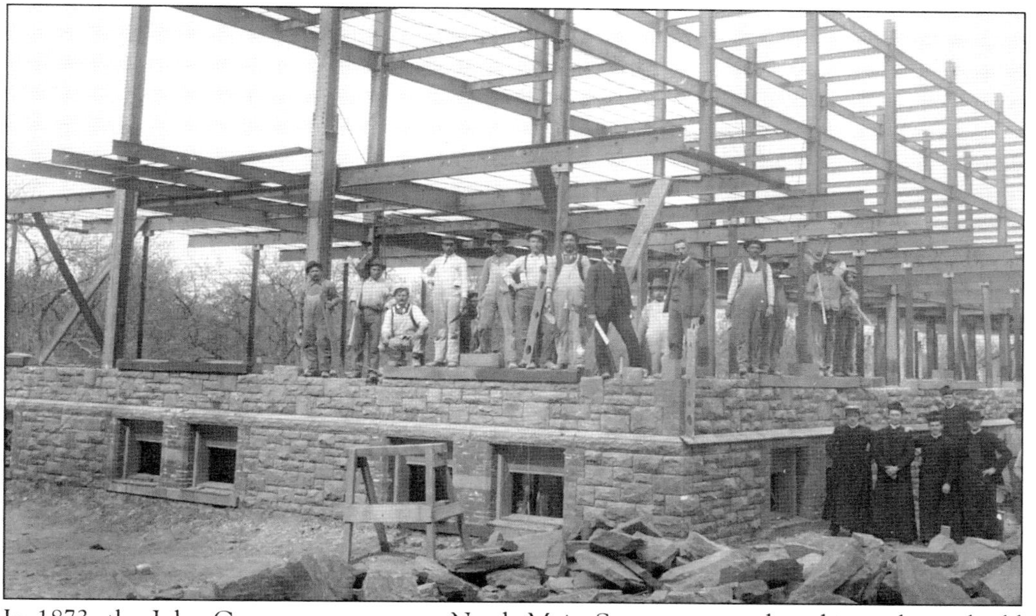

In 1873, the John Granger property on North Main Street was purchased in order to build a school, convent, and rectory. Construction for the church began in March of 1903 for the current St. Mary's Church. The structure cost $99,000 to build. The installation of new electric fixtures, a marble altar, and other renovations took place in 1930.

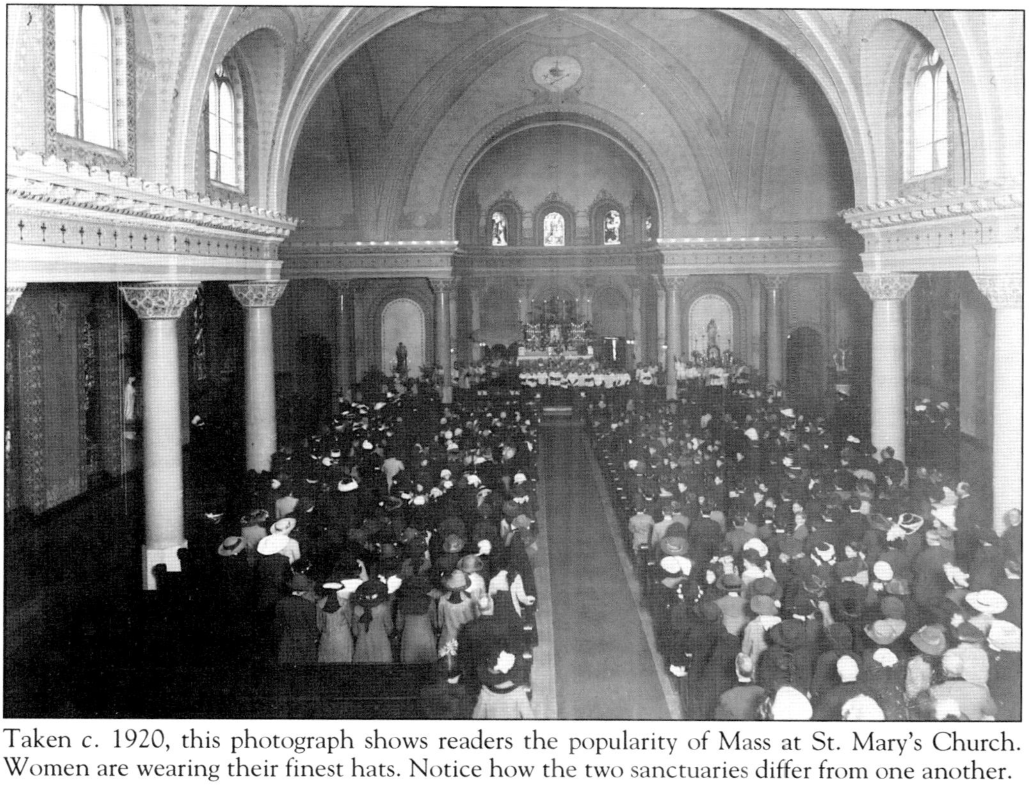

Taken *c.* 1920, this photograph shows readers the popularity of Mass at St. Mary's Church. Women are wearing their finest hats. Notice how the two sanctuaries differ from one another.

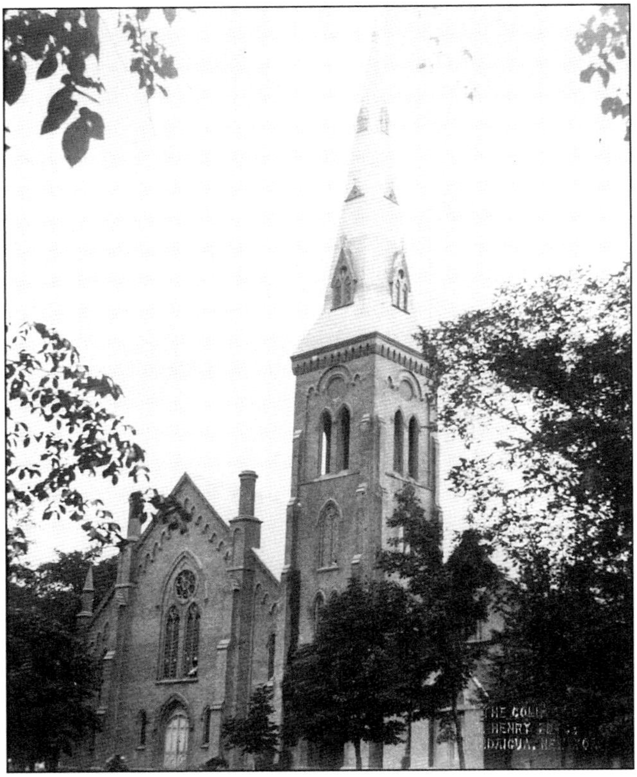

The United Church at Main and Gibson Streets was designed by C.K. Porter in traditional Gothic Revival style and was completed in 1872. The tall steeple was removed in 1928 and replaced with a smaller peak. The sanctuary was redecorated in 1951. The wooden beams in the ceiling are adorned with gold leaf. When the Baptist church on South Main Street burned in 1942, the Presbyterian Church offered its building for worship. The two congregations were later united.

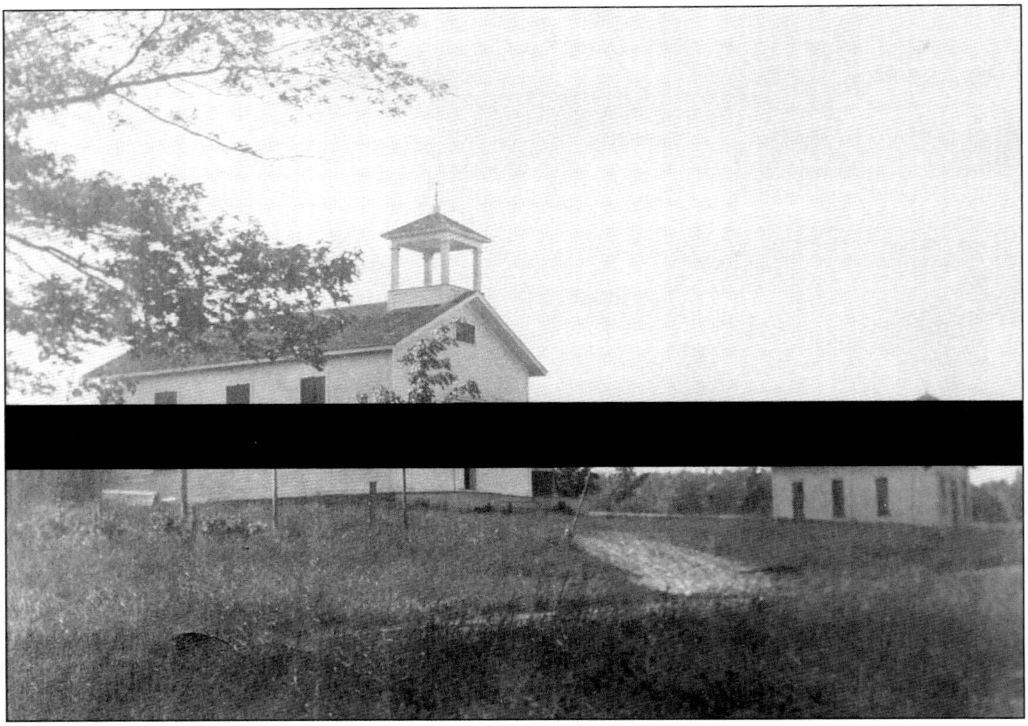

The church and school at the academy were located on Seneca Point Road, south of West Lake Road. The schoolhouse still stands, but the church no longer remains.

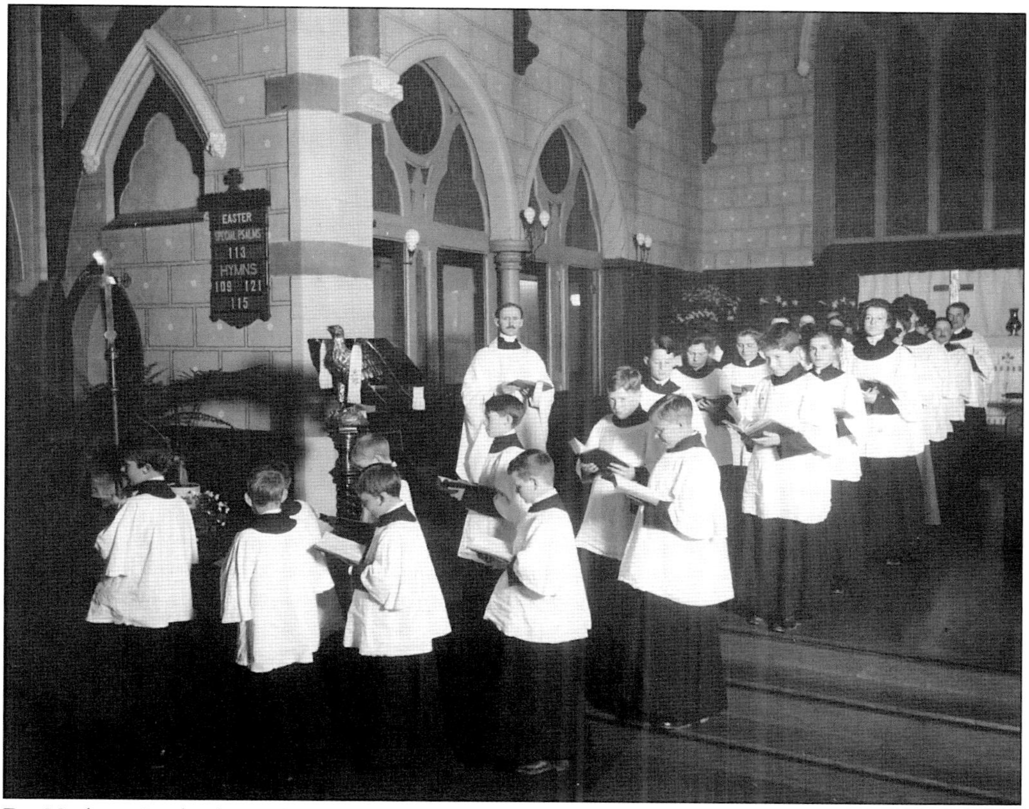

Dr. Herbert Gaylord stands over the choir at St. John's Episcopal Church at 183 North Main. The church was designed in traditional Gothic Revival style by E.T. Littrell of New York City, and built by De John Builders of Newark in 1871. In 1908 a parish house was built to the north of the church. The tall steeple was removed in 1928 and the battlements were rebuilt. The education wing at the rear of the church was constructed in 1965.

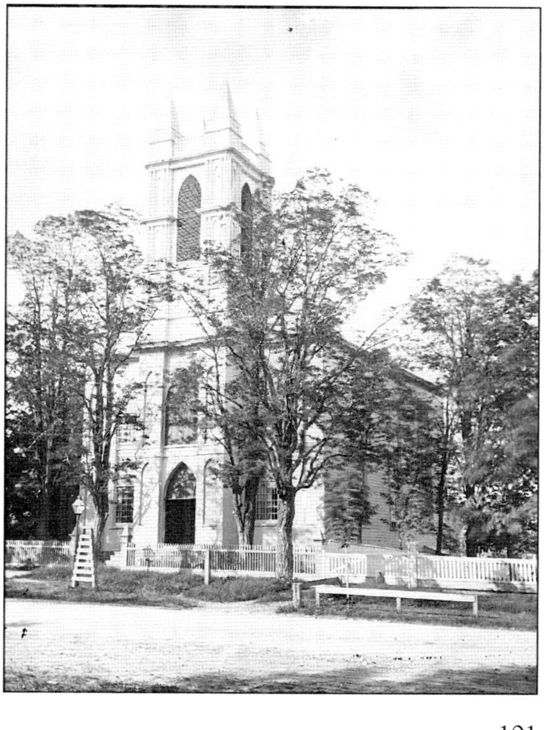

St. John's Church was founded in 1799 and reorganized in 1814. The original St. John's Church in Canandaigua was constructed of wood in 1816. Prior to its construction, services were held in the town hall. An addition to the church was added in 1867. Despite the addition, the church again became too small for its congregation and had to be demolished for a larger structure.

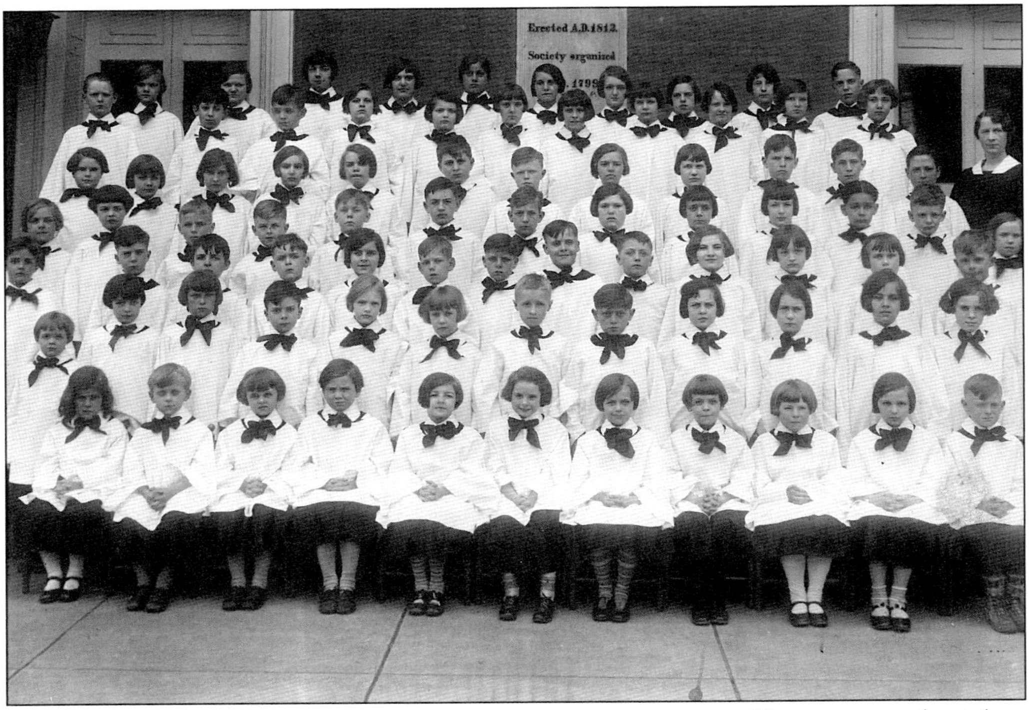

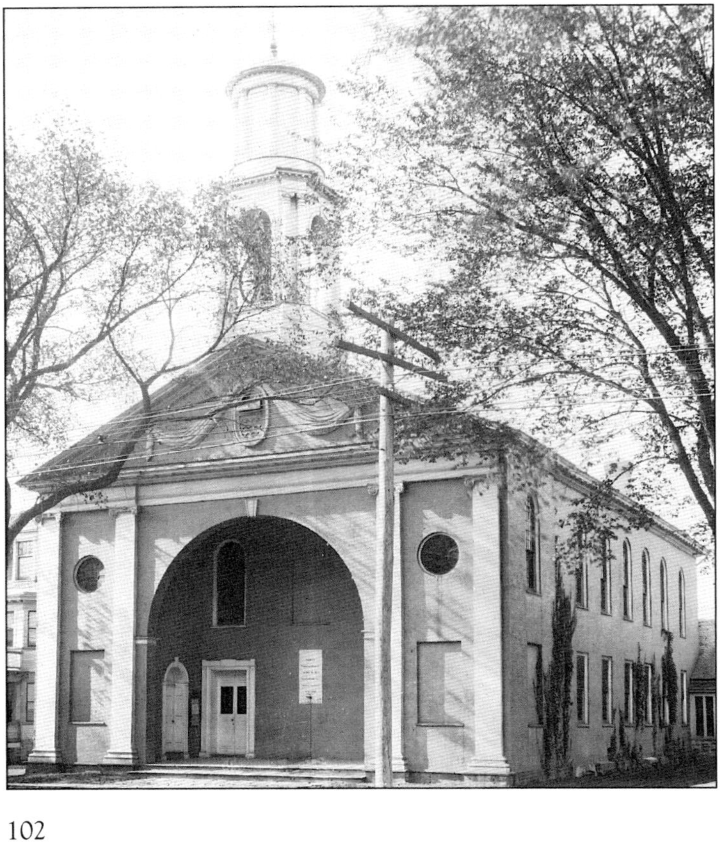

The woman at the right in the photograph of the children's choir at the Congregational church is identified as Elva Johnston. The church was built in 1813 at a cost of $13,000. This money was donated by less than forty members of the congregation. In 1873, the chapel was added with monies contributed by Mr. and Mrs. F.F. Thompson, among others. The chapel met the needs of the growing congregation. This is Canandaigua's oldest religious society, organized in 1799. The colonial lanterns at the entrances were added 1899.

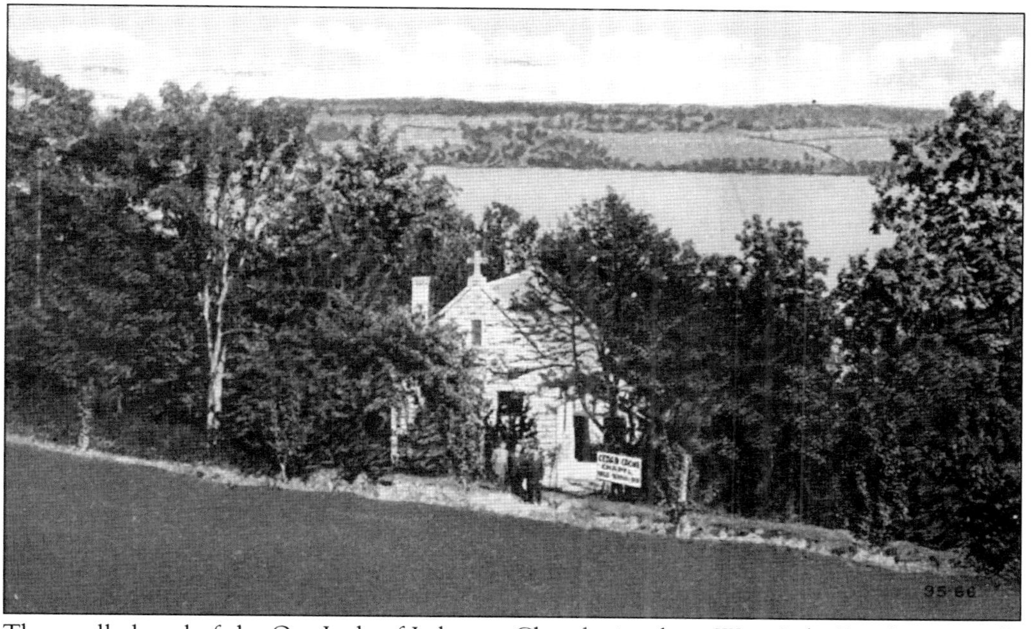

The small chapel of the Our Lady of Lebanon Church sits along West Lake Road near Wells Curtiss Road. At one time, it must have suggested a closeness to God and nature in this beautiful setting, nestled among trees, obscuring it from passersby. The chapel still stand today, and the curious can spot the structure in the now-overgrown trees.

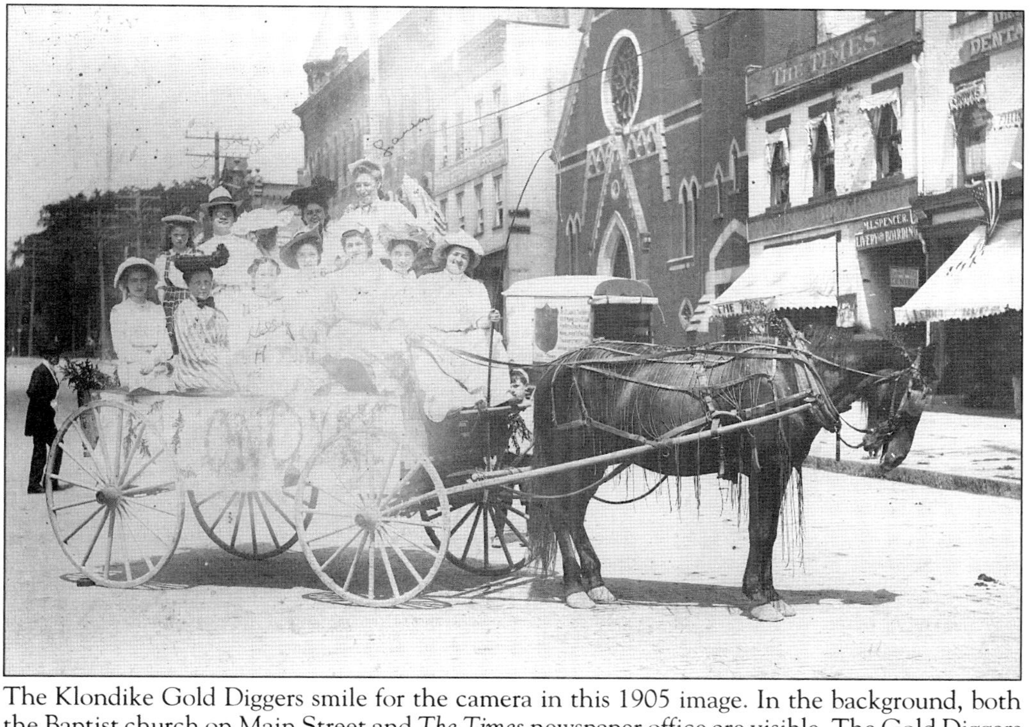

The Klondike Gold Diggers smile for the camera in this 1905 image. In the background, both the Baptist church on Main Street and *The Times* newspaper office are visible. The Gold Diggers were a traveling troupe of Baptist entertainers.

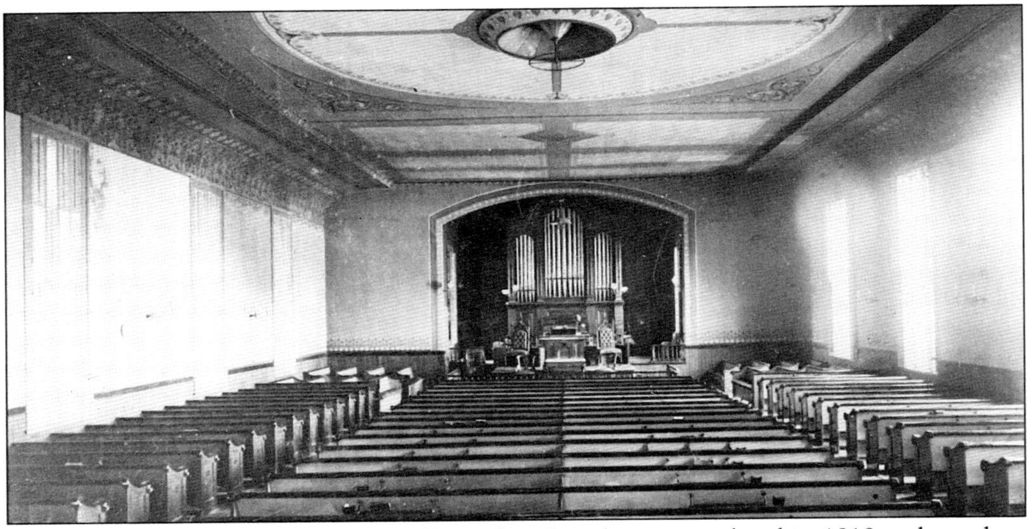

The original Methodist church, a small wooden chapel, was completed in 1818 and stood on Chapel Street. The original wooden building was moved to its present location in 1835. The interior boasted a beautiful and ornate ceiling medallion.

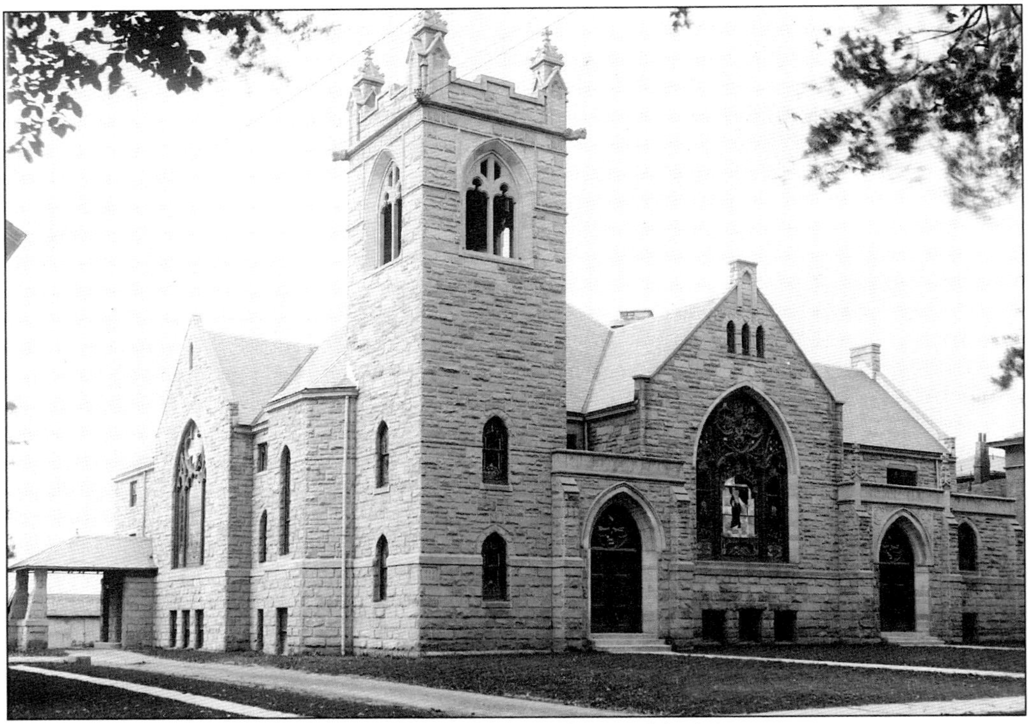

An exterior shot of the Methodist church shows the modified Romanesque stone structure. Constructed of Median limestone, this building replaced the original wooden chapel in 1903. Built at a cost of $52,000, the church features several beautiful stained-glass windows, one of which was donated by Senator John Raines. In 1946 carillonic bells were added, and in 1957 an educational wing and chapel were dedicated. A fire in 1960 prompted the remodeling of the sanctuary.

The First Baptist Church stood at 77 South Main Street, in the downtown business district. The Baptist Church was organized in 1800 in Cheshire, New York, and moved to Canandaigua in 1833. This 1860s photograph shows a modest structure that featured sloping side galleries and a platform on the east end.

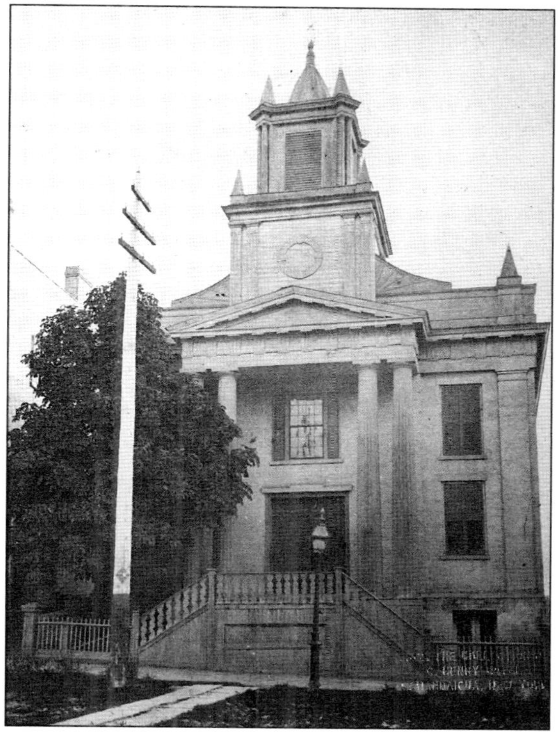

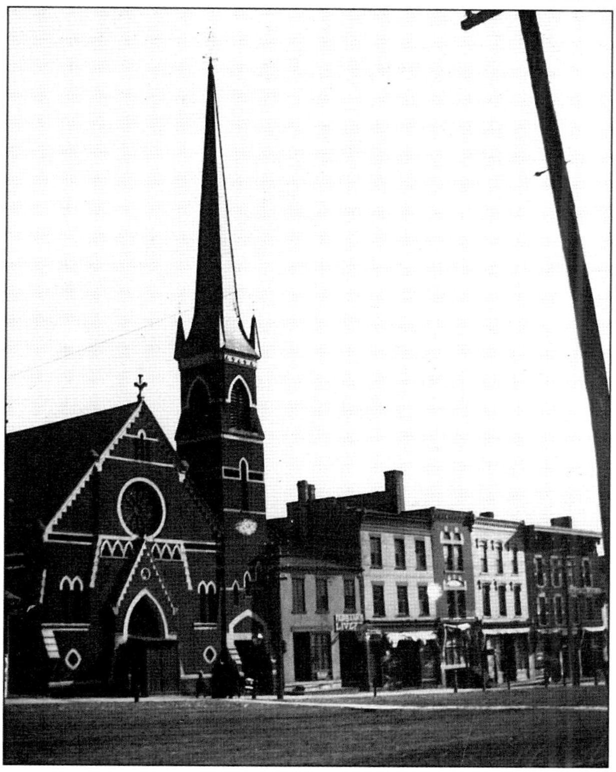

With a spire that reached to heaven, the Baptist church was rebuilt in 1879. The church, located on the east side of Main Street between the present Phoenix and Niagara Streets, shows the ornate exterior gingerbread that was typical of the late 1800s. A fire burned down the church in 1942 and the congregation joined with the Presbyterian church in 1947.

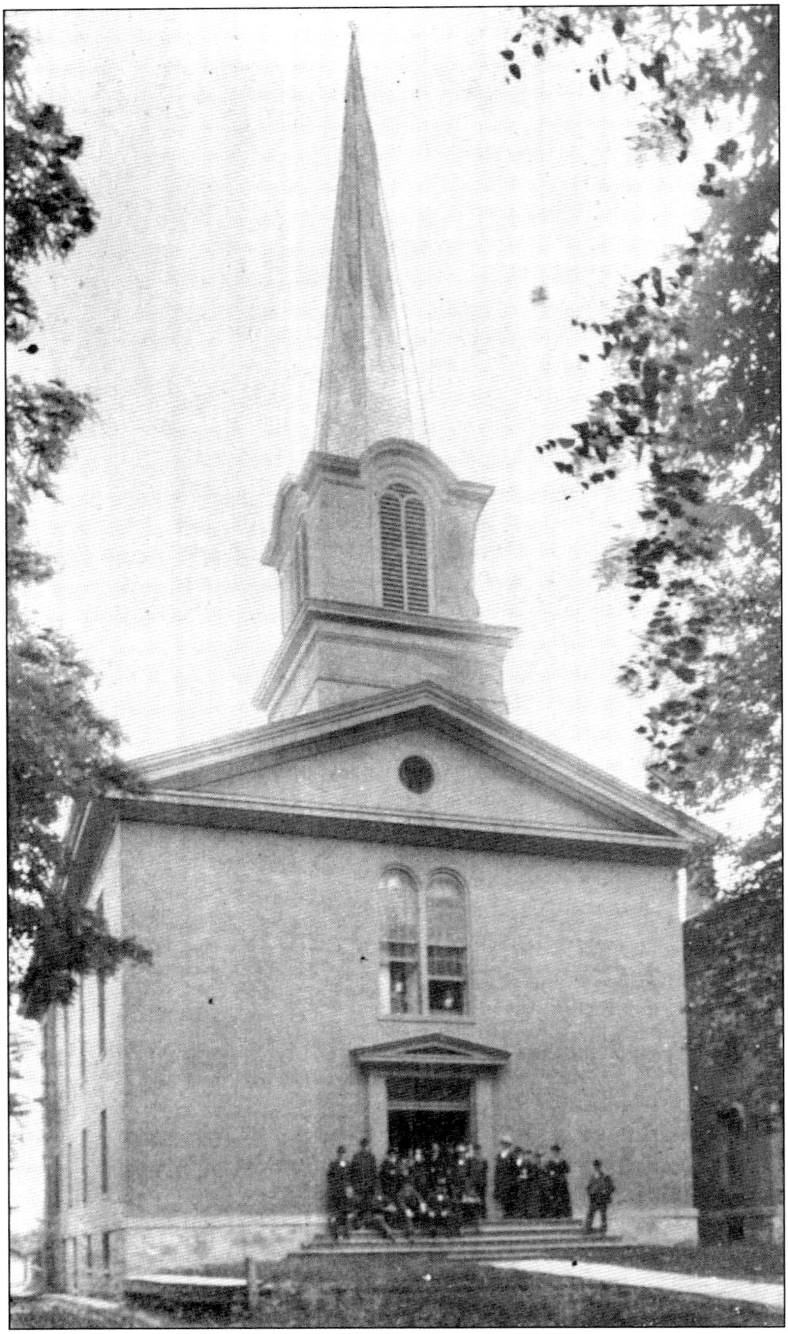

The congregation gathers on the steps of the old Methodist church. This picture shows the church sometime after the extensive remodeling done in 1855. Reverend Benjamin Padock rode the Ontario Circuit, urging the Methodists in Canandaigua to build a permanent chapel after the War of 1812. The Methodists purchased the site on what was later named Chapel Street. The church was constructed in 1818. In 1835 they moved the chapel to the present location for the church on Main Street at a cost of $1,200. The outside was faced with brick at the time of remodeling and the church bell was placed in the tower. The parsonage, partially visible to the right, was built in 1874 and modernized in 1903.

Eight

SONNENBERG

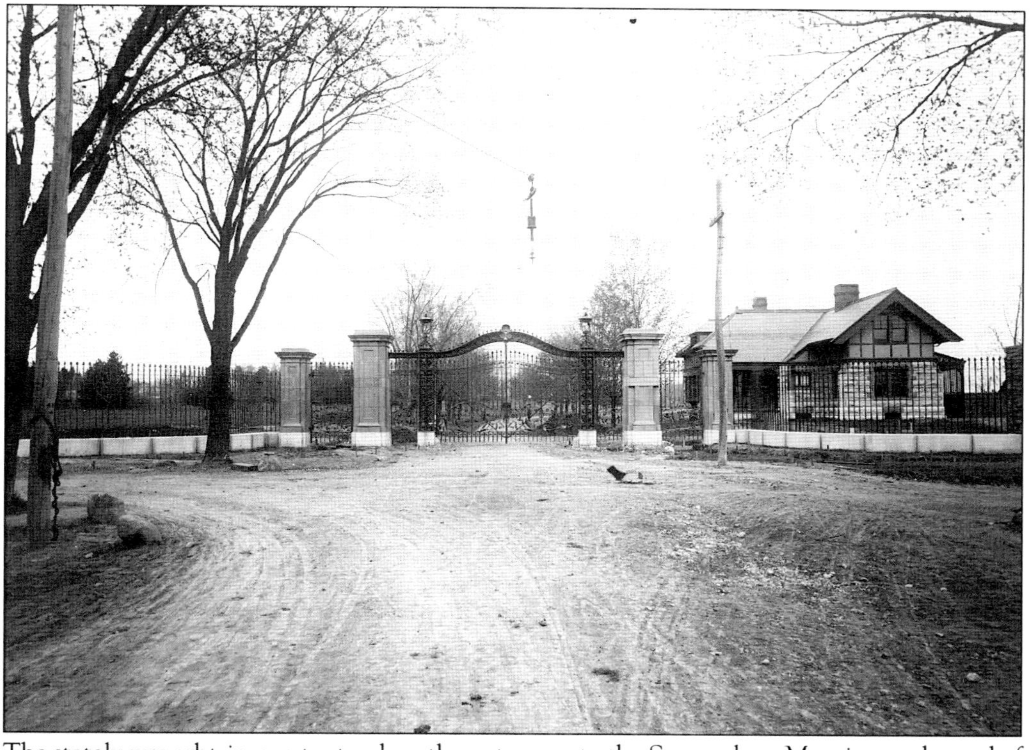

The stately wrought-iron gate stands as the entry way to the Sonnenberg Mansion at the end of Howell Street. Notice how the street has not yet been paved with either brick or asphalt. The intersection at night was illuminated by gaslight.

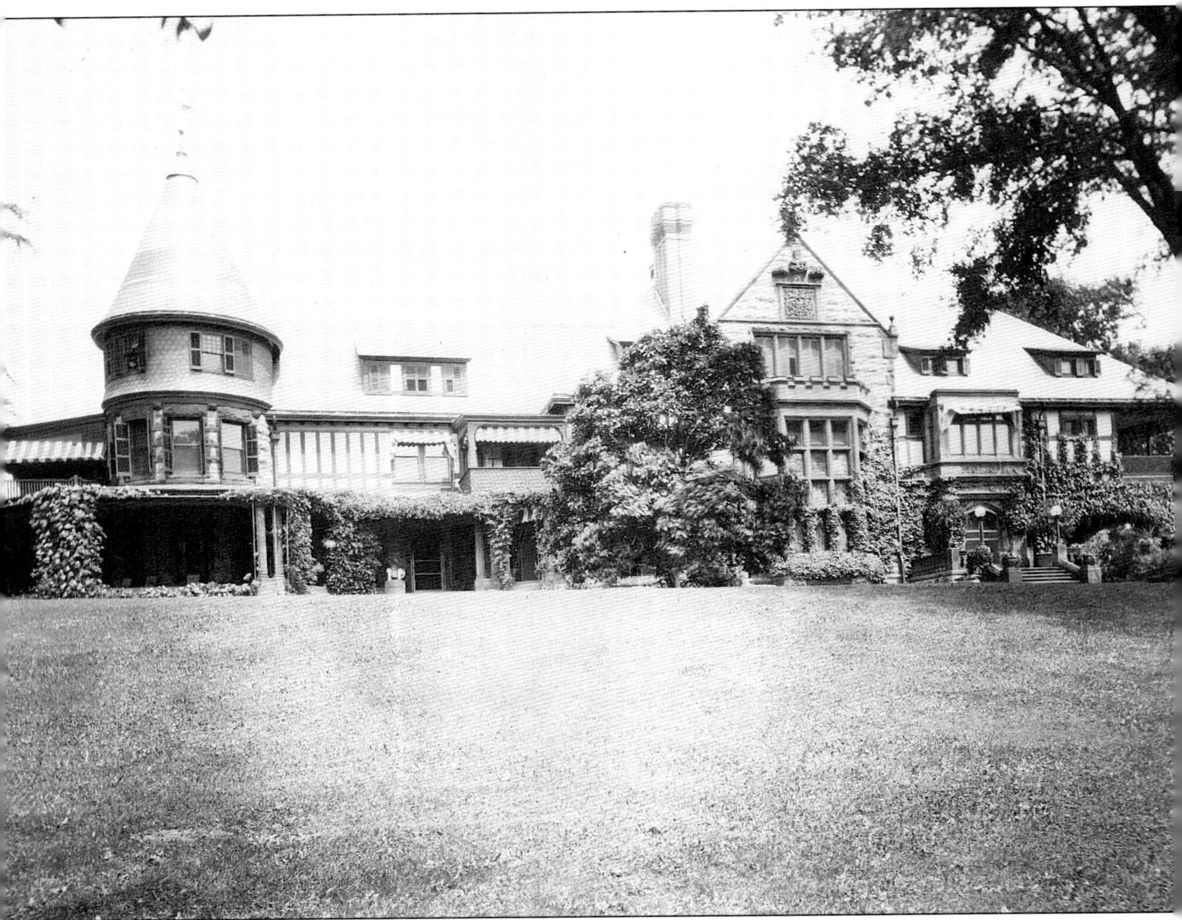

The Sonnenberg Mansion was built in 1887, and was the centerpiece of Mr. and Mrs. F.F. Thompson's 50-acre estate. Francis Allen, a Boston architect, designed the forty-room home. The exterior is constructed from stone. In 1863, the Thompsons purchased the original home from the Holberton family, inheriting the name Sonnenberg. Named after a small town in Germany, this appellation means "sunny hill." The Thompsons' primary residence was New York City, but summers were enjoyed in Canandaigua. They were known as gracious hosts, giving summer garden parties and organizing other events. Mrs. Thompson traveled the world seven times collecting art, antiques, and gathering ideas for her gardens. An extended trip to Holland prevented her from riding on the deadly voyage of the *Titanic*. The Thompsons had no children and therefore had abundant means to help others. They gave very generously to the community.

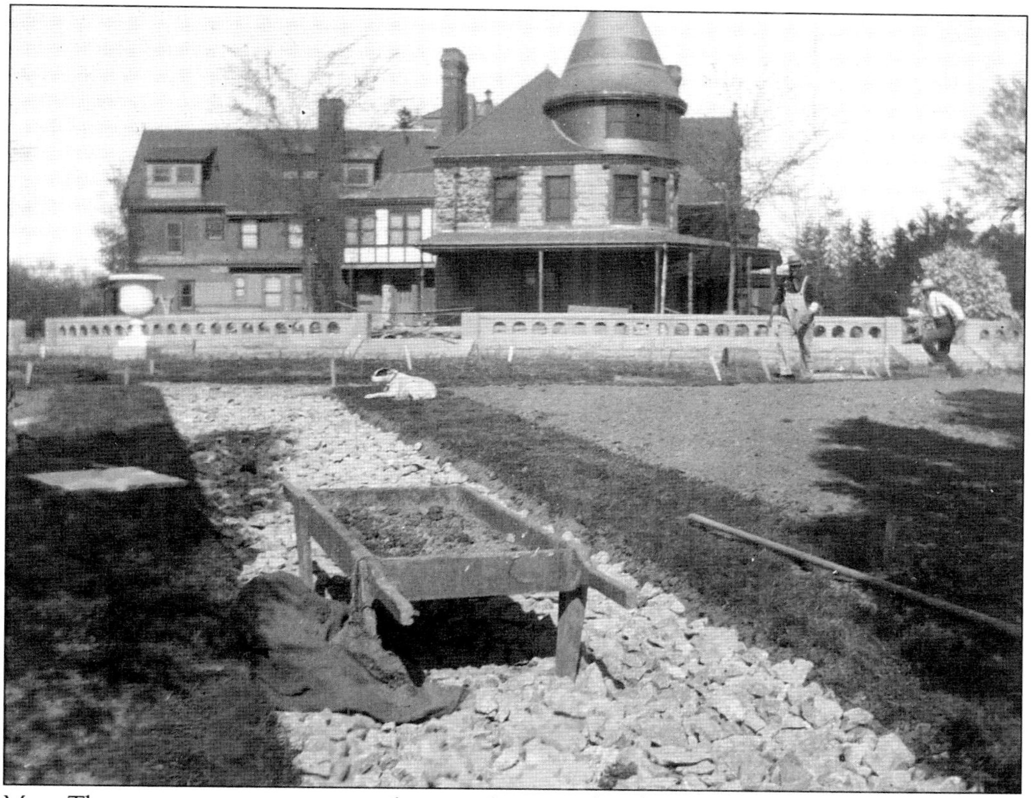

Mr. Thompson, an amateur photographer, took this photograph of a walkway under construction.

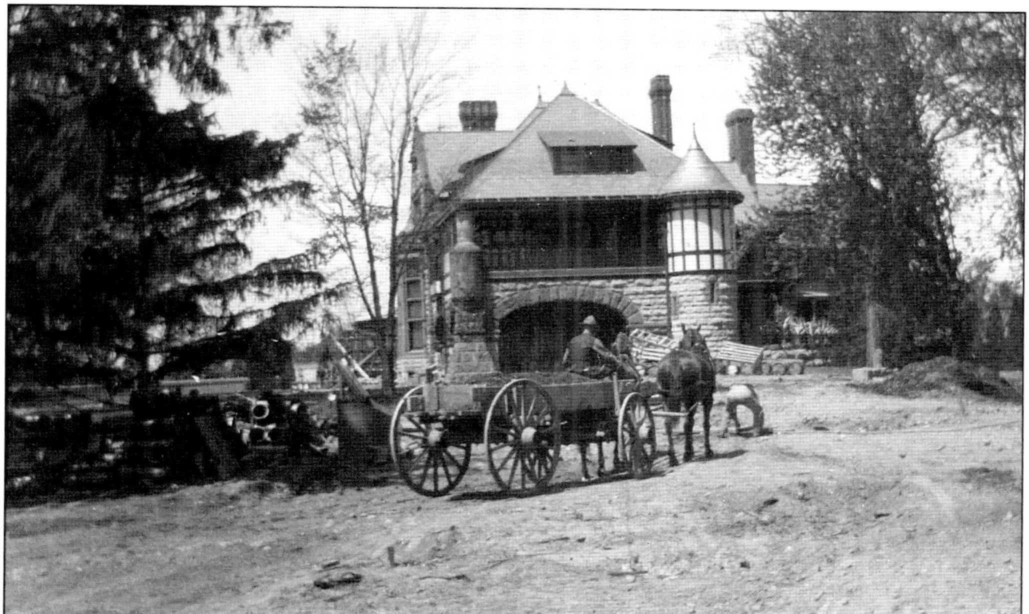

A horse-drawn wagon approaches the Sonnenberg Mansion.

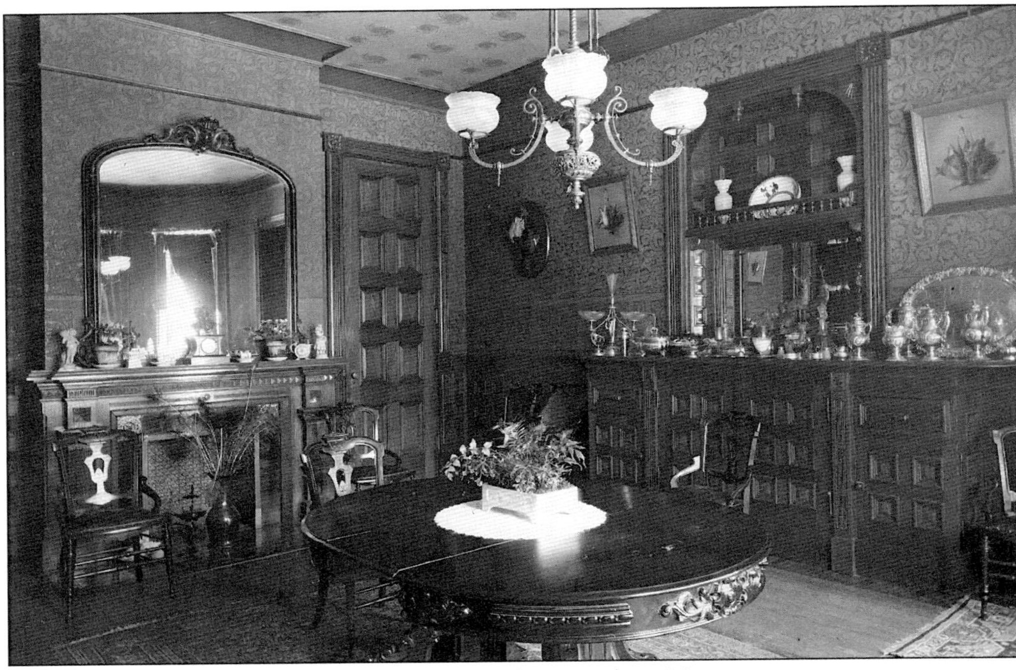

This is the beautiful dining room of the original Sonnenberg Mansion.

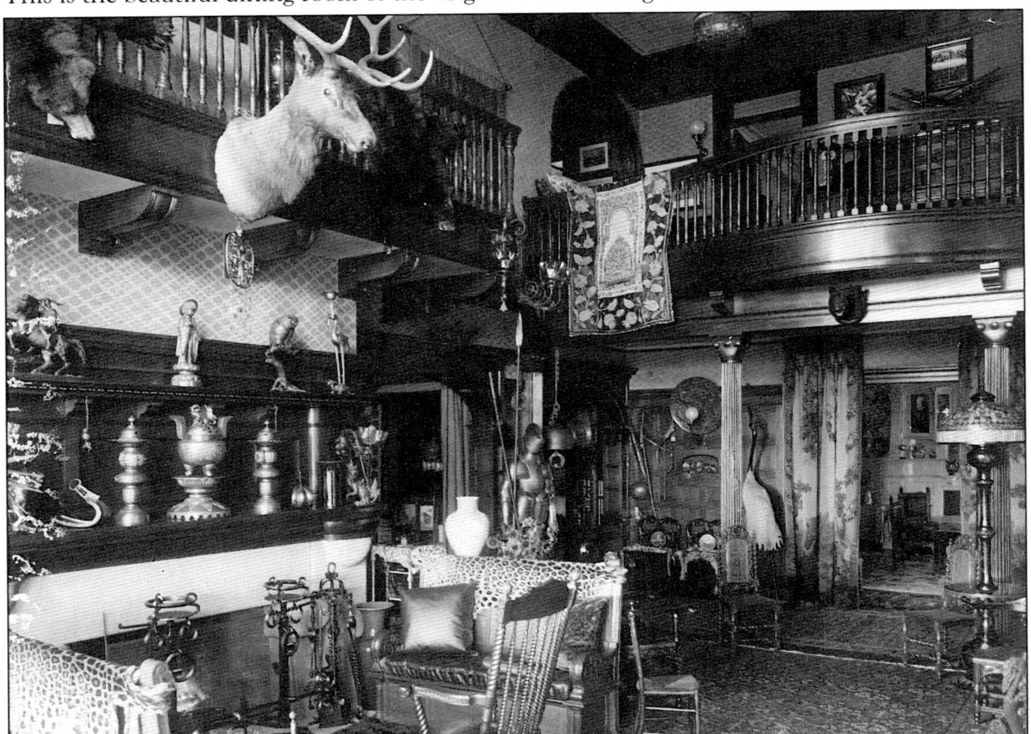

The magnificent great room at Sonnenberg is displayed in this photograph, taken by Stewart Studios of Canandaigua. The great room's ceiling is open to the second floor.

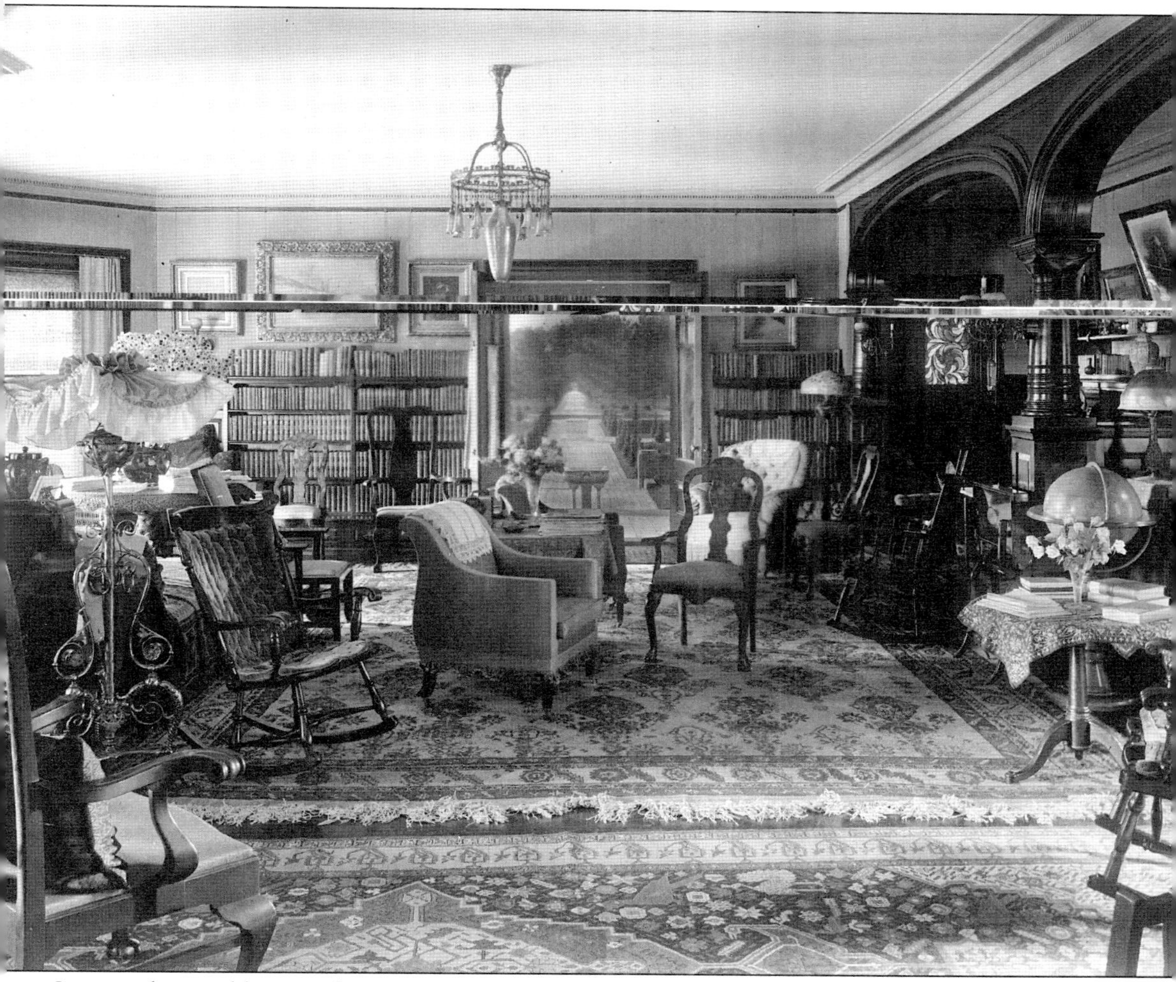

Imagine being able to sit here, in the library at Sonnenberg, and enjoy your favorite book. It would be hard to concentrate with all the visual distractions. Large windows offer the opportunity to view the gardens from inside the house. The abundance of ornamentation was typical of the Victorian era and and suited Mrs. Thompson's penchant for collecting art and antiques.

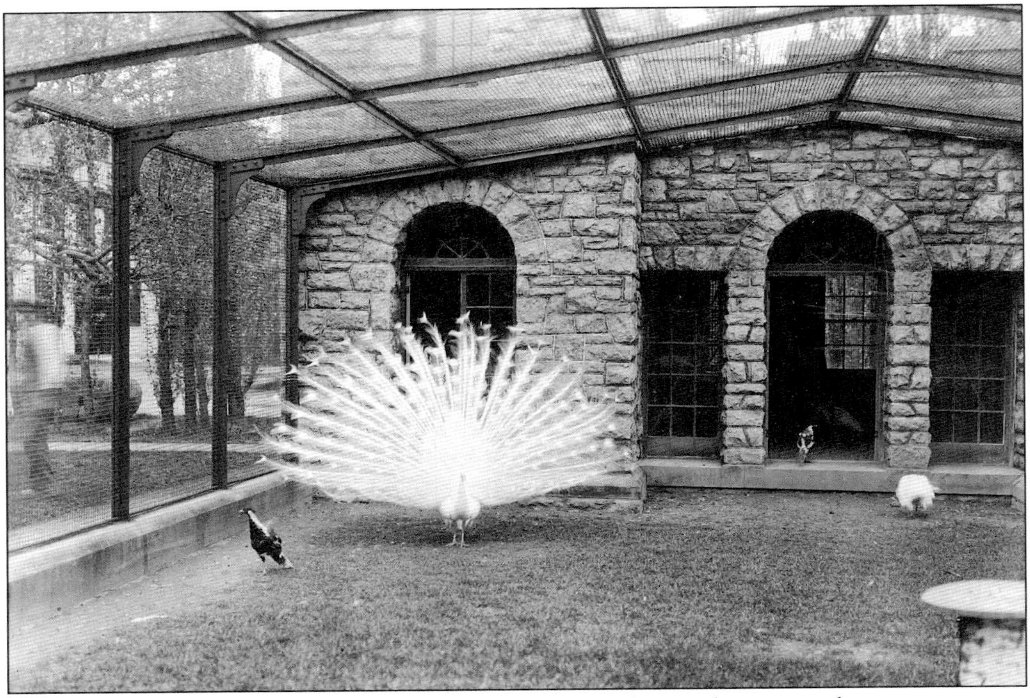

The aviary housed a variety of birds, including this magnificent white peacock.

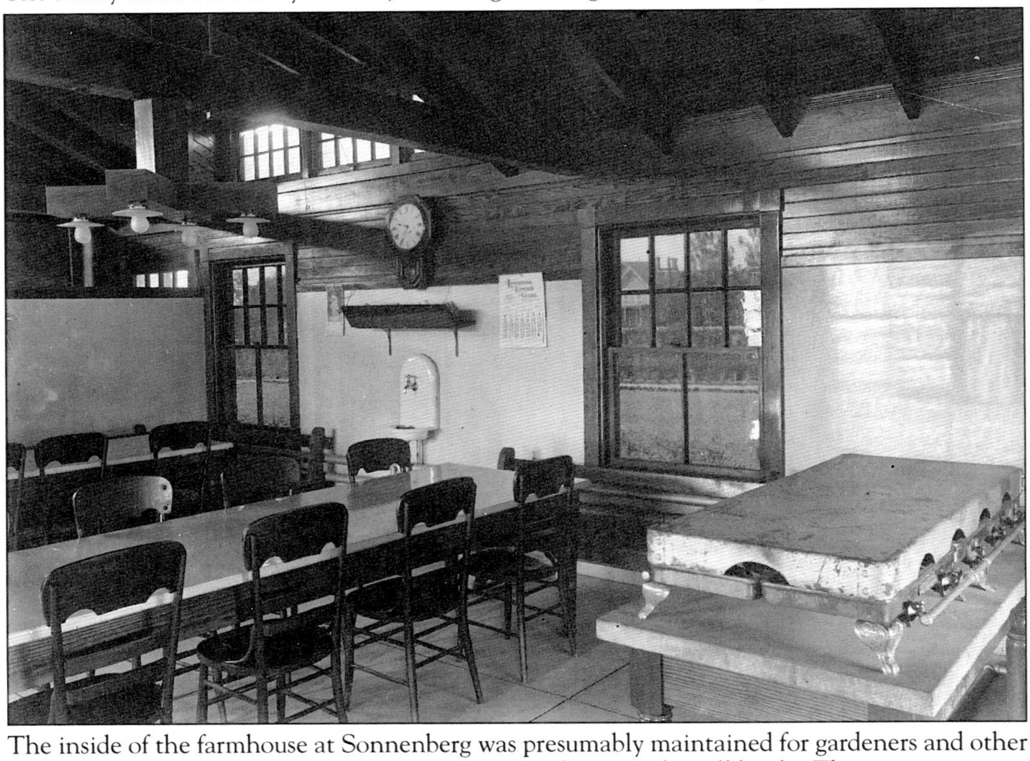

The inside of the farmhouse at Sonnenberg was presumably maintained for gardeners and other workers. Reports say that all employees were treated extremely well by the Thompsons.

A cool path inside one of the Sonnenberg greenhouses shows that the numerous gardens on the estate required many horticultural skills. Many species were raised in greenhouses, later to be transplanted to one of the nine gardens.

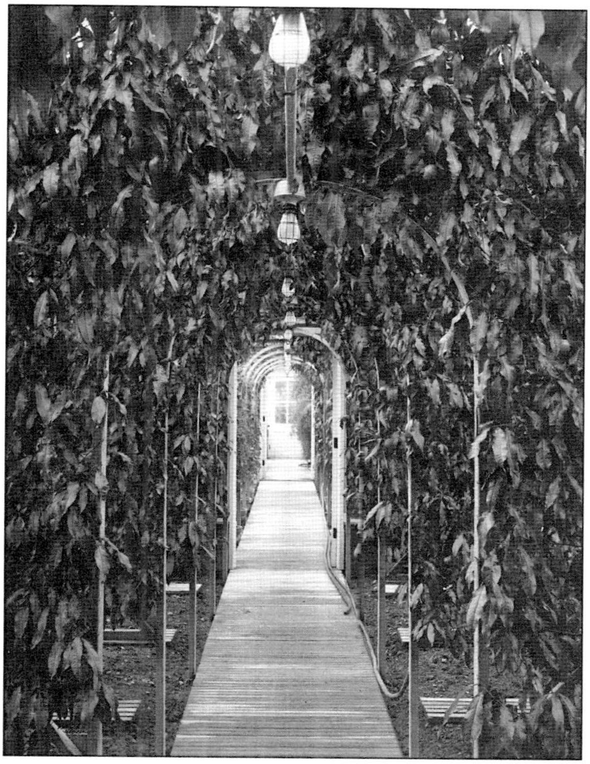

Workers harvest the fruits of their labor from the vegetable garden.

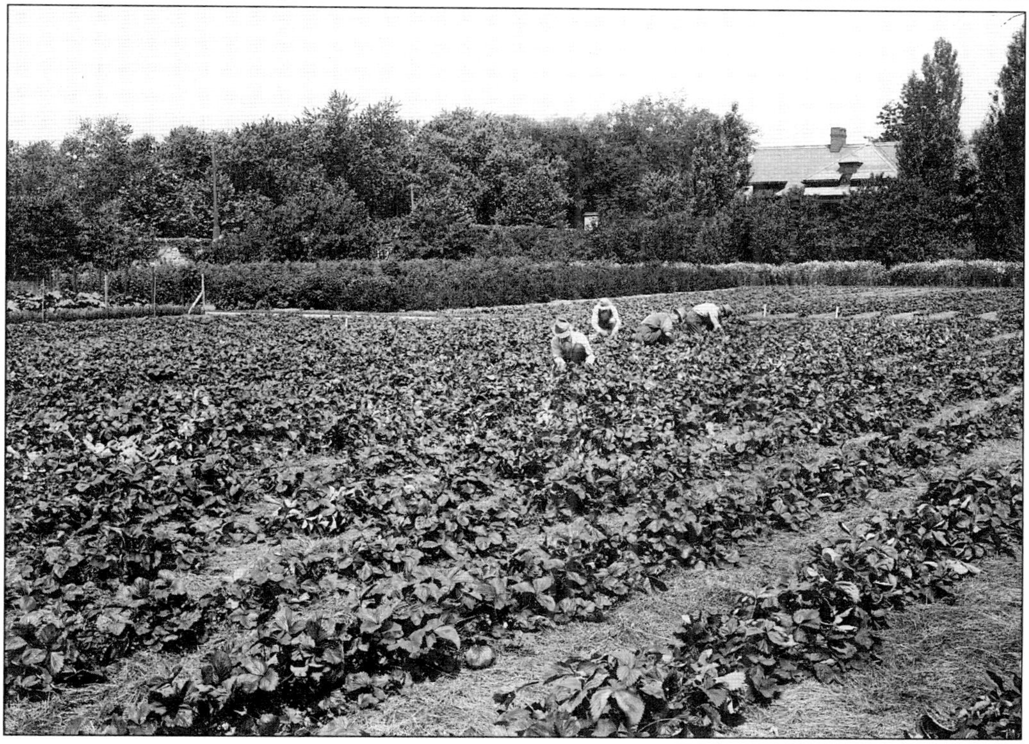

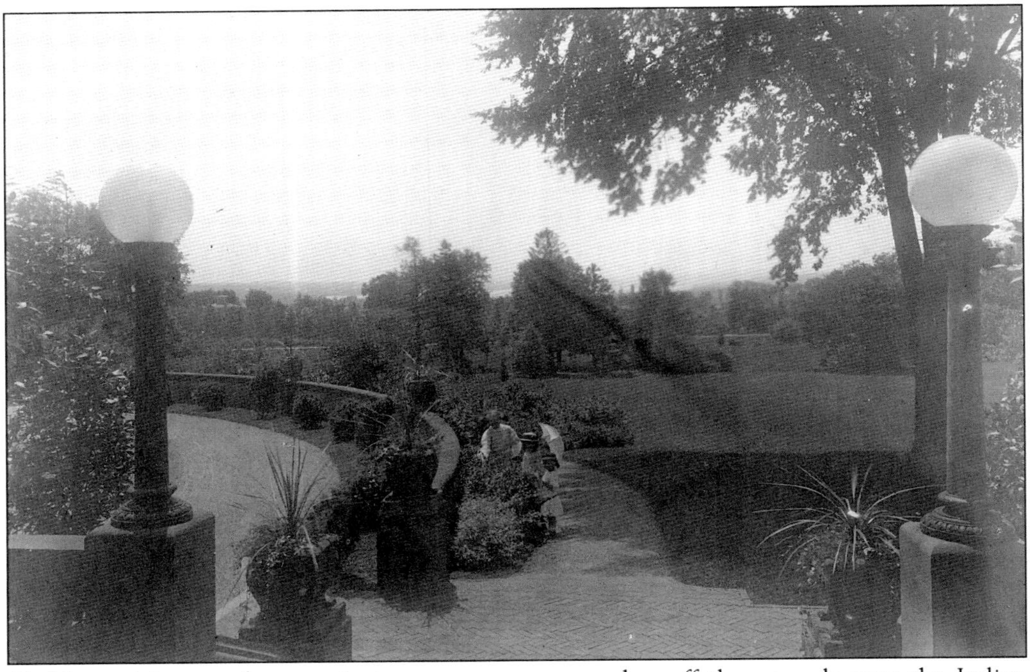

Children with parasols are enjoying a warm summers day, off the veranda near the Italian Garden. A sliver of Canandaigua Lake can be seen in the distance.

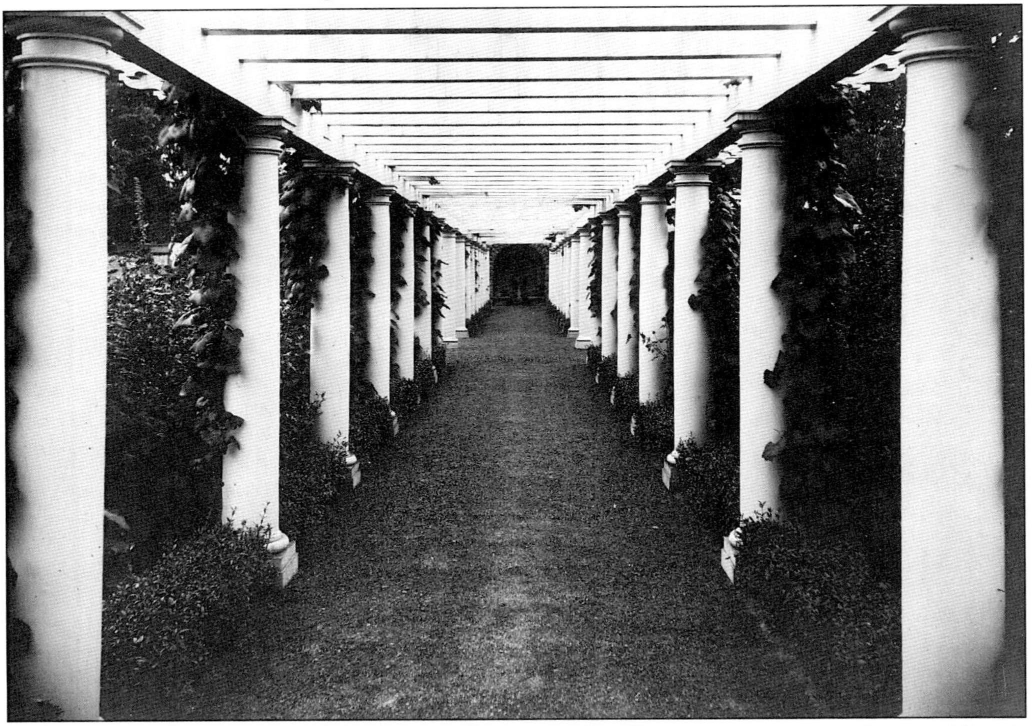

The pergola creates an image of infinity as this covered walkway seems to go on forever. The air surely must have smelled sweet on a summer's evening.

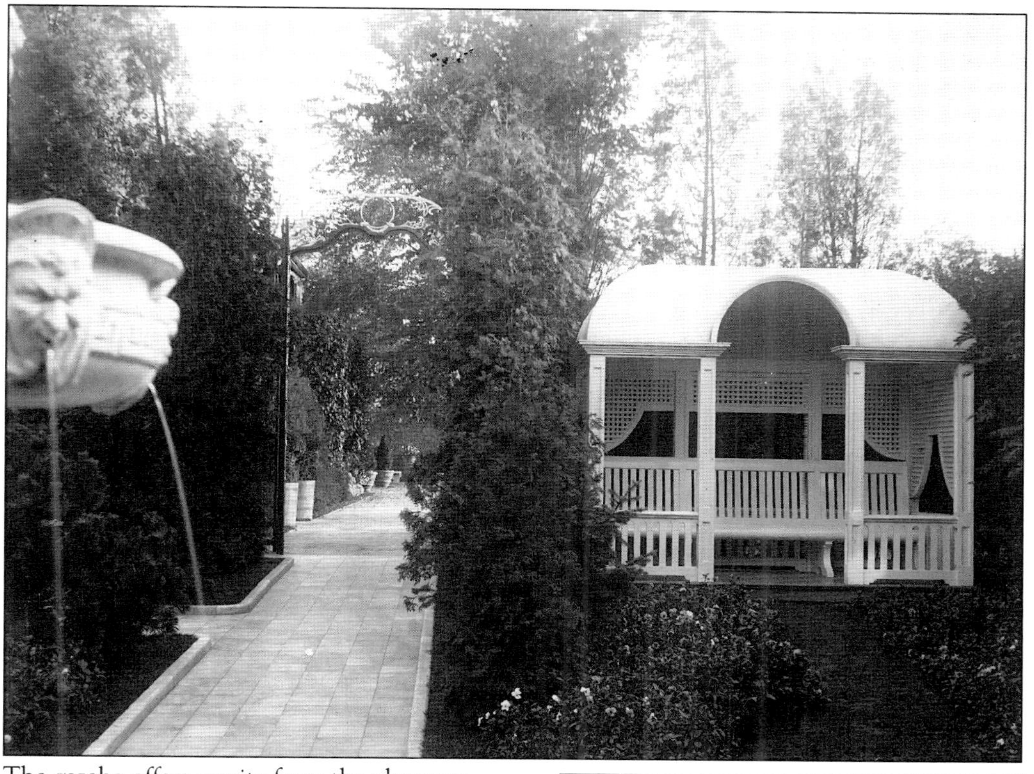

The gazebo offers respite from the elements.

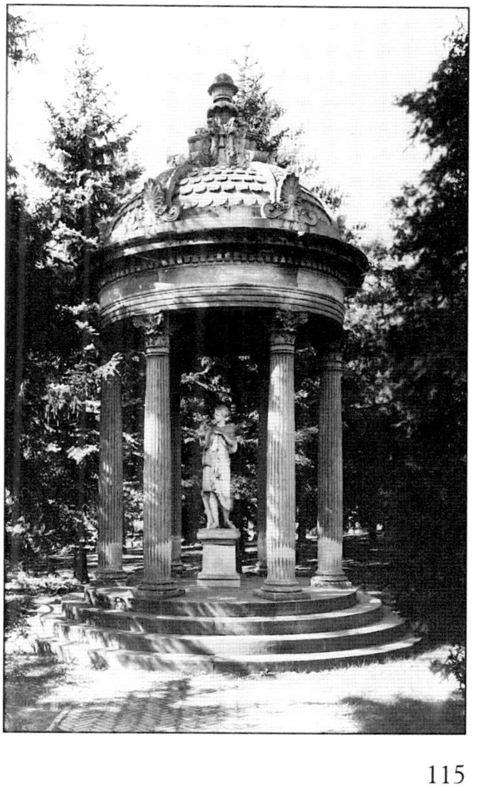

This basic structure is still standing today, although time has rounded some of the edges.

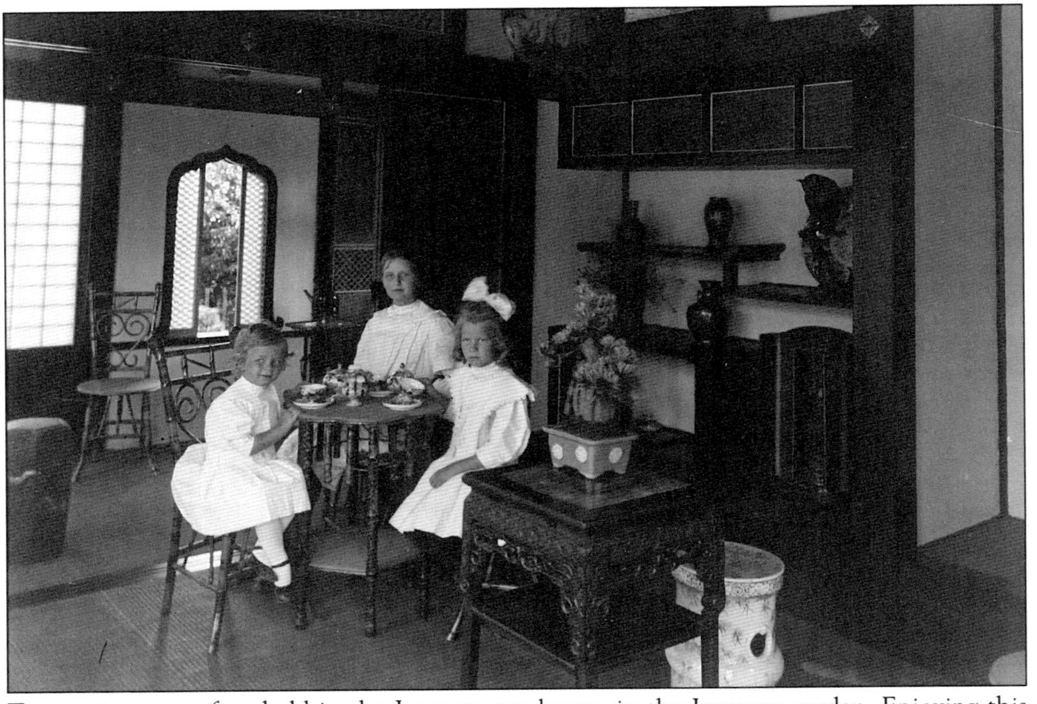

Tea parties were often held in the Japanese tea house, in the Japanese garden. Enjoying this party are the Thompson's nieces and nephew: Bill, Elizabeth, and Martha Clark.

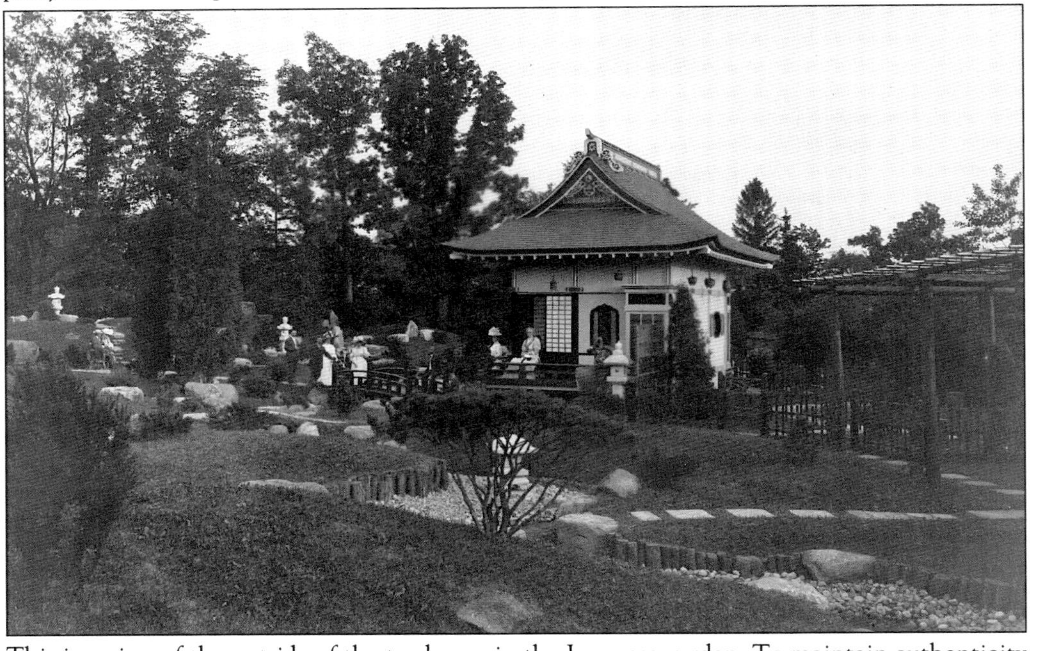

This is a view of the outside of the tea house in the Japanese garden. To maintain authenticity during the creation of the Japanese garden, a crew of designers from Japan worked for over six months. The landscaping, rock work, and water system for the brook and pool were built with painstaking care.

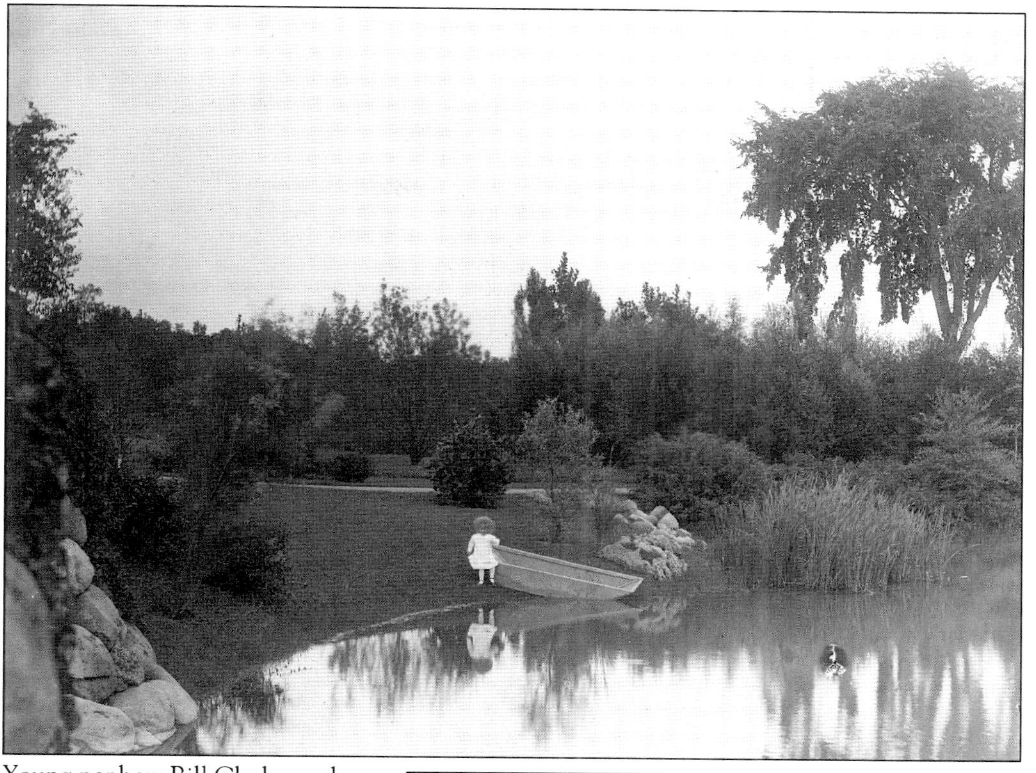

Young nephew Bill Clark ponders a boat excursion in the pond along the main drive to the mansion.

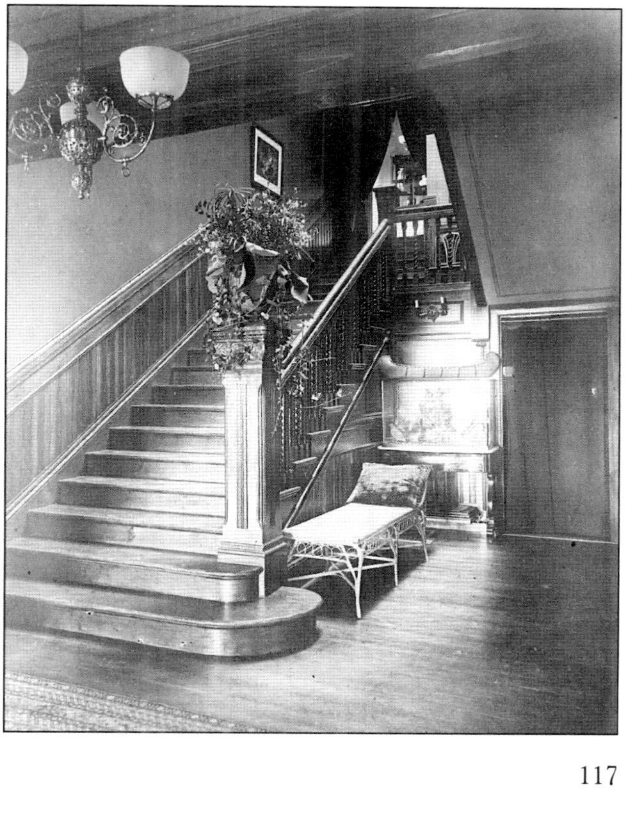

The main stairway inside the mansion was captured on film by Mr. Thompson. Notice the stuffed owl along with other decorating flourishes.

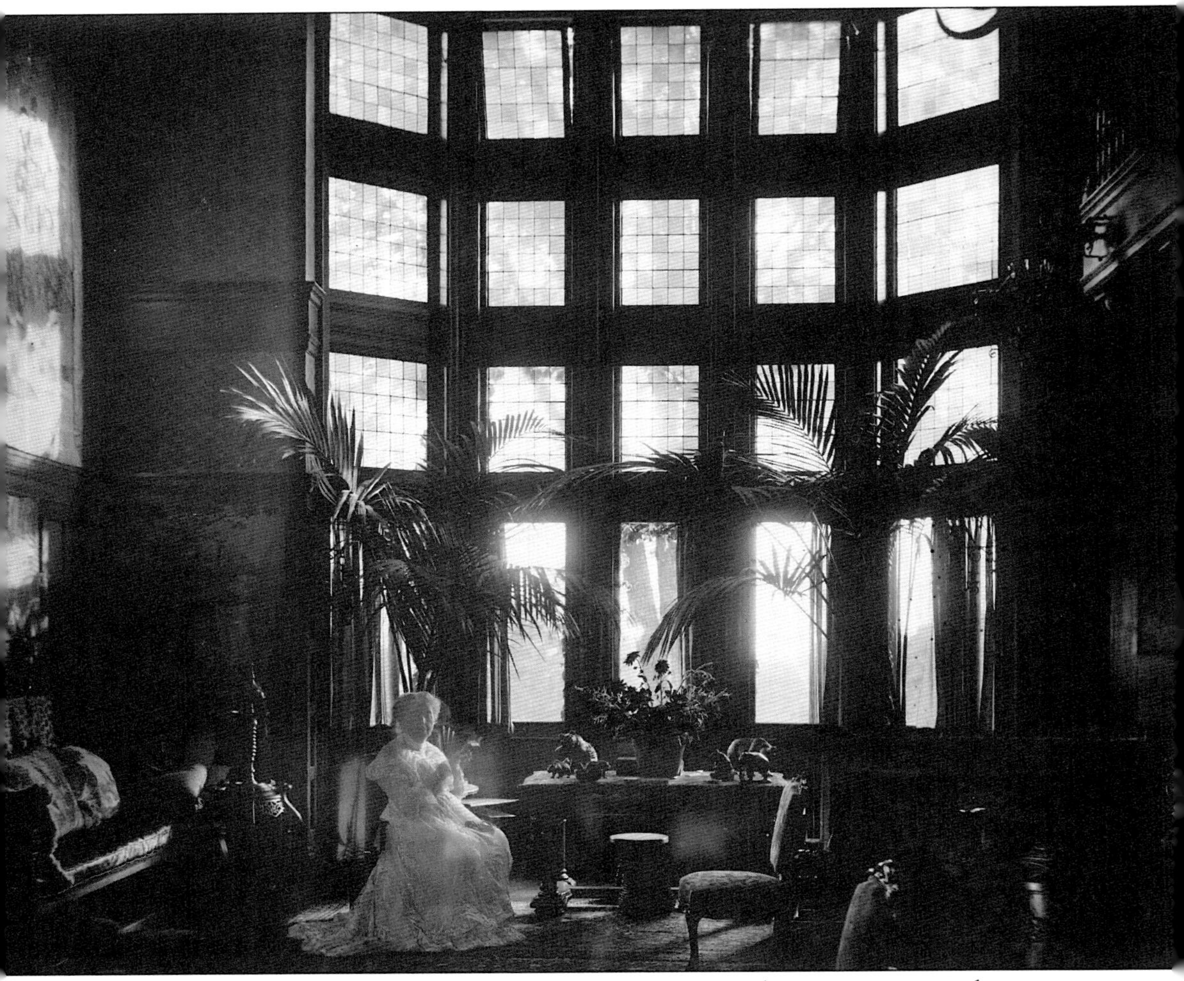

Sitting alone in the great room looking westward, Mrs. Mary Thompson is captured in a moment of quiet reflection. The people of Canandaigua still benefit from Mrs. Thompson's generosity, as her frequent donations advanced the community. Her lasting gifts were felt by the populace through civic enhancements such as the post office, the Sonnenberg Playground, the swimming school at Kershaw Park, the Ontario Orphan Asylum, and the F.F. Thompson Hospital, among many others.

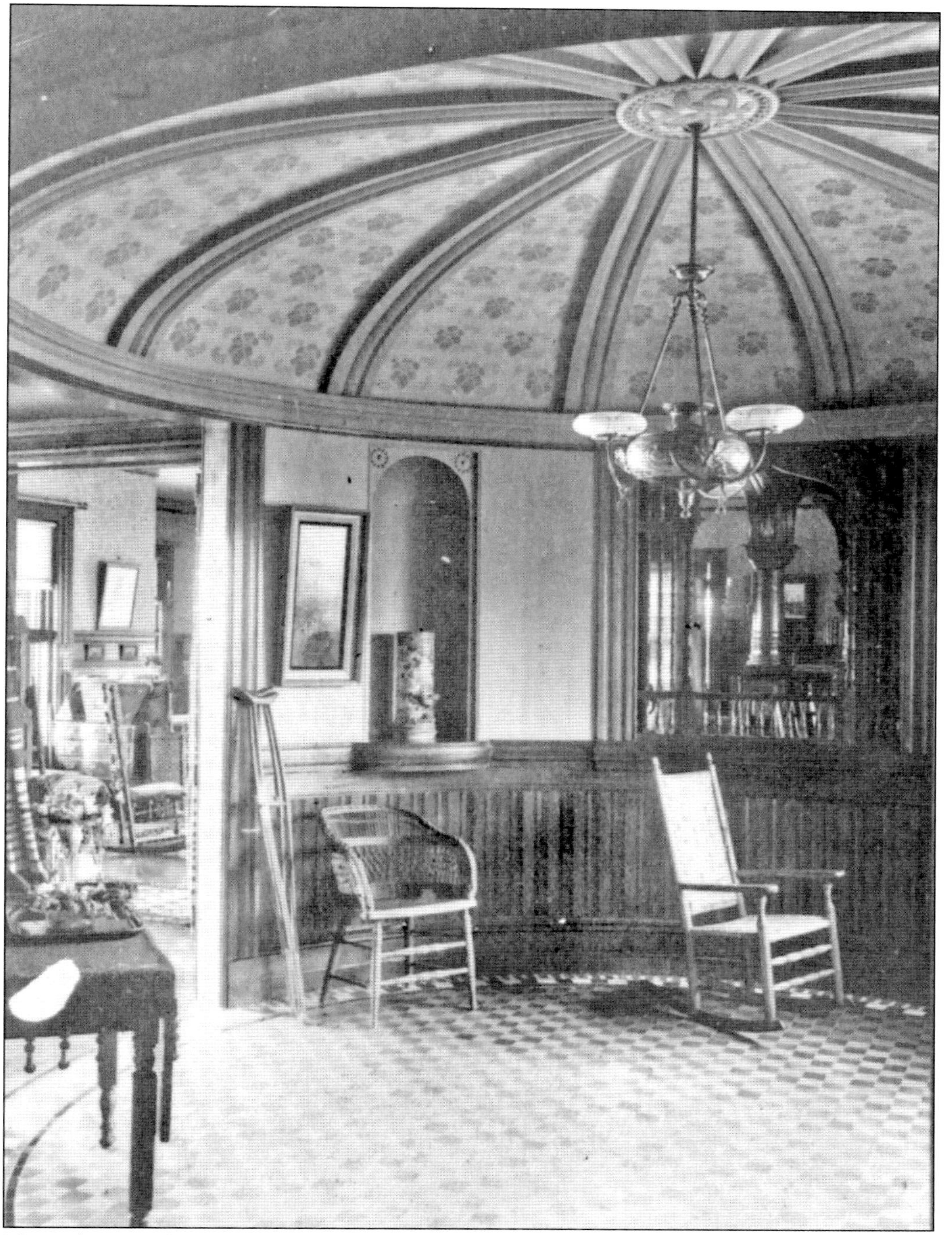

This photograph, taken from the Thompson family album, shows "The Rotunda." Mr. Thompson's photography caught a light-filled round room on a sunny Sonnenberg day. This small circular room is still a favorite of the visitors who come to enjoy and learn about the beautiful estate.

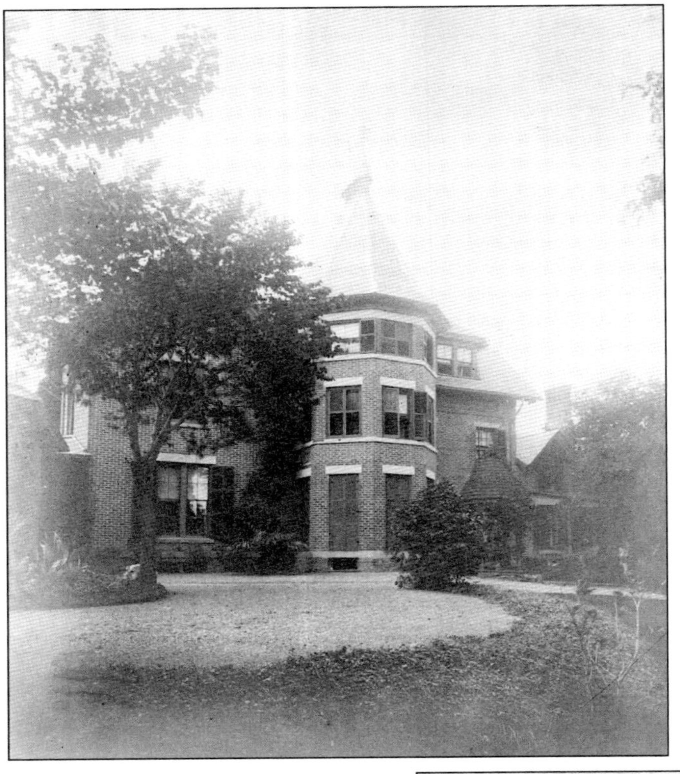

Mr. Thompson took this photograph of the first house on the property in 1885. The new mansion was to be built in 1887. The original home appears to have been very lovely, but it was replaced by an even more magnificent structure.

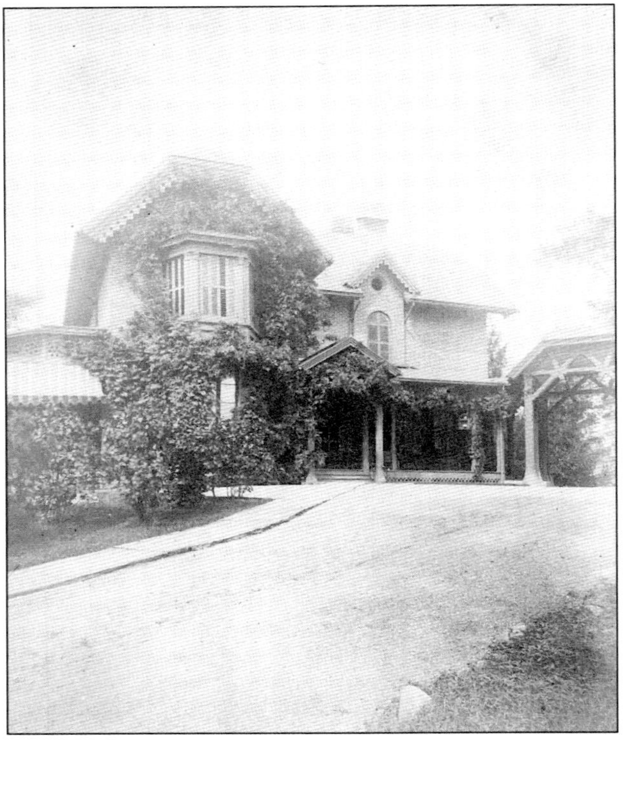

This is another photograph taken by Thompson of the original Sonnenberg.

The burning of the *Ontario* is shown here in a photograph taken by F.F. Thompson. Mr. Thompson was an avid amateur photographer and enjoyed capturing local images through his hobby. The cause of the fire remains a mystery today.

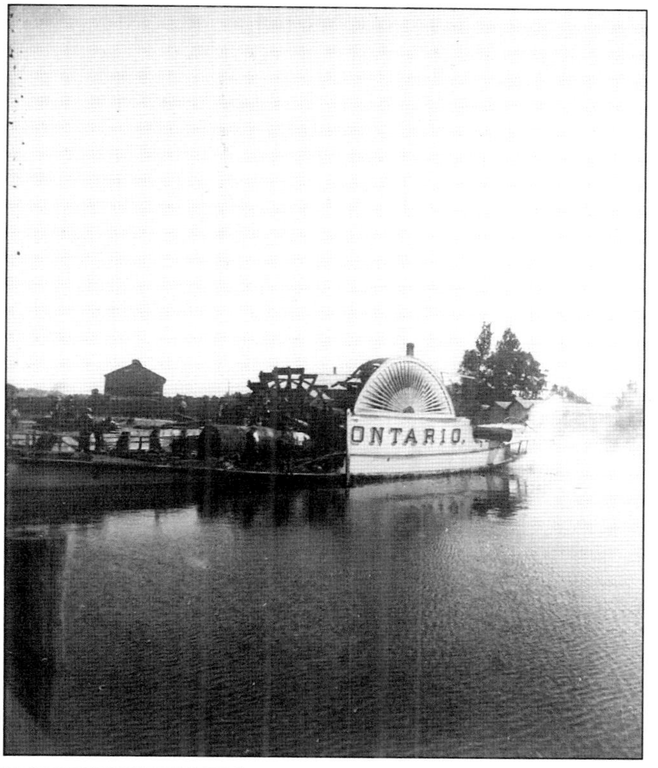

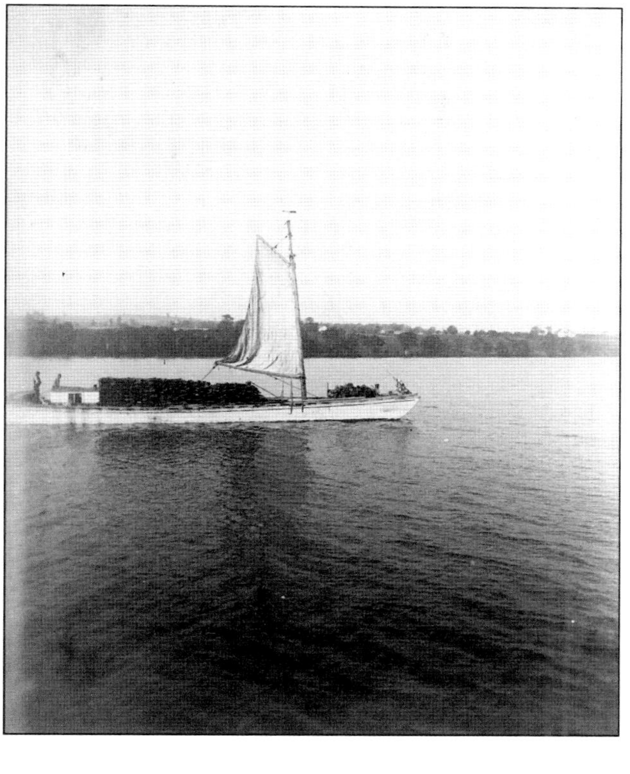

Another F.F. Thompson photograph depicts a scow with a load of unknown cargo on the lake. The Thompsons had a cottage called Pine Banks on the west side of Canandaigua Lake for additional summer enjoyment.

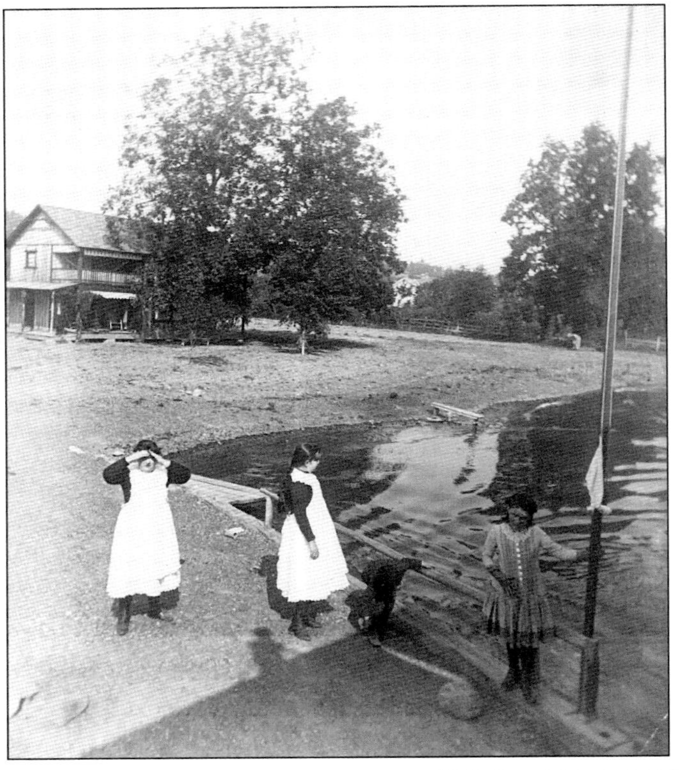

Labeled "The Twins" by F.F. Thompson, this picture shows a group of children by water's edge. The twins are pictured here in pinafores watching a steamship.

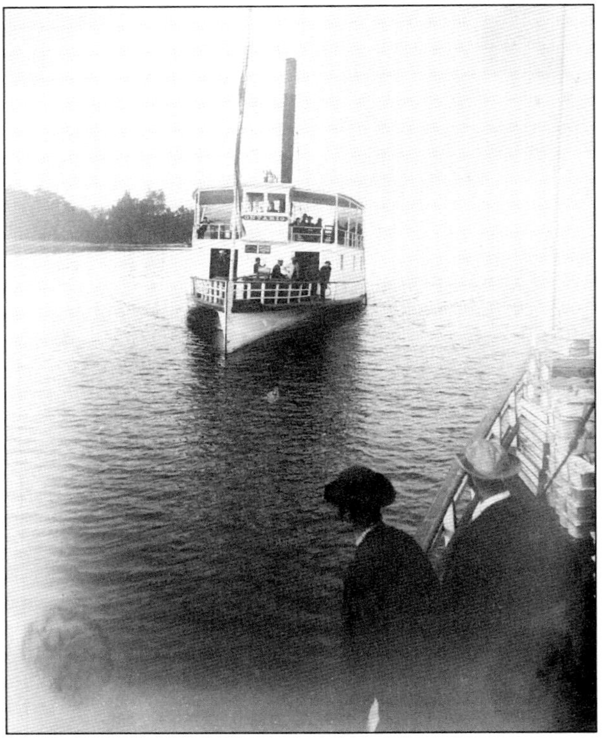

The ill-fated *Ontario* approaches as steamboats pass on the lake. Thompson captured this unique shot from the ship's deck.

Nine

Lisk Manufacturing

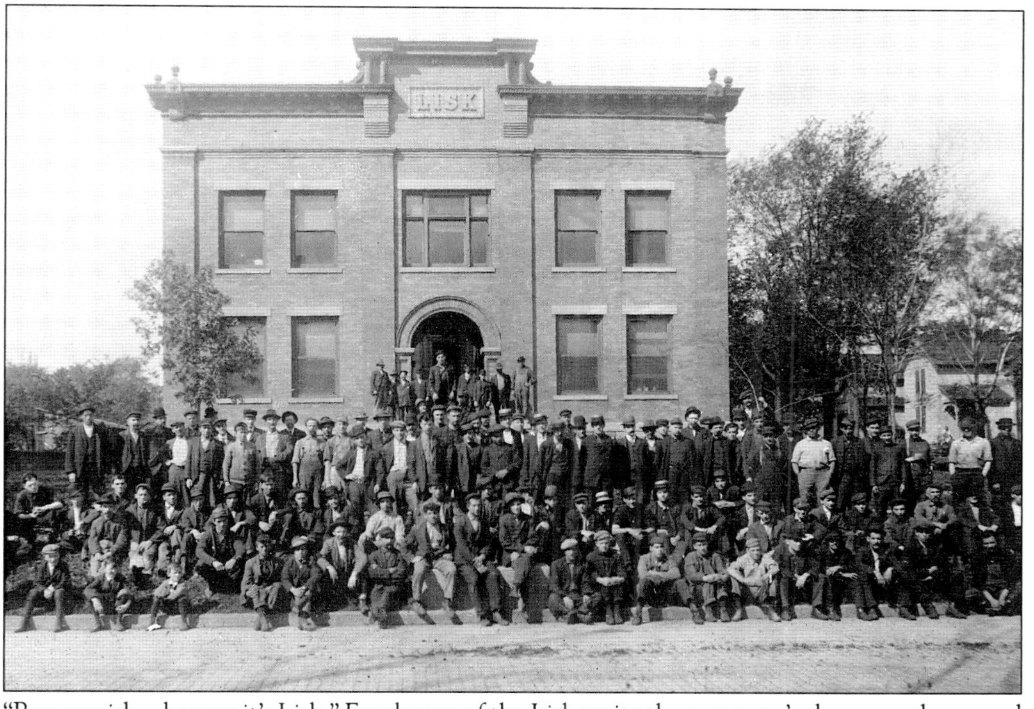

"Run no risk—be sure it's Lisk." Employees of the Lisk recite the company's slogan, as they stand outside corporate headquarters on Gorham Street. Lisk was a manufacturer of enamel ware goods, and produced items ranging from roasting pans to lanterns, funnels to baby bathtubs, farm products to health aids. They were a major employer in this area, featuring national sales of their varied product line.

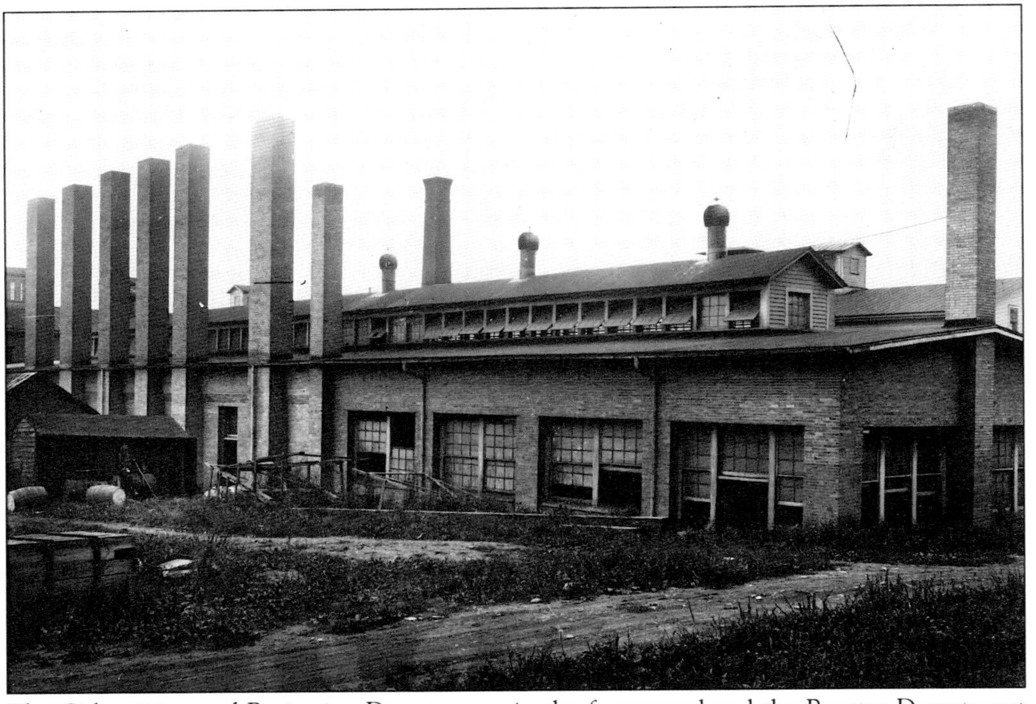

The Galvanizing and Retinning Departments in the foreground and the Roaster Department behind them appear idle in this picture. These were some of the many manufacturing buildings located in the Lisk complex.

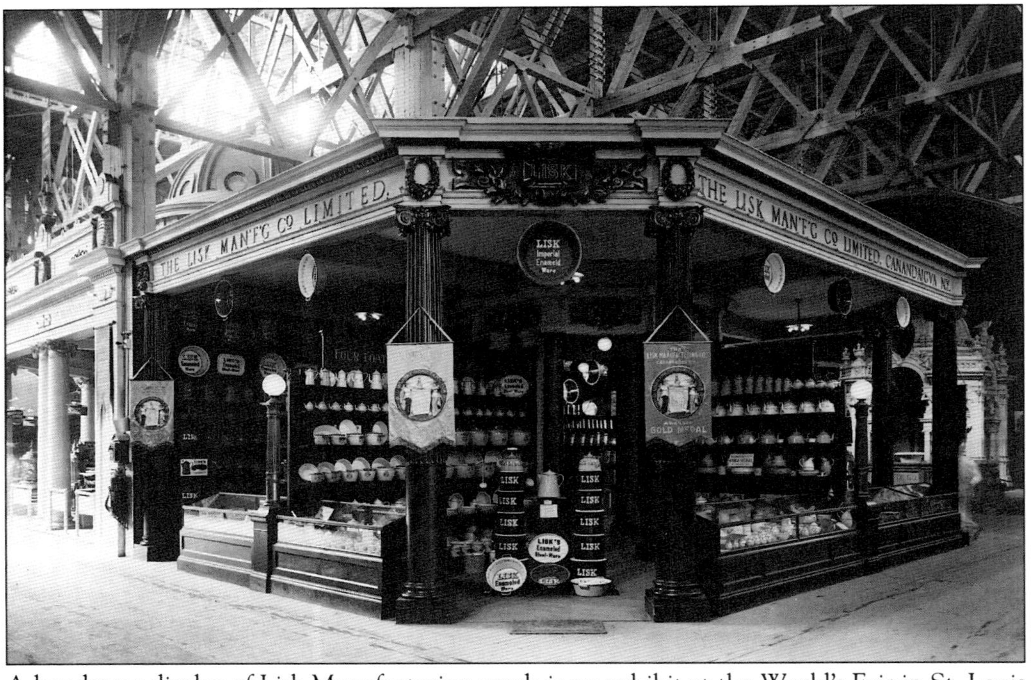

A handsome display of Lisk Manufacturing goods is on exhibit at the World's Fair in St. Louis in 1904.

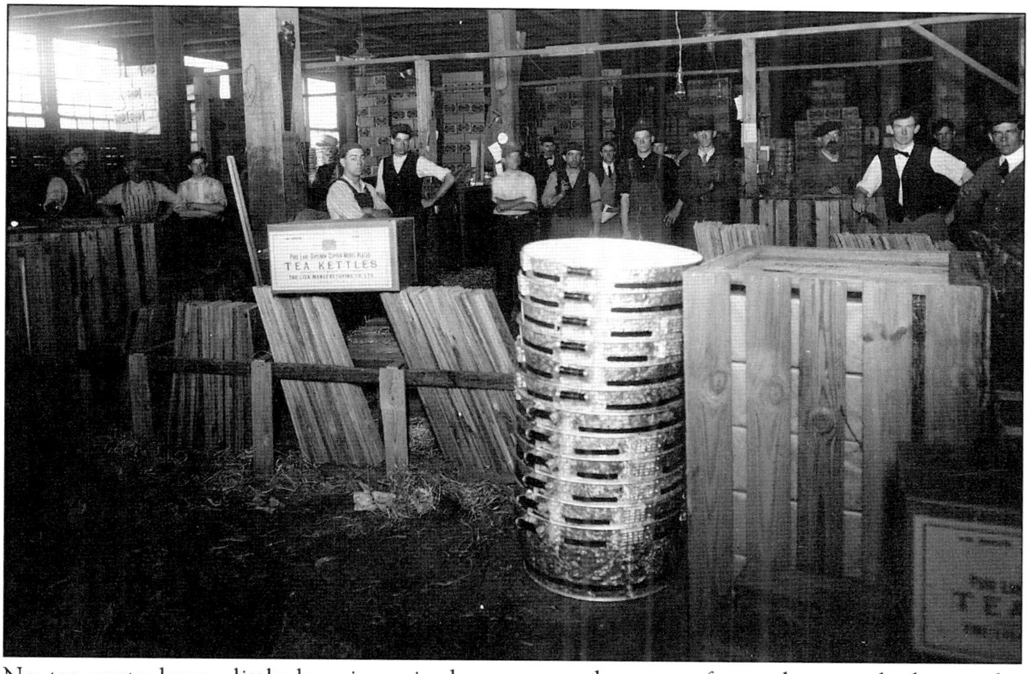

No tea party here—little happiness is shown as workers stop for a photograph during the manufacture of Lisk tea kettles. The work environment seems oppressive by today's standards.

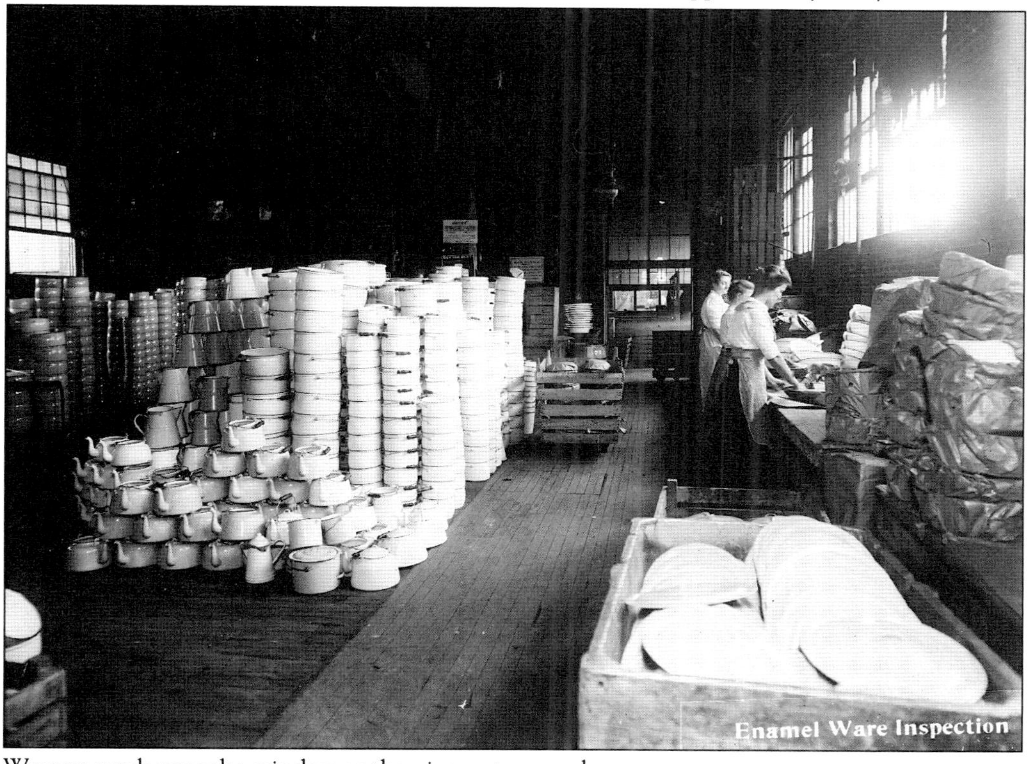

Women work near the window as they inspect enamel ware.

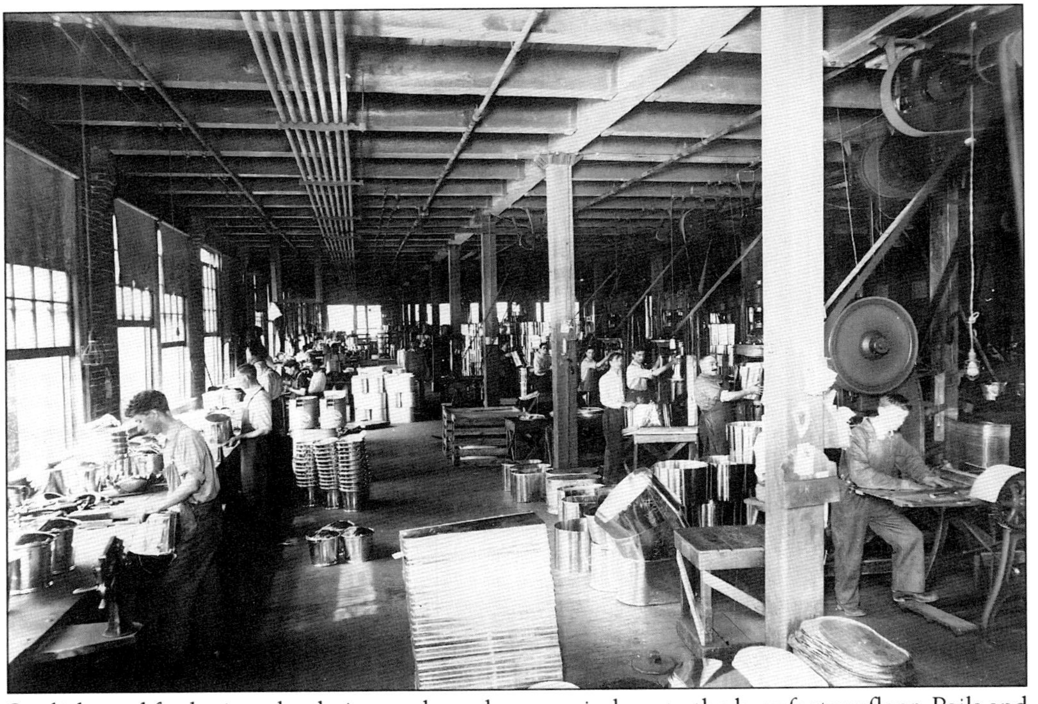

Sunlight and fresh air make their way through open windows to the busy factory floor. Pails and roasters appear to be assembled in this scene.

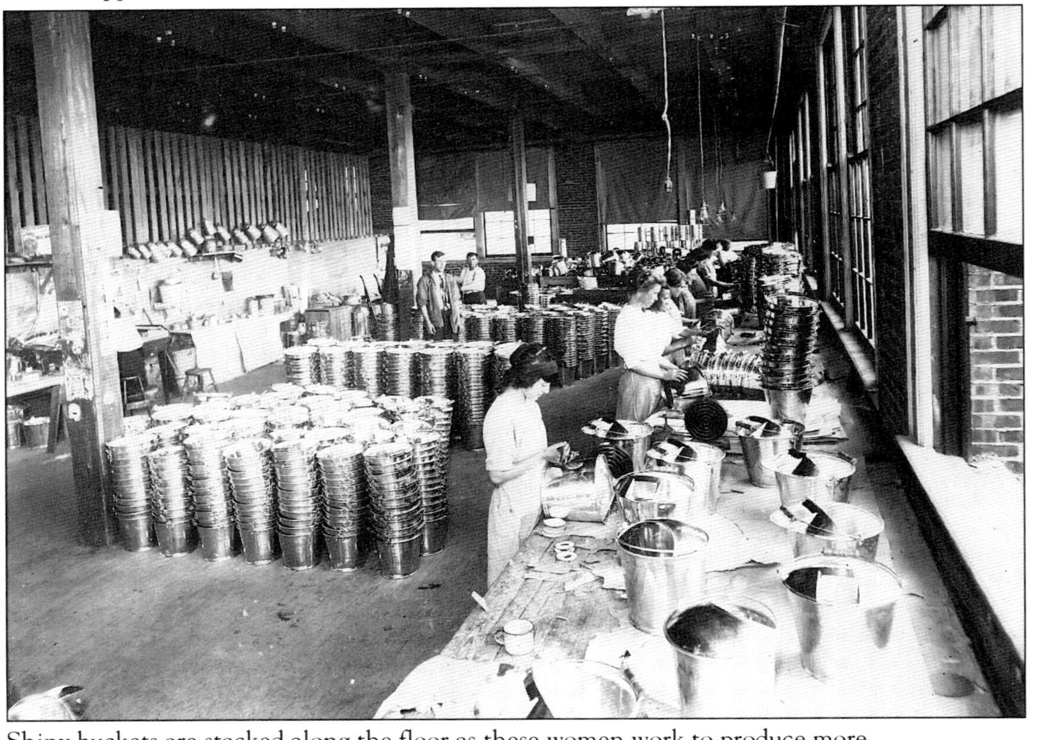

Shiny buckets are stacked along the floor as these women work to produce more.

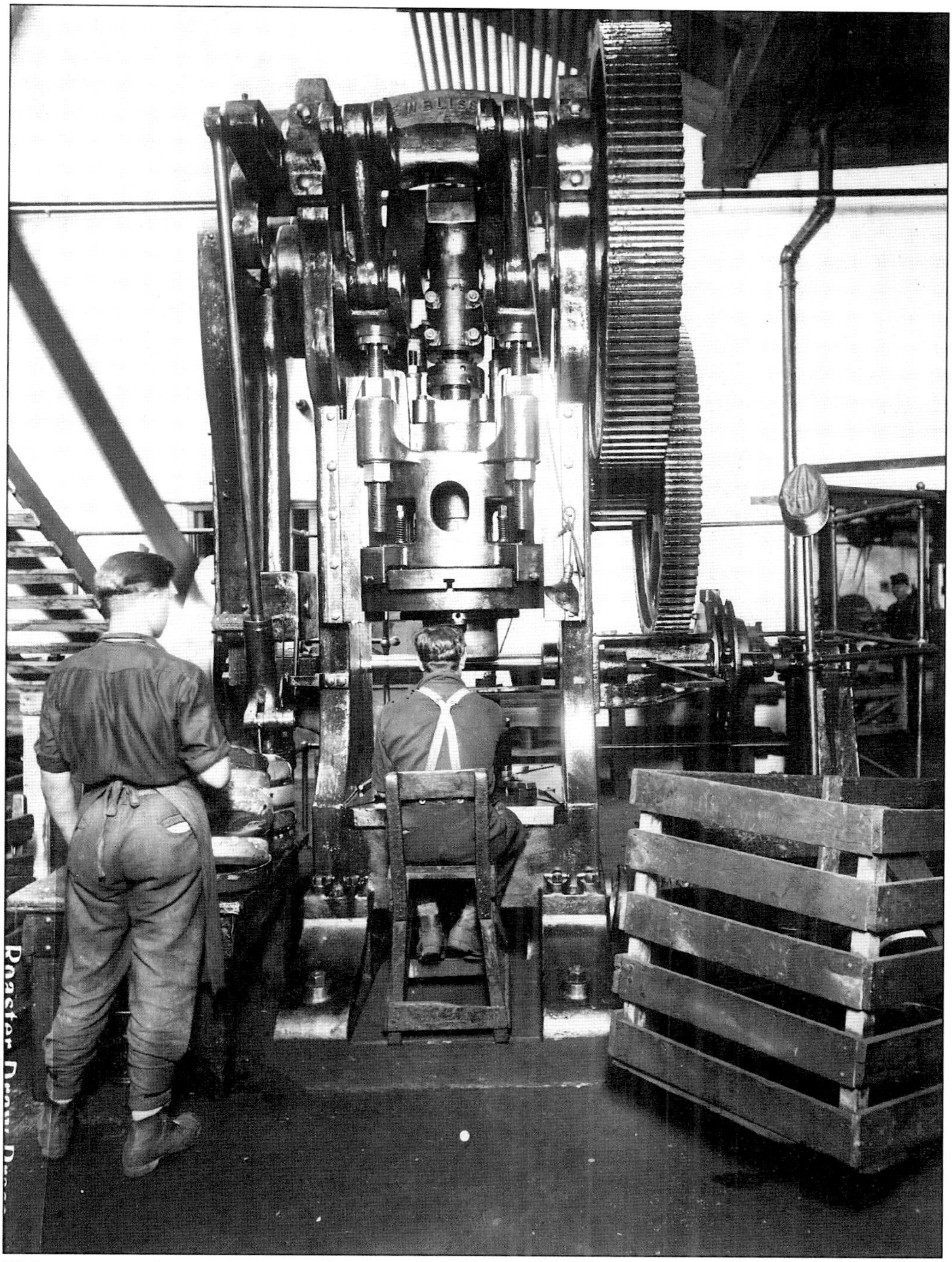

Elaborate machinery was used to manufacture roasting pans. Enormous gears propel the machine.

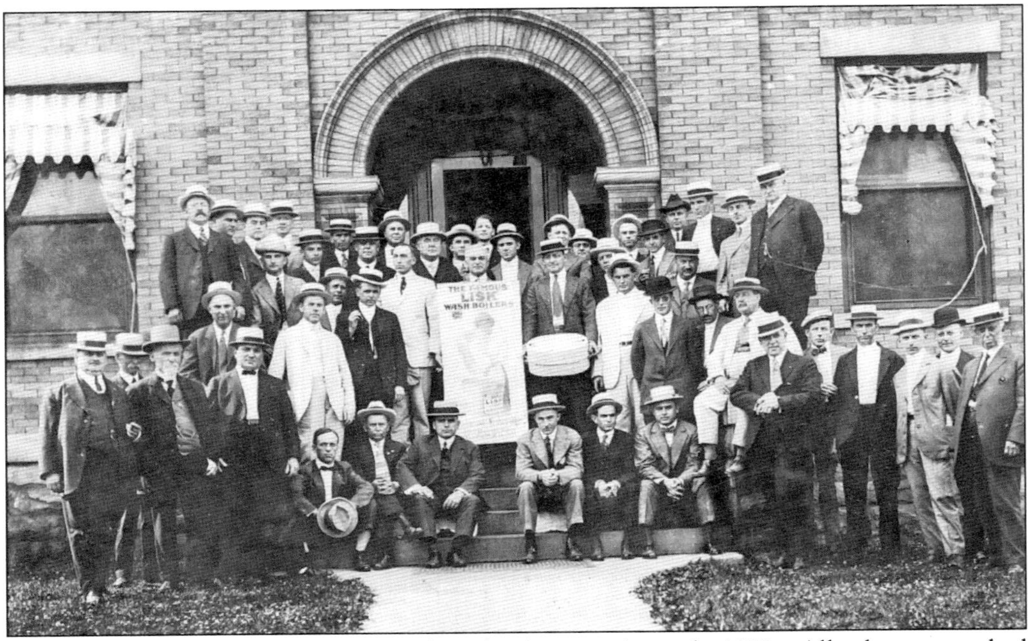

A Lisk salesmen's convention shows the sales force in the early 1900s. All salesmen worked on a strictly commission basis, and were responsible for financing their own selling campaigns. Salespeople were not allowed to discount goods—the sales manual stated, "We have only one price. Don't send in any orders with prices lower than you are authorized to give."

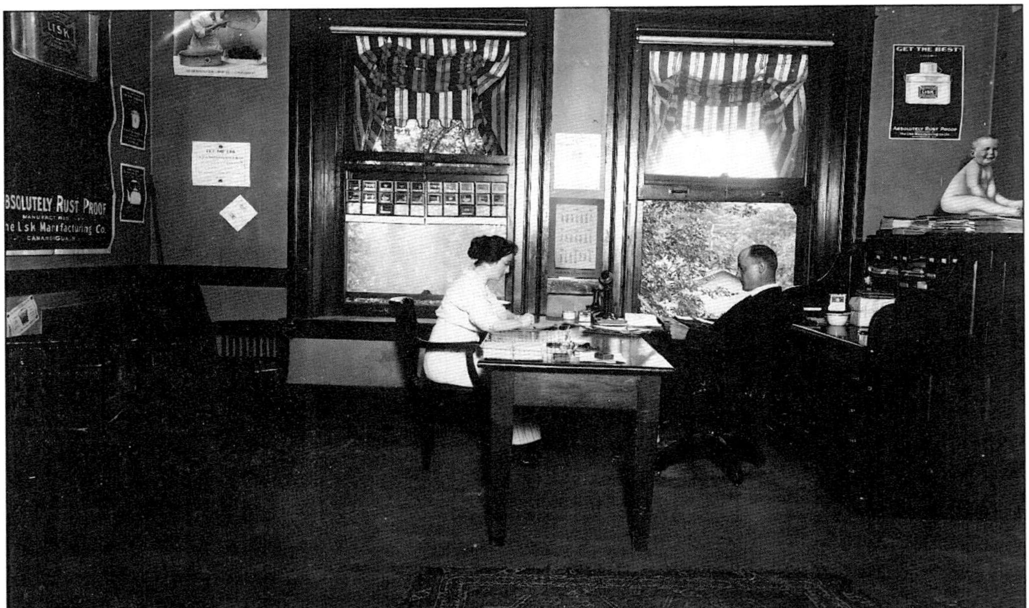

Inside the offices at the Lisk, two somber looking employees ponder paperwork. The cutout baby on the right was used in promotional ads.